Renate Sperling: The Essence of Gemstones

Renate Sperling: The Essence of Gemstones

Renate Sperling

The Essence
of
Gemstones

Bluestar
Communications

Woodside, California

Translated from German into English
by Christine M. Grimm
First published in German under the title:
Vom Wesen der Edelsteine
© 1994 Aquamarin Verlag, Grafing, Germany

This translation:
© 1995 Bluestar Communications Corporation
44 Bear Glenn
Woodside, CA 94062
Tel: 800-6-Bluestar

Anglicized & Edited by Goddess Enterprises, Escondido, California
© Photographs:
Adelheid Siebenbaum
Sabine von Neubeck

Cover photo: Vladimir Grof
Layout: Annette Wagner
Lithos: PHG, Planegg, Germany

First printing 1995

ISBN: 1-885493-12-8

Library of Congress Cataloging-in-Publication Data
Sperling, Renate
    [Vom Wesen der Edelsteine. English]
    The Essence of Gemstones/ Renate Sperling.
                p. cm.
    ISBN
    1. Gemstones & Minerals. 2. Esoteric powers—Gemstones & Minerals.
    3. Talismans, Amulets, & Gems—Religion.
1995

Printed in Hong Kong

CONTENTS

This book is based on
my own experiences and situations I encountered in my life.

Important information
is not always found
where we assume it should be.

I recommend
that you read the entire book.

This book was originally written in German.
Therefore in the American edition,
the gemstones presented in it are not in an alphabetical order.
Please use the index to refer to a particular gemstone you might be looking for.

R.S.
Berlin, 1994

THE ESSENTIAL POWER OF GEMSTONES

All things are energy.
All vibrate at individual frequencies. All resonate at harmonic tones.
Gemstones have energy fields; they resonate with vibrating sound.

When we bring them into our energy field, gemstones give rise to seminal events in our lives. We will either notice this or not—depending on how far we have come in our own development.

By mixing the two vibration fields of body and mineral, a new vibration field forms that affects both the person and the gemstone. Change is the result of this alliance.

Infinitely many moments of change compose the life of a human being (his or her growth process). A human being is change, growth, and life.

Various factors spark our moments of change. In this book, we will deal with the changes that occur through gemstones.

Gemstones are living entities. They are living vibration fields. Nothing is solid; everything is in the process of changing, and everything is life.

Not surprisingly, gemstones possess images of their vibration fields on another level. These images are consciousness. *They are Spirit.* And so, there is naturally no separation between gemstones and spirit—stone and spirit are joined; stone and spirit are one. A stone can then also perform great transformations within a person beyond the small changes.

Wise people know that every stone has a soul, no matter in which manner!

When we live with gemstones, when we consent to their influence, then we have already made a covenant; consciously or unconsciously, we have declared ourselves willing to permit the stone to have an effect on us. Nothing occurs in the universe without agreement and nothing occurs without Divine knowledge of it.

Since we are children of the universe and have free will, we live in a state of exception. We live outside order, but are still completely bound to the Divine Order.

Our path, from its very beginning to its completion, is nothing other than a constant conflict between these polarities—a strife within us. When we relate to gemstones, it is as if they give us the ability to diminish, change, or put an end to such struggles. We naturally feel inclined to make use of any assistance offered in all of the possible forms.

This is how gemstones can be our helpers, accompanying us through more than one life. Sometimes we give more honor to them, sometimes less. At times, they can be very important to us, and at other times, not at all. The stones are always willing to help us. It is our individual prerogative to decide whether or not we want to accept their help, as well as when and how frequently we accept it.

If we love gemstones, they will reveal their true nature to us, extending far beyond *magnetic fields* and *energy potential*. Gemstones can connect with the highest spiritual vibrations and are therefore spiritual helpers. An angelic helper is aligned to each type of stone; we can contact the angels through the stones. The stones are an expression of God.

When gemstones entered my life, I was unprepared for them—at least, not consciously. It seemed to me that I had never even had a particular interest in them.

Then I set off to see a healer who worked with stones, among other things. I took a blue stone in my hand and saw with my *inner eye* a direct line to my heart. Then I selected a yellow one and saw a line to my forehead. She later gave me a crystal that *spoke* to me (I heard inner phrases as I held it in my hand). I felt quite suspicious about this, and I hardly ever used that stone.

Afterwards—apparently by coincidence—I participated in a seminar on the effects of gemstones. I gradually became interested in the stones. I acquired small handstones; what I read about them in books fascinated me. Subconsciously, I had always asked myself, "Why? Why do the stones have this effect? Why do they influence us? How is it possible? What do they want to tell me?"

When we love life, much will be given to us. My present was a trip that my girlfriend urged me to take with her to Idar-Oberstein, a German stronghold for trade in gemstones.

"Why should I go there?" I asked in a bad mood. "I don't have any money anyway."

As if a lack of money could stand in the way of our development! I had always wanted to move forwards and had done so during the previous years. I had been an executive secretary for thirteen years. Afterwards, I made the effort to learn a new profession and was working as a teacher for word processing. After a physical breakdown, I started a new life. Meanwhile, I possessed the ability to see my past lives and those of other people. I worked as a healer. I had developed these abilities through years of deep work on myself. I had given up everything that I had in order to follow my spiritual path.

Therapy and healing sessions, my training as a naturopath and reincarnation therapist, further education and advanced training had cost me a fortune. But I did not have a fortune to spend. For the purpose of following my spiritual path, I had forsaken all the things that had been dear to me. I sacrificed my financial security by quitting my career; and working on the side, which I had been temporarily forced to do. I gave up my privacy by renting out some of my rooms. I had to sell cherished possessions. I gave up my pride because I had to ask for help. I also had to give up people—those who were afraid of my path and my development and who no longer understood me. I wanted to progress; I wanted to be conscious.

God helped me. At first I learned about myself—my behavior, nature, fears, despair, deepest pain, joy, and desire. Then came a remembrance of my past lives. During a psychotherapy session, I suddenly experienced myself as a different woman. I relived things that seemed incomprehensible to me; I felt extreme pain while knowing that this was still myself. From that point on, I worked with a reincarnation therapist on my past life. I later learned to do past life regression on my own. The resolution of my memories from a past life freed me from pain and suffering; it explained my life to me; above all, it gave me profound knowledge, understanding, and strength. Afterwards, my abilities developed.

After I had already been working as a psychic healer and reincarnation therapist for a period of time, the gemstones came to me. I very quickly perceived their greatest gift—

Lightness and Joy. Until then, I had not admitted to myself that my work drained me of strength, and that I suffered in empathy with the people who came to me. With the help of the stones, I could finally allow myself to confront my needs.

I asked God for help—once again, without awareness that I had done so. I had consciously asked Him for the ability to see and feel only what is absolutely necessary for my work with people. I no longer wanted to share the entire pain of others—their despair, panic, fear, inner conflicts and all the repressed feelings from past lives. These remain within us and need healing.

"Father," I called, "Help me! Please!"

So, I started to use the gemstones. Consciously, I had no idea that we had made a pact.

"Work with the stones," said God, *"and you will be happy. I will help you. You are my child. I want you to feel happy."*

"How wonderful," was all I said, "I love stones. Thank you, God!"

My girlfriend became active as my helper in the outer world. She urged me to go to Idar-Oberstein. *En route*, it dawned on me that I should buy more than a few handstones there. I sensed a sum of money and idealized the possibility of borrowing this money.

The stones have always challenged me to overcome my limitations. They love me and I love them. We are friends. Friends help each other. I expand their knowledge about human beings and they impart divine knowledge to me.

In Idar-Oberstein we bought stones. An enormous challenge arose because of a brilliant cut diamond [See THE BRILLIANT CUT DIAMOND, p. 385]. In debt, yet with open hearts, we returned home.

The universe always rewards us for courageous deeds. The stones had spoken to me. I had listened to their counsel. I had obtained them, although I had no funds. I had trusted and trust is rewarded; this is how we learn.

Shortly after this trip, I began giving seminars on gemstones. The knowledge was suddenly there. Just as I had been clairvoyant about certain matters before then, I also became clairvoyant about gemstones. The stones initiated epic learning processes within me; I grew and grew.

I slowly gained interest in the material side of the stones (for example, mineralogy, value, jewelry, etc.). This also helped me to progress as my gemstone skills multiplied and developed. Abilities lie dormant within us all; they wait to be awakened. The stones help in the process.

Gemstones are great helpers. They produce changes within us. How can such a process manifest itself?

Once, I recommended to a woman that she wear two necklaces—crystal for clarity and citrine for confidence. Fourteen days later, she returned.

"The necklaces are not good for me. I have red spots on my neck, and I sometimes have feelings of fear. When I remove them, this all goes away."

I saw the reason; she was desperately repressing a past life memory that greatly disturbed her. The crystal gave her clarity of insight; she must resolve those memories in order to feel better. The citrine gave her confidence; she had to trust in herself—her misgivings were exaggerated. Knowledge versus fear struggled within her. Her fear and the repression of these feelings manifested as red spots. We worked on her past life; 11

afterwards her life went smoothly for her, until the next learning cycle. She now enthusiastically wears the necklaces. They no longer cause any symptoms and they contribute only to her happiness.

In my practice, I work exclusively on the esoteric causes of illness and negative states of emotion. For this purpose, I use reincarnation therapy, which involves my abilities as a psychic healer, training in past life regressions, and gemstones. In this calling, I work with the laying on of hands, whereby karmic blockages dissolve.

A mother had successful sessions with me; she brought her twelve-year-old daughter into my office.

"The laying on of hands doesn't help," the girl told her mother before her treatment.

I gave her a pyrite to hold and then worked with her.

On the way home, she excitedly said to her mother, "Imagine! The whole time, the stone said, *'It helps, it helps, it helps!'*"

Gemstones may reveal negative thoughts and feelings so that we can expunge them and move onward. For example, at a time when I still knew little about stones, I bought myself an aventurine necklace and immediately put it on. Some hours later, I found myself in a terrible mood. Everything seemed gray and hopeless to me. I thought about my life and saw no prospects.

I asked myself, "How I could think such negative thoughts?"

In the course of several meditations, I experienced the sensation that my life was happiness and my task was to be a lively, loving, and happy woman. This deep perception of my calling overcame me and tears ran down my face. I was ashamed to have so little trust in myself and my task—for not trusting God enough! I immediately established a bond with God and devoutly embraced Him. All at once, everything felt lighter—much lighter than before. The necklace suddenly occurred to me. What effect does aventurine have? I looked it up in a book. The words that jumped out at me were HAPPINESS and SUCCESS. This necklace had made my calling clear to me; it gave me strength for a long time afterwards. The three above examples show us that stones can use very different ways to help us.

It is very important to know that we should never choose a stone listed in this book in order to experience specific qualities. Under the influence of one type of stone, it is possible that three people could have three different reactions.

For example, we desperately want to feel peaceful. We read in this book that jade provides peace. We should differentiate here. Jade does radiate a vibration that is capable of creating peace within us; it does not necessarily have this effect. Person A might perceive how removed she is from peace and weep in despair; this is liberating. Person B may understand that she needs harmony in order to achieve inner peace (that requires different stones) and that she must reconcile with her husband! Person C may become restless and aggressive; she might feel annoyed by the jade and perhaps would not have a high regard for the power of stones. Had this person used another stone—such as a carnelian—she would have felt its power to bring order to her life, or to the
12 most important aspects of her life; she would have experienced peace indirectly. The

carnelian has absolutely nothing to do with peace but in this case it would have created it.

Very seldom does jade bring on a perceptible sense of peace. For instance, jade would seem ineffective to someone who is unfamiliar with a peaceful state of mind; this person needs to become familiar with it and learn to strive for it as a future goal. However, jade can mean the final return home to someone who has already achieved much on his spiritual path, and it can cause deep joy now and then. We gradually grow completely into peace.

Although every stone emits a particular vibration, its effects can vary on each individual and during different situations in life. Its vibration is normally consistent; its effects can be very diverse! It is therefore important to look more deeply than most books can show us. How can we achieve this? *We depend on our intuition.* If we cannot trust it, we must train it.

Why? There is one authority—our Inner Knowledge—that knows exactly what is good for us. It knows that type of help we need at the moment and what types of help are optimal for us. This inner message wants to penetrate into our consciousness. This can occur through dreams, happenstance (for example, someone might call me to tell me about a stone), meditation, prayer, various Light techniques, or in similar practices. It has also happened that someone has given me a stone as a present, or that I felt the inner impulse to visit a mineral shop.

When we then stand in front of the stone, what should we do then? Listen to our feelings! We will feel drawn to the stones that we need at the moment. They will be beautifully attractive to us. This works almost every time!

In my practice, I often work with a large pyrite. Pyrite creates the breakthrough. I usually ask patients how they like this stone. Many find it beautiful. New patients often reject it, and remark that it looks cold. After three or four sessions, I present it again. It is almost humorous that most of these patients burst out in enthusiastic exclamations when they see the pyrite again. They wonder why they didn't like it right away or do not even remember that I have already shown it to them. When a person is ready to experience a breakthrough, he or she perceives this stone as beautiful.

We also need to pay attention to stones that repel us. If I wholeheartedly reject a stone, I should ask myself what its effect is. Then I can usually understand what inner issue I am avoiding. It may remind me of a past life that I do not want to remember.

A woman once said to me, "I cannot stand these stones! When I touch them, they make me sick!"

The stones did not trigger the symptoms. The gemstones had a connection to the woman's memories.

Although I love all stones, there have always been some that did not especially capture my attention. They seemed uninteresting or inconspicuous to me. When these stones became important to me, there was no limit to my enthusiasm for their beauty. I suddenly found them infinitely important; I became mature enough for their help!

Gemstones influence the vibration of our auras, and can also effect changes in our bodies. Let us first understand the meaning of *healing*. The Light said to me:

The person is healed
Who can say of himself,
I am love.
I am life.
I am sun.
I am happiness.
I AM.

There is more to healing than just being free of symptoms. People often come to my practice who had shown strong symptoms a day or even an hour before the treatment. We work through a past life and the complaints disappear. These people created short-term symptoms because they wanted to remind themselves of something.

Many years ago, I saw a pair of lovers kissing in the corner of a house. I had often seen scenes like that before but then I suddenly sensed a question within me.

"What do I really feel when I see a kissing couple?"

At that moment, a strong pain in my heart shot through me; it took my breath away. After it had passed, I felt as though nothing had happened. Since I was rather ignorant at that time, I let the matter rest, but I never forgot this experience.

We become ill when we deny an inner truth. We create symptoms for ourselves when we ignore the voice of the heart for a long time, or do not even want to hear it. We have great powers. We create our own circumstances in life and it is easy to make ourselves ill. An inner no precedes an illness. Every therapy, every treatment, every prayer can only have one effect—to transform the no into a yes. This inner yes is the precondition for our healing. Here lies the answer to the miracle when a terminally ill person suddenly becomes healthy. His yes was strong and his body not yet destroyed. This is also the answer to the incomprehensible occurrences when healthy or slightly ill people die suddenly and unexpectedly. Something happens within them and they speak an absolutely strong and vehement NO.

IN THE BEGINNING WAS THE WORD. Part of our maturation is learning to understand this sentence for ourselves and our lives. We are the creators of disease and health; we are never the victims. If we feel victimized, then the misunderstanding is within us; we have not yet perceived our own truth. When we recognize this truth, the key to holistic healing lies in our hands. Through reincarnation therapy and other forms of illumination, we learn that life is always just—absolutely and unerringly just; this knowledge is a gift of mercy. Injustice is a misconception; misunderstanding, ignorance, and conflict, are the real sources of illness.

With this awareness, we can understand the effect of gemstones on the body. If someone wants to die, he has abdicated from life. This resignation is usually subconscious. A precious stone can influence it. Stones with the vibration of courage, hope, and love can be very effective here. Under certain circumstances, a few particular stones can influence the physical body directly .

Here is an example. While on a vacation, I rented a lovely room. The landlady looked into my room and asked if I needed anything. We exchanged a few words, and she then left. My eyes began to itch intensely. I rubbed them, and within a short time they swelled shut with all the signs of a virulent conjunctivitis. It occurred to me that blue helps infections. Fortunately, I had an aquamarine necklace and a large amazonite. I put the rolled-up necklace on one eyelid and the stone on the other. Surprisingly, the symptoms had completely gone after half an hour and my eyes were clear once again.

Some time later, the landlady stopped by the room in order to explain a few more things to me. Almost immediately, the eye problems started again. I had attributed the first occurrence to a physical allergy; after the second occurrence, I had to ask myself, "What do I not want to see?"

I realized that I did not want to see this woman; unpleasant experiences from a past life connected us. I worked through these experiences, used the gemstones, and became free of the symptoms. We can see here that although the stones had an effect, they only had a *lasting* effect when the *cause* had been eliminated.

I once had a vision; naked people were lying in the warm sand of a beach. Surrounding them were stones the size of a fist; these were laid close together and then were covered with sand. The stones drew negative energies out of the bodies. A woman standing next to them spoke to me.

"We have been healing in this manner for a long time, but the world does not want to know about it."

Next, I saw a truck that transported fresh stones to this place. They took back the used stones, which they returned to the earth for purification. It was clear that the healers exchanged these healing stones in a certain rhythmic timing, until all the negative vibrations drained away.

People became healthy in this way. After their healing, they learned to use gemstones to prevent illness. Only jasper, lapis lazuli, malachite, onyx, and sodalite affected the physical healing. Many other gemstones helped to advance spiritual development.

This vision made me very contemplative. There is always knowledge that we do not use. We do not want to use it—even when we are desperate for a cure. We could, for example, create energy in a very simple manner—through prayer. We do not believe it. We cannot imagine it. One day, when we are utterly without recourse, we will try it. During a meditation I learned that, sometimes in the future, every person will be able to generate enough electricity to run a house. Groups of people will provide industrial electricity. How will we do this? By laying our hands on a type of drum, in which is a type of transmitting device that converts human vibrations—evoked by prayer—into electricity. It's that simple! Why haven't we made use of this? Because our paltry imaginations have limitations.

Wernher von Braun told my father that he would one day build rockets taller than a church tower and send them to the moon. My father laughed. Von Braun added that these rockets would one day be manned. My father turned away, shaking his head! He respected Wernher as a scientist, but this idea was simply too crazy for him.

In the past, the general public feared and laughed at inventions that, today, we take for granted. To learn from the old and discover something new, we only have to let our fantasy play a little. We are too comfortable, and invent most achievements during times of need or tension. Frequently, individuals or groups of people created an external demand. What pressure do we need to put on ourselves in order to turn off the nuclear power plants?

Fortunately for us, there are individuals who change the world. The power of a single person can be endlessly immense on the spiritual level. For this reason, we 15 should never permit ourselves to become discouraged. We must find our own way, and thereby benefit all people. The world may not understand these individuals, but their work is significant.

Mahatma Gandhi is such an example. One could say in somewhat provocative terms that one can thank him for the German unity. We are gradually learning that everything is one; everything that we think, say, and do influences every one of us. At some point, individual people create a power field in the universe and from that field the rest of the world receives impulses. Gandhi's life has affected us within. Through him, humanity has come to understand an important principle: peaceful revolutions are possible and nonviolence is also a *force*. Germany's unification occurred through this principle.

We will gradually learn to understand the power fields of gemstones as well. In the process, every experience that we have with gemstones will help us. Where love is, there is discovery. The spreading of knowledge about gemstones in our time occurs through love. One day, we will do everything out of love. This is our path.

Hildegard von Bingen was one of the great, loving people. Even today, many devotees follow her teachings. The gemstones have taught me that all energies on this earth change through us. We have changed ourselves. The vibrations of the earth become different as time passes. As a result, some of Saint Hildegard's counsel no longer applies to our age. It is important to collect our own experiences, listen to our inner promptings, and to act on them.

People who are open to the idea of conversing with gemstones should ask the stones for advice. They respond with vibrations. Even those of us who are clairvoyant normally only grasp one aspect of a truth. We always experience only partial truth because personal vibrations distort the pure translation of reality; also, we have biased interests in any topic. This is why various people can preach divergent spiritual messages, even though they have dedicated themselves to their work with pure hearts. Each experience is important and every person is important. Everything is only a part and it takes an infinite number of parts to form the whole.

WHAT DEFINES A GEMSTONE?

A gemstone or a precious stone is a mineral, distinguished from the abundant variety of other minerals because of its purity, rarity, beauty, and radiance. In this book, I call all minerals stones or gemstones—including organic materials that serve humanity and have outstanding characteristics. Expert lapidaries no longer use the term semiprecious stone.

A precious stone embodies a vibration; it is a manifestation of compressed *spirit*. It can have the effect of a helper, a brother, or a friend. It is a child of God or an expression of highest Divinity. What I perceive within a gemstone depends on the stone and on my own consciousness.

Gemstones affect changes in us when we wear them, lay them on our bodies, hold them in the hand, look at them, or use them in a multitude of other variations.

HOW WE RESPOND
TO THE ENERGIES OF GEMSTONES

Gemstones that influence us through the vibrations of their energy fields are important. This happens in a unique manner; it is a type of transference.

Drops, ointments, drugs, and essences affect us directly; in contrast, stones influence us in an indirect manner. What occurs is an exchange of vibrations on the spiritual level. One could say that the stones work through enlightenment. They affect a specific contact between Inner Knowledge and Divine Wisdom. From this perspective, we can see that they influence us through perception.

If I were in deep despair, and reached for a precious stone, its message might be this: "TRUST—life is simpler than you think. Everything has been prepared, everything will change. Trust."

This information would then enter my subconscious mind. There, it would integrate with the collective knowledge belonging to my higher self. Until that time, I would not let this Higher Self express itself often enough. Now this double information reaches me with emphasis, perseverance, and conscientiousness. I can no longer ignore it; it permeates my being. It begins to have an *effect* within me and creates an *impact*. The impact can vary greatly in nature, depending on where I stand in my life process, what I allow myself, and what I would like.

One hundred people can achieve inner peace with one hundred different stones. In addition, time is also an important element. If the amethyst brings me peace through perception today, it is certain that another stone will bring me peace some time later; weeks later, a different stone will help me, and a year later, another. When I become more mature, completely different stones will be appropriate.

This is why I always ask myself key questions:
- What do I need at this point in my life?
- What is good for me today?
- What will help me further right now?

When I select a precious stone, I ask myself the next questions:
- How should I use it?
- For what length of time will I need it?
- What else should I consider?

We eventually develop a feeling for all of this. Some stones want to be worn while others do not. For the latter, it is perhaps more suitable to lay them on the body for a limited period of time. Some stones are most effective during the day, others at night.

Do not jump to conclusions; I must not decide about a stone's overall effect just because it has told me something, or because I have a certain experience with it. The influence of an individual stone can be far-reaching and comprehensive; we are possibly glimpsing only a very small detail of its possibilities. The more open we are to gemstones, the more we will learn about them; they will become true friends. As spiritual helpers, gemstones are inexhaustible! I cannot say this often enough. Every judgment means limitation and stagnation. 19

How Should I Use the Stones?

The most common practice is to keep them with you. I carry the so-called tumbled stones in the pockets of my dresses and pants. I wear the small or intense stones in a little silk or leather bag close to my heart; I wear my favorites as necklaces, pendants, and rings. It is good for the stones to touch the skin, which is why I have jewelry set in such a way that the underside of the stone contacts my skin. A little bag made of thin leather, silk, or cotton is porous enough for a stone to affect the body; these little bags are very easy to sew. The cord on that they hang should—of course—be unbreakable. In addition, it must be secure so that no stones can fall out, if one bends over for example. Now and then, replace the cord and wash the bag.

We can also wear necklaces as arm bands or as belts around the waist. When I use them frequently, I can also wear them on my clothes and do not necessarily need skin contact.

I make a habit of taking a rest at noon. While doing so, I often lay stones on my clothes—over the energy centers—and in my hands. After twenty minutes, I feel fit for the rest of the day.

When I have new gemstones that are small, I tape them over my heart chakra for three nights, and then on my forehead for the next three nights (with surgical tape). During those nights, I almost always dream about the power of the stones and their nature. Sometimes, I also sleep with necklaces or larger stones.

People with the ability to perform remote, or absent, healing agree that this absent healing works as long as they hold a stone in one of their hands. I understand that absent healing is the neutral sending of Light energy. For this purpose, I use a special healing system that has a holistic effect (The Radiance Technique®—Real Reiki®), without applying my will or personal wishes.

Many people use gemstones in meditation. They may place the stones in the palm of each hand, or directly in front of them, or between their legs. They might also tape small stones on the forehead or the heart center. Those who meditate in a supine position may prefer to place the stones on the forehead or the heart.

Be careful about a suggestion to suck on the stones or put them in drinking water! I did try this at the beginning of my explorations. However, if you do not know exactly what you are doing, you should forego this experiment! Some minerals are poisonous. The body would automatically absorb certain trace elements, which it then cannot expel. If one active substance can harden my bones over a longer period of time, then another can soften them. Which dosage has what effect? How much information do you know about it?

I also used to be enthusiastic about ointments containing powdered gemstones; some of them seemed to work. However, we are no longer dealing with the spiritual energy of the stone in this case, but merely with its chemical substance. The same caveat also applies here; we are not certain about what we absorb through the skin. The wonderful thing about wearing gemstones is precisely that there are no chemical side-effects; the spiritual effects occur for our benefit.

Gemstones in the home can exert their influence on the dining-room table, in the working space, in the sleeping area, and other places. They may clear the energy in rooms, or they may invite you to touch them. We should remove them before renovating a room; since the paint vapors can harm us, they can damage the stones, too. Quartz crystals are suitable for neutralizing such odors and vibrations but the stones must be large enough to do their work. They need cleansing after a short period of use, and they possibly may lose their virtue.

Every time you use one: THE STONE MUST BE CLEANSED AFTERWARDS!

Gemstones radiate their pure vibrations and affect us within. They absorb information from us and draw negative vibrations away from us; the stones store this within themselves. If we do not cleanse them, the stones will eventually exhaust their positive energy. They will then return our destructive energies to us. They would then reflect our dark sides, and no longer heal.

The easiest way to cleanse is with cold water (warm water binds energies). I put several stones together in a cup or a bowl with water, wait 2 to 5 minutes—sometimes longer. Then, I quickly rinse the objects under cold water once and lay them to dry on towels. This includes necklaces, although jewelers disapprove of this practice. What use is a necklace to me if it lasts for a longer time but cannot develop its power and possibly even harm me!? To protect the stones from cracking, no pieces warmed at body temperature should go into cold water. For example spodumene (kunzite, hiddenite) can crack by merely cooling from body temperature to cold air. Inspect new minerals before putting them in water; some of them do not tolerate it. A stone can crumble because the parent rock turns out to be sand. Water can turn very soft stones unsightly (phosgenite, ulexite) and pyrite can create rust spots. Luckily, there are very few exceptions that need special care when cleansing with water.

For a period of time, bury stones that have not been cleansed for a long time in earth that is as pure as possible (not in a flower pot). Some stones simply need to return to the earth with thanks. This is an opportunity to learn to let go.

We can cleanse the stones through spiritual means, when we have advanced on our path, and feel confident. One possibility is prayer, but there are other spiritual techniques that will work.

I would always recommend the water or earth method to beginners. I cleanse many stones with water, because it appeals to me. I completely reject the practice of cleansing gemstones with salt! This can only be harmful! In the long term, a mineral could even change as a result. We should also know specifically whether stones can withstand an ultrasound bath at the jeweler's. I had a turquoise set, which a goldsmith put into an ultrasound bath. I didn't know that it had been varnished and ugly spots appeared immediately. Never clean turquoise, coral, pearls, and other very soft stones in this manner!

It is not necessary to charge stones in the sun. If we love them and carefully cleanse them, they will always retain their full power. As a part of nature, they welcome every natural element. If you so desire, you may lay them in the sun. Conversely, it is entirely detrimental and especially degrading to keep them in safes and bank vaults. Gemstones live; they want to serve; they love and want to be loved. We should surround ourselves with them. Only in this manner they can have an effect.

Some gemstones reveal to me that their wearer has gone through a long phase of depression or illness, which I can sense when the stones have not been cleansed. It is also 21 the reason that nobody will buy some old jewelry, or wear certain inherited jewelry. One instinctively recoils from it, although the jewelry is appealing. I usually have been able to cleanse such stones; they were then worn or sold promptly.

One time, I held an emerald that had passed through many owners. It had a sublime aura, which affected me very deeply. Certain stones have reached their absolute perfection; they are impervious to illness or moods. They radiate such a magnificent vibration of perfection that every human problem pales in comparison. I will be able to remember such a stone for many lifetimes.

Gemstones teach all the divine laws. Two important principles are letting go and giving. The gemstones first truly came into my life when, in obeisance to an inner urging, I gave away all my jewelry. I gave away everything that had given me pride and that I had held onto for my entire life. I seriously believed that I would never again be able to wear jewelry; it seemed to be incompatible with my work as a healer. With some of these pieces, separation was very hard for me, but I felt that I had to do it.

The universe loves us. In my case, this experience was a test and a help. The test was my willingness to give up possessions that I loved when I felt the inner call. This helped me; I knew enough about energy circulation at the time to recognize that these old things constrained me. This was my breakthrough to my own healing and to the healing of other people; my life began anew. Only a very few pieces remain in my possession from the time before my transformation. The principle of letting go conceals an enigma.

"The human being who overcomes himself
sets himself free from the power that binds all beings."
—J.W. von Goethe

The universe reacts immediately. I had just given away my last piece of jewelry, and gone on a trip—where I found my first simple necklace of gemstones.

Owning minerals and gemstones presents quite a different challenge. These valuables cannot really be insured; one can only pray, request their preservation and protection, and then let go at the proper time.

Gemstones teach the important values in life—development and growth. For example, I might buy a stone that costs a thousand dollars; I am permitted to keep it for three years before I give it away or possibly lose it. It has given me a boundless wealth in those three years and the money is no longer important. It gave me far more than thousand dollars worth of value.

Whether or not we believe in them, gemstones can influence us. When we love the stones and feel convinced of their influence, they can do even more for us. I have experienced direct physical impact from gemstones, but I am more fond of the spiritual impact. A precious stone is a companion, guardian, and helper; it is just as real as my Guardian Angel in its presence and help. It touches me time and again. What touches and impresses me even more is the selflessness and the quality of joyful service that these children of God express. This energy puts me to shame as I consider my constant struggles to walk the path of God in complete devotion. The moss agate, which I place in my left hand during writing breaks, speaks to me in a friendly manner.

"That's just how you human beings are."

22

UNDERSTANDING THE EFFECTS
OF GEMSTONES

Gemstones have an effect every time we employ them, but we cannot always understand their full impact.

The more sensitive we are, the more we perceive their influence. Many opportunities for learning and developing await us upon our path of growth. The better we understand ourselves, the more alert we will become. We will choose the correct stones more quickly. I recommend precious stone seminars in any case; the energy is very intense there and the chances to learn are great. Try it! Get to know different teachers. Learn, and listen to what others have experienced during these seminars. If a seminar did not appeal to you, try the next one! In my courses, I hear about the most astounding experiences! Some people have experienced entire epics. Some participants at these seminars see and hear a great deal; others do not, but still feel marvelously well. Sometimes, a student will tell me about occurrences that resulted from a gemstone seminar.

One of my favorite stones for beginners is the honey calcite, because it has a tremendously fast effect. People who hold it feel understood, warm, comfortable, relieved, *joie de vivre*, and much more. This stone works quickly and has a lasting influence.

Some stones work more slowly. I have gained insights from a higher plane in many cases; however, a completely different kind of experience caught me by surprise. I once put a stone in the hand of my six-year-old nephew. At my request, this mercurial little fellow even lay down on my sofa and closed his eyes. I asked him to focus his attention on the stone.

After a while, he said, "This stone goes tack—tack—tack." I gave him another stone.

He said, "And, this one goes tack, tack, tack, tack."

Astounded, I gave him six stones, whose energy he described in a similar manner.

"Can I go now?" He asked cheerfully. I naturally allowed him to do so, and I felt enriched by his different perspective.

We each have a personal way of perceiving the energy of gemstones. This is the lovely thing about them. Each stone brings a new experience and various ways of experiencing it.

At a school for naturopathy, a woman listened to me for hours. She later told me her impressions.

"I sat there and thought, 'Gemstones can't work! Nonetheless, there must be some truth in it if this woman talks about them so seriously.'"

She had a son named Willi, who was four years old.

"What happened at your school?" He asked her.

She told him a little about it. He begged to have a stone, so she bought him a green one. Willi took it to bed with him. The next day he said, "Mummy, I dreamed about the stone, and it said, 'Willi, you are a lucky boy!'"

I laughed when she told me this. "Aha, you bought him an aventurine!"

"Yes, I did," she confirmed.

"You know," I said, "children relate much better to their inner voice than adults do. The five-year-old son of a friend selects his minerals with uncanny sureness. In addition, he sometimes says, 'Back then, when I was an adult.'" I work with reincarnation therapy and so I wanted to make her aware that children often remember their past lives.

Surprised, she looked at me, and then said shamefaced, "So—we've never taken it seriously—but Willi often says, 'Back then, when I was retired'!"

The energies of the stones vary greatly, particularly in the ways that they enter the consciousness. For example, a sapphire never works as quickly as a honey calcite. Instead, it has a deeper and broader effect. Despite this slowness, I can have important experiences with a sapphire the first time I wear it, when it often shows me where it would like to lead me. It can take months before it affects a change. Some stones affect one immediately; others can take weeks, months, or years before they fulfill their task. The padparadscha that came to me requires fourteen years to work along with me.

To become familiar with a gemstone, you should carry it with you for three days and three nights. This will develop a feeling for the stone. You should open up to it for the next six weeks. After that, you will sense whether you want to set it aside or whether you would like to continue wearing it. Please, only use six weeks as a relative reference; this is too long a period for some situations and stones. If you ought to use the stone for just a very short time, you will quickly become disinterested in it. The general wisdom is to wear a stone for too long a time rather than for too short a period.

Stones have energies that are quick-acting, sharp, clear, heavy, effervescent, stable, gentle, distinctly slow, or have other peculiarities. An energy field always surrounds a stone, which belongs to it. This energy field can be measured with scientific methods; the vibrations can be recorded.

Sometimes the size or purity of a stone is important. Valuable gemstones are sold in size increments called carats; one carat is 0.2 gram. To achieve a quicker effect in my healing work, I prefer minerals that are as large as possible. Now and then, a patient will show me a gemstone that he or she has bought. Once, such a stone was very small. I was about to open my mouth to say that it could not possibly have an effect; then I noticed that it indeed had a very intense effect, because its owner loved it very much. Small stones usually are too weak to have much influence. Of course, on the other hand, some gemstones only are available in small sizes; their crystal structures may only achieve small dimensions, or larger sizes might cost an astronomical price that be unattainable for most people.

Gemstone or size, it is completely your personal choice. It will have an effect in any case; this is what is important. It does not matter very much whether I wear a stone, lay it upon myself, look at it, or meditate with it.

Gemstones are our friends. When we sincerely become involved with them, when we love them, they will reveal their secrets to us. They can guide us in learning processes and usher us. When we love them, they will become our helpers.

The intensity with that we surround ourselves with stones is in proportion to how much we will learn about them and the degree that they will open to us. Stones also learn from us; we should never forget this. In this aspect, we enter into a partnership—a relationship—a love with every stone we acquire. Love endows everything with a living soul; more precisely, everything has a soul, but love elevates everything—above all, the person who loves.

SELECTING GEMSTONES

It is simple for me to find the suitable precious stone—I listen to my feelings. Why? Because I know what is good for me from my inner being.

Do not be tempted into selecting a stone on the basis of its description! Choose a stone—and then read about it! First allow your present condition to express itself; your choice reveals the vibrations that you require at the moment. Learn about a stone after making your choice. Through this sequence, you can perceive your momentary learning process, understand more about yourself, and increasingly learn to trust yourself by recognizing that your choice was good.

One other fact is very significant. When we become involved with gemstones, the spiritual world knows and we will, therefore, receive support. The many types of spiritual assistance probably take a different form each time.

For example, my girlfriend might call me about a gemstone, but I listen with only one ear. Later, I hear about this stone for a second time.

"Why? Does this have something to do with me?" I should finally ask myself.

If I am a beginner, I should then go to a rock shop and take a look at this stone. How do I feel with it? Am I enthusiastic about it or do I feel repelled by it? In either case, the stone is important to me. Now I can decide whether or not I want to acquire it. If I feel nothing, the stone is not significant to me—at least not now. Sometimes, the world of gemstones merely beckons us into a store this way, where completely different stones want to come to us.

Gemstones are our helpers. They remind us of their presence. To do this, they choose countless ways and are absolutely resourceful! Thus a stone can come to us through other people, through stories, through advice, or as a gift. We may feel a distinct click when we read about an appropriate gemstone in a lapidary book; other descriptions might be interesting, but we would feel no connection to them. We can dream about a stone or its name. We can happen on it somewhere, and find it to be infinitely beautiful or feel ourselves intensely attracted to it.

In addition, we can arrange stones in an ordered list. From this very book, we can number the names of gemstones, add the terms PRAYER and OTHER METHODS, and number them on the list as well. Then we pray, asking "What stone is important for me right now?" A number should come to mind or appear to the inner eye. We can likewise pray for guidance, and then open this book to a page at random, which is also a way of finding the right stone.

Sometimes a person asks me, "Is it possible to make a mistake choosing a stone?"

NO—there are no mistakes. Either the vibration of a chosen stone has a good effect on you or you need to go through a certain learning process. In that case, you might select a stone that no longer applies to your needs, but through that you will have a necessary experience. When you select incompatible stones, then you begin a process in that you must examine your values and judgments, how you treat yourself, and many other issues. When you feel depressed, you may gravitate to a stone that can drive you even deeper into your depression; perhaps it will depress you so much that it can serve as the catalyst for your redemptive moment, when your feelings become brighter within or when you can accept help. Even a wrong stone allows something meaningful to happen within you.

Trust your feelings! In all these years, I have only experienced three occasions when someone picked a stone that seemed to be surrounded by a gray fog; naturally, which also had its purpose. I assume that people interested in gemstones always make a good selection. A chosen stone always corresponds to the current condition of the person. Sometimes I perceive that a person has not selected the shortest path to a goal; I have observed this at my seminars now and then.

I once saw that a woman needed pyrite to break through her feelings. This person chose rose quartz (trust).

At a later time, she asked me, "Would you now recommend that stone for me?"

In this case, she first surrounded herself with a vibration of trust before she could face a more intense step in learning. How wise!

The following experience impressed me very much. A woman came to a seminar with her sister and sister-in-law. She had no therapy experience; she did not want to discuss her feelings. I felt that I should leave her alone. On the first day, she selected four stones: rose quartz, hematite, malachite, and pyrite. These stones worked for her in the ways of truth, courage, strength, comfort, and breakthrough. Every stone ushered her into its energy vibration, which affects inner processes with great intensity.

The next day, she once again chose pyrite (breakthrough). At last, she could cry but she still refused to discuss her feelings. Then she picked amethyst and she discerned her reasons for sorrow. Afterwards, she reached for rose quartz (trust) and finally for aventurine (happiness). In the vibration of trust and then happiness, she realized that there was no true reason for sorrow. She could forgive herself and others for the memories—the experiences and feelings from the past—that she had processed during that weekend. She only reported surprise that this memory had resurfaced at all; she had thought it finished and no longer important. She ended the seminar with a sense of great relief, happiness, and peace. I feel fascinated that she, with absolute consistency and without hesitation, chose the stones that, well and reliably, led her through her learning process. She had trusted her feelings.

Through my clairvoyance, I perceived that she had worked intensely on herself. Her problem concerned children in her current life, but her sorrow was from the pain of losing children during past lives. She feared to speak of it, especially in front of family members, who were karmic participants. Time and again, I feel surprised and thankful for how gemstones gently help us to heal our wounds!

We need to trust both our feelings and our ability to make a selection!

If we feel uncertain, we can reinforce the connection to our feelings by holding a suitable precious stone over the third eye (in the middle of the forehead, right above the root of the nose) or over the spiritual heart (at the level of the heart, in the center of the body). We are then more likely to feel that stone we should choose.

Above all, it is important to learn trust in the inner voice. This not only applies to choosing an appropriate precious stone; it is relevant to one's entire life. We risk foregoing our task, our path, and our happiness; we can have these things when we learn to understand the inner voice, and thereby speak with the Light, with God, and with the angels. Unfortunately, our society does not yet teach this truth as it teaches us to read and write. In our elementary schools, I wish that we as children could learn to deal sincerely with our feelings. We would have no difficulties with politics and daily life if we could have training with the inner voice and the benefits in listening to it. The person who has direct knowledge of the laws of karma will find it very hard to commit a crime—not even a small indiscretion, which many people disregard (karmically, they count a great deal!).

Nothing should be more important to us than our spiritual development. When this is the primary focus, everything else in life resonates with it. We also cannot expect to hear our inner voice after one self-realization seminar, when we have not learned this through years or decades of living. The way within is a life assignment. We need training to contact our spiritual nature and our inner Light directly. It can take years, many seminars, much patience and long practice. We should therefore pray, asking for these qualities. The effort is worth it! Later we will say, "I was nothing without this contact. At last, my life has a purpose."

We should then make use of everything in order to train what we call *feeling*. This will change your life; it will change you. Portals will be thrown open for you; the vastness and the Light will dazzle you; every help will be granted to you. You know yourself and God. In completely normal everyday life this means: there is nothing more to fear if you listen to your inner voice. Life becomes a joyful and relaxed experience when you observe that the Light accompanies you every moment and communes with you. You will never again feel loneliness or failure. Life has become an adventure.

A very popular way of trying to select gemstones for oneself is by using a pendulum. I want to warn you about this practice. Pendulum energy is very frequently misinterpreted. If I do not exactly know what energy speaks to me through the pendulum *per se*, if I do not know what its motivation is, I am not clear as to whether or not the pendulum reacts for my best interests. Until I am sure where and how I can use it, I should avoid its use. People who use the pendulum should see this as a temporary learning process; they should be aware that it can often misdirect learning; one can misunderstand its impulses.

Following is an example that has nothing to do with the pendulum, but is still quite appropriate. At the beginning of my spiritual quest, a fortune teller gave me a reading from the tarot; she told me that I would marry in three years. This made me happy. I hoped for a fulfilling relationship, and this prediction helped me at that point in time. One year later, I heard from another medium that I would marry in two years. Finally! This had been my lifelong wish; through the double confirmation, I now really believed that it would come true. Since I was experiencing a very difficult and painful phase of development, the prediction comforted me very much. Time passed. When the third year was almost over, I again felt overcome with doubt. I prayed devoutly. The wedding will take place in seven weeks, I heard. Seven weeks! Did I already know the man? Would I risk making such a quick decision if I didn't even know him yet? Thousands of questions descended on me.

Three weeks later, there was still no man in sight. I already felt very defeated. Then I heard a date in response to my question about the wedding: June 7. June began. I slowly let go of the message. Had it only come to give me encouragement when I had bitterly needed it? In the meantime, my life was going very well; there was a less desperate fervor to my longing for a relationship. I was happy by myself; I could wait for the right time. Could I really do this? I felt disappointment along with doubt. Although I trusted that my life would turn out well, how could I trust wholeheartedly when such messages were unreliable?

The seventh of June approached. A woman I had met during a Radiance Seminar visited me. She could create Light—an ability that was not familiar to me at that time. She treated me for half an hour. During this energy work, I saw myself in the Light. Jesus—as a radiant Light Being—came to me and gave me His hand. Together we stood before God, the Highest Light. God blessed our union.

It was only days later that I comprehended the magnitude of this experience—the true gift. The Holy Wedding had taken place. Quite incidentally, I also recognized the truth from the message of that time. I had experienced my wedding at the promised time—only in a different manner than I expected it to be. Our thoughts, our ideas, and our desires are also the only things that can prevent us from correctly choosing our gemstones. We must listen to heart and feeling. We must ask for help; the gemstones that are important will come to us.

At this point, I would like to emphasize that it is not necessary to possess many stones. Those who love gemstones, and who make a pastime of acquiring them, will gradually have a considerable collection. An intense growth process is possible with just six stones, which—except for possibly two—are still reasonably affordable. I would recommend that you buy a clear rock crystal about as large as a finger, a citrine and an amethyst of similar size, a diopside as a mediator for other stone energies, and two stones that feel extremely attractive over a long period of time or that clearly force themselves on you. One of them should belong to "the great stones" (see p. 393). If this is too expensive, ask the diopside for mediation here (see DIOPSIDE, p. 118). Choose one from the stones that you already have to be your very personal helper (see p. 34).

In this manner, we can use the energies of the gemstones for years to come and attain a high level of growth. Gemstones are for everyone. They also come to those who do not have much money. Remember that just reading the description of a stone can open your heart and have an effect, even if you cannot afford to buy the stone. The same thing can happen when you look at a photograph.

Do not be tempted into buying nearly all the stones that I have described in this book. Stones draw attention to themselves but this does not mean that you must have them. Of course, you could also possess a magnificent number of stones, if this is your path and your joy. Carefully scrutinize this desire. Ask the world of gemstones for help. Then you can sit back, relax, and wait to see that stones come to you. However, you should also examine your request.

Do not approach the gemstones by saying, "I want a stone now. See that it comes to me!" This is not a request, but a demand. Can you make a request and be thankful? Then the proper events will continue. Never say: "The description is just great! I must have this stone!" Ask instead, "What stone corresponds to me and my current situation in life? What stone should I seek?" Perhaps you will hear or see something as a response to your question; perhaps you will not. You can be certain that you will soon find your stones.

PURCHASING GEMSTONES

When we love gemstones, we naturally would like to possess some of them. The purchasing of gemstones is a matter of trust. It is therefore sensible to buy them from a specialized dealer—a store or company mainly concerned with the sale of minerals and gemstones.

Displayed gemstones frequently have signs describing them. They usually include the mineral names, places of origin, and price. Loose goods are less well labeled. Here we should trust the judgment of the salesperson. However, the sales staff is not always well informed! Many salespeople do not even make an effort. Some of them do not care to know the name of a stone—they only want to sell it. It is unbelievable how many sales clerks invent fairy tales about stones for the sake of a sale.

So we need to learn the information, and not rely on others. When we are knowledgeable, we will be careful. We can develop a sense for truth or lies. Asking specific questions, we can very quickly establish the qualifications of a sales staff.

Personally, I like to buy in specialty stores and at companies with that I am familiar. I sometimes pay higher prices there than elsewhere, but I can feel confident that I will really get the stone that I want to have—not a substitute, glass, or synthetic one. On the other hand, gemstones always guide me to new experiences and various companies.

I also like to buy at mineral exchanges. The abundance and the variety available for comparison appeal to me. With some luck, I can buy gemstones there at very reasonable prices. The same caveat about salespeople applies here; there are experts, and there are others who have barely held a stone. This is a reason to be cautious. We are always on the safe side when the stone itself gives us a message. This may be a different stone than a sales clerk claims it to be, but we know that it will affect us and how. Again, we must depend on our own feelings.

We can find very rare stones at an exchange. I have sometimes found them in certain mineral stores from some companies in Idar-Oberstein, Germany. Always talk to company representatives. Take a risk. Most companies can officially sell only to wholesalers—but many also have a soft spot for collectors! When I am looking for a certain stone, I never let myself be put off by a no. I always ask, "Do you know where I can find such a stone, such a necklace?" This can result in another no, but it usually gets me new addresses.

When I want to give myself a treat, I visit an elegant jewelry store. I select a piece from the showcase that I believe the clerks will think is in my price class. Then I request to have this piece shown to me.

We do not always have to possess gemstones. An important lesson from them in any case is that we never really possess them, even when we have bought them. Gemstones are free agents; they have their own laws about their coming and going. I cherish lasting memories in my heart of at least a dozen gemstones that I was lucky enough to hold in my hand for a short time or see in a museum. I will never forget them; they still have an effect on me. I will meet them again after my death.

Lapidaries with a special love of gemstones like to show their best pieces. When they sense this kindred love—and perhaps even professional knowledge— in the person they are dealing with, they will fetch their rarest stones out of the safe. For most of these stones, the price is not even important. Lapidaries have often shown me stones that they knew I could never buy. To be permitted to hold such a stone in your hand is a gift, and the stone has an effect! It affects us through its qualities, its beauty, its size, its radiance, and this influence remains with us.

Sometimes I recommend that you inspect the best stones first in order to develop a feeling for the energy of a stone; then buy yourself one that is less expensive.

Gemstones are living beings. Buying them is ultimately not a problem because gemstones best know to whom they want to go. They choose us; we do not choose them. This is why finding them is just a matter of openness.

The more intensely we occupy ourselves with gemstones, the more experiences we accumulate, and the more we learn.

Life with gemstones is an adventurous growth process. Risk it! Try it! Gather your own experiences! Listen to your feelings! Validate yourself through this opportunity!

THE CHARACTERISTICS OF GEMSTONES

Color

The color of a precious stone influences us just as its composition does; it is part of its nature. Each color represents a special task and message in the superior minerals (see THE ENERGIES AND GROUPINGS OF GEMSTONES, p. 37). Color plays more of a subordinate role for the remaining stones. For instance, calcite always has the effect peculiar to calcite minerals. Depending on the color, it also has a special vibration. The colors always affect us in the following ways.

PINK . . . . concerns opening the heart and symbolizes holistic love.
GREEN . . . signifies healing and a connection to nature.
YELLOW . . represents the principles of the sun and Light
—also the sun and the Light within us.
RED . . . . . indicates vital energy, vitality, and physical love.
BLUE . . . . upholds perception and spiritual knowledge.
LILAC . . . . connects us with the Highest Spirituality.
BLACK . . . supports self-communion and connection.
WHITE . . . brings in joy and Light, perfection and happiness.

The color of a precious stone depends on the color-giving trace minerals in nature, natural or artificial heating procedures, or artificial radiation. These are the essential influences. These forces also determine the impact of a stone.

When we love gemstones, we also love the variety of colors. Every color influences us; we feel their effects, depending on where we place them on the body. A common recommendation is to assign certain colors of stones to their corresponding chakras. The classification of the chakras (energy centers) is as follows:

Base chakra . . . . red
Spleen chakra . . . . . . orange
Solar plexus chakra . . . yellow
Heart chakra . . . . . . green and pink
Throat chakra . . . . . . blue (light)
Third Eye chakra . . . . blue (dark)
Crown chakra . . . . . . purple

Naturally, I recommend trying this system. At certain times in life, we experience a great increase in energy and purification if we lay the corresponding color stone on each energy center.

However, for me it is more essential to look into the *depths*. A woman who had heard about the above mentioned color classification asked me for a blue stone for her throat chakra because she wanted to heal a blockage there in order to be able to sing better. I recognized that this blockage could only dissolve through a red stone. She had forbidden herself to sing because she had not healed an experience that concerned love. She required a ruby, which she wore for six weeks, so that she could risk letting her love flow more freely. Afterwards, her voice was more powerful and beautiful. Again, my advice is that, if you cannot clairvoyantly perceive these connections, then rely on your *feelings.*

If you feel particularly attracted to one type of stone and have a number of specimens in the house, I recommend the following experiment. For a number of weeks, lay one of these stones on every chakra for about twenty minutes or longer, then cleanse the stones. Apply this method once or more often everyday. Not all stones are suitable for this purpose. It is preferable to begin with rock crystals, aventurines, or honey calcites. This requires six or seven stones (you can leave out the crown chakra). If you have selected honey calcite and buy it at an exchange, this will cost about $35 to $55; you will have gained friends who will let you have a sunny vacation in your bed.

You might also apply many different stones. Sometimes, I think it is better to open up completely to one precious stone or just a few. You should then choose them very deliberately, but also experiment with them sometimes. In any case, limit yourself to one stone if you want to become more familiar with it.

Form

The natural diversity of form for minerals and gemstones is vast. Gemstones are available in raw or treated states. Treated stones come in the following types.

- **Tumbled:** Rocks or gems that tumble in drums for days, weeks, or months. A slurry of abrasives fills the drums. This process first removes their sharp edges and then, with a second mixture, polishes them. Tumbled rocks are also called handstones.
- **Faceted:** A jeweler cuts precisely arranged facets (polished surfaces) onto a gemstone. Faceting achieves the highest degree of brilliance, as light reflects off the gem's surface and refracts through it—if it is clear.
- **Cabochons:** A jeweler sculpts and polishes a gemstone into a halved egg or a halved sphere shape.

Some raw stones, such as rock crystals, are cut in their natural form. Others are shaped into spheres, drops, figures, eggs, rectangles, pyramids, and all possible fantasy forms.

The shape of a precious stone can absolutely influence its effect. However, this book concerns the essence of gemstones, which do not really change by appearance.

Some people only like gemstones in their raw state; I think that is unfortunate. Beauty opens the heart—be it the beauty of love or a stone. An impeccably cut precious stone radiates completion, maturity, and perfection. If it is of the best quality, it has achieved its highest goal—it lives its perfection. Through the faceting process, people make its perfection visible; this opens other people's hearts. Many times the beauty of a precious stone affected me and touched my heart so deeply that I had to weep. There are gemstones of such sublime beauty that just looking at them or briefly touching them changes something within us. Yes, there are even stones that I held in my hand thousands of years ago—and have not forgotten to this very day!

During some past civilizations, we altered gemstones so that nothing remained of their essence, and we used them to destroy people and animals. We designed and programmed the etheric crystalline structure to a certain degree. The stones, as tiny balls, were inserted under the skin or in the veins; they caused rapid decay of the cells. Emerging memories of these types of manipulations were very painful to me; I immediately became ill. Although I was able to heal the horror, the shocking certainty remains with me that we are working with comparable experiments today, although we seldom use gemstones for this purpose.

On the basis of experiences repeated by other people and by myself, I can say that we feel endlessly guilty for every interruption of life. Many lifetimes ago, we destroyed and manipulated life; we felt justified and appropriate in our actions. This inner horror, this boundless feeling of guilt, and the compulsion to punish oneself for it is great; people find countless ways to keep themselves small in this life, to torture themselves in many manners, and above all, to be unhappy.

All of us can heal these experiences from past lives. Our life will change as a result, although this requires courage and will be shocking for us in any case when it deals with such traumatic experiences as these. We will become freer after healing a greater portion of the self; we will rise up to our potential. I did not want to deal with altered gemstones until quite recently. Subconsciously, I always had these experiences in mind, where we had misused gemstones to such an extent. There are books that deal nearly exclusively with natural mineral forms or their artificial alterations and their alleged effects. My hair always stands on end when I see them. Whether this is a justified premonition of the future or just a memory of the dreadful history of humanity, I cannot say as of yet.

Where They Are Found

A multitude of factors influence the energy of a gemstone. For example, all green tourmalines have the same basic nature; however, they carry the imprint of their country of origin—its history and the karma of the country; they also record how they were mined and handled.

Green tourmalines from Africa, therefore, express the qualities of persistence and endurance, power, and strength. In contrast, similar tourmalines from Brazil radiate a more lively energy; they also impart a feeling of joie de vivre, laughing, and lightness.

A stone also stores its country's negativity. African tourmalines have a fatalistic vibration; the Brazilian tourmalines have a vibration of shallowness. If we need these vibrations to learn a lesson, these characteristics will affect us.

I have cleansed stones possessing a strong aura of hatred. These had absorbed the feelings of miners who had felt unjustly exploited as they struck, extracted, or collected the stones.

One can say that everything constituting the earth is stored within a stone. This is because stones are part of the WHOLE and they know this. They not only share the   33 karma of their country, but also the experience of the entire earth. The information of the earth and all its inhabitants—plants, animals, and people make up this comprehensive knowledge.

We must expand our thinking processes at this point. Meanwhile, science has perceived that everything is *energy* and we are all *one* in this energy. I have worked through an unbelievable number of past lives; the day came when I no longer questioned whether my past life memories were of my own personal experience or a sensitivity to the collective human experience. I have released them and accept the learning process of these memories for myself.

One stone can contain all the information of the earth and humanity within itself—and if it accords with my path, I can learn everything worthwhile from this single stone. It depends on the relationship between the stone and myself.

Although I always recommend a large variety of minerals for people, you should, however, select one stone as a *personal precious stone*. This stone should be a friend and helper, influencing you much more than the others. Such a stone will tune itself completely to your vibrations, which facilitates a better understanding of its message. It stores all your personal information in order to reflect it back when necessary. You can learn from this. It is important not to let others hold this stone. If it completely attunes to you, information from other people disrupts your direction. With the help of this stone, you can select all the other stones with a greater degree of certainty.

Metals

Of course, we can buy gemstones set into rings, pendants, brooches, and other pieces of jewelry. The setting material also affects us. Metal can increase or reduce the effectiveness of a stone. Following are a few examples of the different metals and their influences.

- Copper—flexibility
- Bronze—a cure for aggressiveness
- Gold—the principle of the sun, warmth, and Light
- Platinum—endurance and tenacity
- Silver—wisdom
- Titanium—stamina

When choosing the metal for a setting, ask advice from the stone or listen to your feelings. Do not fall for the mistaken idea that a tiny piece of bronze can change your life. Instead, this is a matter of principles and vibrations. Any great changes through bronze's vibration would take a large piece of bronze worn or kept nearby for years. Before trying this, ask your spiritual helpers whether or not it is worth the effort.

Degrees of Hardness

Gemstones and minerals can occur in forms that range from relatively soft—and therefore not very resistant—to very hard. The diamond is by far the hardest stone. The hardness of a stone naturally has an influence on its effects. The harder a stone is, the more concentrated and focused are its vibrations; this proportionately affects its ability to advance our learning processes. In addition, the hardness of a stone concerns us in case we want to wear it. Never set extremely soft stones into rings; they become unsightly after a short time, or could possibly crack. The hardest stones are best for rings. This is not quite as important for pendants and brooches. We can naturally also have a soft stone set; we expect that its beauty may suffer—but it will continue to have an effect. This is not considered a problem by jewelers who set new stones or polish those that have become marred; it tends to be more a question of cost for us.

The mineralogist Friedrich Mohs compiled the Mohs' (scratch) hardness scale. His system was developed and used before the invention of modern measuring equipment. It differentiates degrees of hardness from 1 to 10. For example, talc has the number 1 and can be scraped off with a fingernail. The list continues with "can be scratched with a copper coin" and "can be scratched easily with a knife." The degrees of hardness between 7 and 10 are of particular significance for us.

Degree of Hardness	Example
10	Diamond
9	Ruby, Sapphire
8.5	Alexandrite, Chrysoberyl
7.5-8	Aquamarine, Emerald, other Beryls
7.5	Uvarovite
7-7.5	Grossularite, Tourmaline
7	Amethyst, Aventurine, Citrine, Rock Crystal

Ring settings might harm any stones beneath the seventh degree of hardness. Also take into consideration that tiny quartz particles float in the air, which means that malachite with a hardness of 3.5—4 and fluorite with 4 can even become dull through exposure to air.

On the other hand, however, nothing prevents us from having soft stones set as rings if we feel a strong need to do so. We should be aware only that soft stones—such as a hauynite, for example—can even crack while being set. Reject certain settings completely; only a jewel smith who has experience with these stones should attempt working with such stones. In Idar-Oberstein, I know of experienced Goldsmiths who perform this type of work. You could also inquire of the local jewelers guild for an expert who lives nearby. Sometimes, I have found rarities such as hauynite set in rings or pendants at mineral exchanges. Precious stone and mineral exhibitions are worth visiting precisely for these types of special finds.

The stone will not survive for long if we wear such a ring in a normal way. We could limit the wear of such sensitive stones to times of sleep and then occasionally, with appropriate caution, during the day.

Additional Characteristics

Other characteristics—such as purity, rarity, brittleness, rivability, and special sensitivity—can be significant for evaluating or wearing gemstones. If you care about gemstones, you should consider these aspects. There are outstanding precious stone and mineral books on the market that can help us in this process.

I always also recommend courses for becoming better acquainted with gemstones. Apart from seminars on the essence of the stones and their effects, there are gemology courses (for example, in Idar-Oberstein, at universities or corresponding institutions). Gemology, naturally, is the science of gemstones.

These seminars consolidate our knowledge about the stones; they give us a feeling for them, and help us to differentiate between them. In addition, such courses always influence our spiritual growth. In such a workshop that I have taken, sheaves of illustrative material were distributed; for two weeks, I felt immersed in the energy of gemstones for many hours a day. The enormity and duration of this experience created enormous growth. I can wholeheartedly recommend such seminars!

Synthetic Gems

Jewel manufacturers are always inventing new ways to simulate gemstones. Man-made versions come in a wide range of quality and price. Their one common factor is that they have nothing to do with gemstones.

Baubles are pretty, fun for children, and obviously fake. These imitations are often made of glass, plastic, or other materials.

Reconstructed stones are created through the joining of mineral wastes (which are often ground into a powder) and artificial bonds (glue, paint, resin, heat, etc.). Coral and turquoise are often imitated through this procedure. Many stores misrepresent them as genuine stones. Their uniformity and molded shapes reveal their composition.

Cubic zirconium and synthetic stones are artificially grown gem crystals. Their chemical composition, their crystalline structure, and their physical characteristics generally conform with true gemstones. Spinels and zircons are often mistaken for this type of crystal, but they are genuine gemstones mined from the earth.

In any case, all these products are artificial. At best, they please the eye and attest to the inventiveness of humanity. They do not possess the spiritual qualities of gemstones. None of these have the ameliorating qualities of living gemstones.

THE ENERGIES AND GROUPINGS
OF GEMSTONES

Gemstones possess different types of vibration fields. One could almost say that they vary in temperament. I have described the gemstones in this book through my knowledge and experience. The energy designation rangesfrom 1 to 3. Some gemstones are beyond this classification. We differentiate between the following vibrations thus:

- 3—very earth-related; almost always show quick effects
- 2—mediators between the worlds
- 1—connected to the highest Light energy

All stones with the energy designation of 3 connect closely with the physical world. To a certain degree, they need direct contact to human beings or work within the earth.

Stones with the energy designation of 2 affect earth and human beings that are nearby. They possess a wider vibration radius than class 3 stones; they also influence the atmosphere of this planet more extensively and will therefore take on greater significance in the future.

The stones with the designation of 1 represent the highest Light energy. They channel the forces of angels and other important entities who work to cleanse the earth and who influence our personal lives very much (even if we put the stones away and do not wear them).

The alacrity of a gemstone's effectiveness has nothing to do with this classification, which only restricts the way we use a stone in subtle ways. This information will have meaning in the future, when the condition of the earth becomes more precarious. People will then recall the possibilities offered by the realm of gemstones. We will request their help for a great cleansing and transformation of this planet's magnetic field.

Not included in this classification are the following gemstones and their symbolic temperaments:

- Sapphire, Emerald, and Ruby—perfection
- Diamond—absolute perfection
- Tanzanite—learning processes beyond perfection
- Paraiba tourmaline—the Angels of Modern Times

The effects of the sapphire, emerald, and ruby concern us universally; these stones represent superior energies. Without the help of other stones, they enable us to master our learning processes on this planet. They contain the characteristics of all other stones together. This does not mean that we should ignore the rest of the stones! Many other stones have a much quicker influence, which takes immediate effect. In contrast, the three stones mentioned above set a remarkable effect into motion. They give rise to a holistic change within us. Although their effect is obvious at the beginning of their use, their actual inducement is often too gradual for us to notice—*we simply grow*—and we seldom give the credit to these stones.

In moments of despair, it is more sensible to reach for a rose quartz, a dravite, or some other stone that can comfort us within a matter of minutes. We should therefore not underestimate any of the simple stones—they are the direct helpers in our lives (in so far as we want help from stones).

However, the more intense our relationship to the Creator—the closer we feel to God—the more significant His holistic helpers (sapphire, emerald, and ruby) will be. It is something you should experience yourself; the learning processes go into the depths.

Finally, the brilliant cut diamond, as the expression of absolute perfection, contains the power and the energy of all stones and can make great changes within us if we accept it as a teacher. If we do not do this, it can present us with dramatic learning processes. It intensifies all the energies within us. If we accept it as a teacher, it will still clearly show us our darkness but will provide comfort and help at the same time. Its method is to dissolve all our inner obstacles as expediently as possible and this can be quite painful at the start. The process becomes easier afterwards and our progress becomes discernible. In addition, it offers us the highest level of protection.

If we do not recognize it as a teacher, it might harden itself; if we resist its effect, many difficulties can result in the life of the person who wears it. Since the diamond intensifies all characteristics, it also intensifies those of hate, jealousy, envy, and more.

You should acquire a brilliant cut diamond with a sense of trust, when you feel drawn to one. You have made an inner agreement that serves your best interests, whether you know it or not. A diamond will give you assignments that you can master with success. It may even whisper to you, "Get an analcime; you need it at the moment." It may advise, "A hessonite necklace would be the quickest help for you right now. Trust."

Tanzanite has a completely different approach. Its purpose is beyond present understanding. In any case, one thing is certain—when human beings have achieved everything possible, the learning process will continue!

Hopefully, we become reconciled to a perpetual learning process; we will no longer feel a false sense of spiritual accomplishment, feeling that we have achieved mastery long before it becomes reality. When we become humble and persistent in our quest for spiritual growth, our paths will seem better and easier. Life—our development—is love, joy, happiness, and *continual learning*. It is an eternal adventure!

God is with us! What more do we want?

Paraiba tourmalines are the first of an entire series of stones that are still being discovered. They call themselves Angels of Modern Times. These stones exist to preserve the planet earth for humanity. They are great helpers. They awaken an appreciation for the earth as a being—a living being. The earth is God's creation that has imposed such a great task on itself in order to evolve.

We fight the earth; we want to conquer it! When will we finally recognize it? When will we grow-up? We should apologize to the earth for the many crimes that we have committed against it. It comes to our attention only through what we call catastrophes; it supports us continually. Does it not give us protection and nourishment? We reply, "No, thank you, we would rather die!"

Gemstones in their infinite wisdom, as direct children of this earth, will help us to survive. They not only will do this, but they also will help us to recognize and realize our birthright—*happiness and joy in harmony with God and this planet.*

Mineralogy categorizes certain gemstones into groups. These minerals have similar chemical compositions; the degree of hardness is also usually the same. These are the corundum, beryl, garnet, quartz families, for most part. In my experience, I have observed that the spiritual characteristics relate to one another within the families of stones; also, the mineralogical similarities correspond with the vibrations. All gemstones encourage us on the path toward holistic love; each individual stone represents a very personal task and message. In addition, specific groups of gemstones share certain mutual factors.

Diamonds provide the clearest and quickest development for the entire personality. They help us to evolve with obvious results, but we may experience great pain in the process.

The corundum group (rubies, sapphires, and padparadscha) applies expression to the principle of holistic love. All of the corundum stones have a special way of encouraging the maturation of love; they also strengthen connection to God. Their absolute straightforwardness may seem severe. We develop very quickly with them.

Stones of the beryl group (aquamarine, bixbyite, emerald, golden beryl, goshenite, heliodor, morganite) exude a gentle energy; at the same time, they guide us to magnificent spiritual progress with the greatest determination. They are very special friends of humanity; they ease the path for us as much as they can.

The spinels personify different tasks. What connects them is a great determination.

Topazes represent Divine Fire. Learning with them always deeply moves our hearts and touches us to our depths. As a result, we change very rapidly.

The beryls, corundums, diamonds, spinels, and topazes are single-minded when it comes to our swift development; everything is dispensable to that purpose. We should definitely connect them with very earthy stones (type 3 energy) when we begin our relationships. Type 3 stones are fast acting; they radiate an energy of trust, comfort, and warmth.

I have devised the name "the great stones" for the gems listed up to this point, as well as for all unusually powerful stones (see THE EMERALD JEWELS, p. 392). To use a metaphor, the great stones represent a sublime angel world whose only occupation is praising God. The other stones are like active, working angels in the foreground and background of the universe. The above group of stones only looks to God; the group mentioned below vibrates more intimately with the material world. We should love, respect, honor, and thank both for their help. They make available to us an unbelievable variety of energies, which aid our evolution.

The stones listed in the following text provide an earthly equilibrium to a certain degree; they offer inspired, immediate aid for all earthly difficulties.

The garnet group connects with the principle of earthly love and its expansion. Its stones always impart strength and confidence. Almandine, andradite, demantoid, gros- 39 sularite, leuco garnet, melanite, pyrope, rhodolite, spessartite, topazolite, tsavolite, and uvarovite are members of this order.

Zircons lead us into an extensive process of purification. This family includes green (low zircon), hyacinth (yellow-red to red-brown/brown), jargon (yellow to colorless), starlight (dyed blue), and violet zircon.

All tourmalines radiate a great deal of lightness and warmth. Their forms include achroite (colorless), dravite (brown), indigolite (blue), rubellite (pink to red), schorl (black), siberite (violet), and verdelite (green). The paraiba tourmaline has a special position.

The spodumene group expresses the principle of giving love. It teaches devotion to humanity. Belonging to it are hiddenite, kunzite, and spodumene.

The entire quartz group is a very earthy team of helpers. It always connects with the earth power within us. It encourages courage and joy in life. This classification includes agate, amethyst, amethyst quartz, ametrine, aventurine, bloodstone, blue quartz, carnelian, cat's eye, chalcedony, chrysocolla, chrysoprase, citrine, falcon's eye, girasol, heliotrope, jasper, moss agate, parrot-wing, petrified wood, praseolite, quartz onyx, rock crystal, rose quartz, sard, sardonyx, smoky quartz, tiger's-eye, and more. We recognize quartz by the formula SiO_2 or $SiO_2 . nH_2O$.

Chloromelanite, jadeite, and nephrite radiate repose and calm. Serpentine possesses a similar vibration, but it is not a true form of jade. As a group, these are usually sold under the name of jade.

An energy of joy and gentleness surrounds the stones from the feldspar group. Amazonite, labradorite, moonstone, orthoclase, spectrolite, and sunstone belong to its phylum.

Most of the other gemstones are designated as independent minerals. They do not belong to a group representing specific characteristics. The harder a stone is, the more intense and resolute is its usual influence on our development, when we permit it to do so.

I am not aware of any outstanding characteristics that can be perceived from chemical compositions. Some time in the future, I am sure that chemists who are committed to their spiritual path and to understanding gemstones will investigate their molecular significance. In homeopathy and the Bach flower remedies, the individual treatments are grouped to show similarities in their effects. Gemstones will be similarly categorized. The classifications will not limit their meaning (for example, "such and such stone is good for coughs"). Instead, their typing will reveal their outstanding principles (for example, "all XY compounds effect a quicker release of the need to suffer because these compounds influence people in such and such manner").

I am Mates, a guardian of the gemstones.
This book has been created for the joy of humanity.

This book is a gift from God
for courageous deeds
and the love of Light that gives everything.
It is a gift for one person,
yet also for all those who seek the path to God.
It was written for those who yearn for Light and Truth and Life
and those destined to feel
the overflowing and all-embracing love of God.

It has also been created
for those who carry doubt and fear in their hearts
so that they may rise
to the plane where only joy and love count.

Finally,
we wanted to give a gift
to those who love gemstones
and see them as children of God.

The world of gemstones greets all people as God's jewels,
and wishes them an ascent into the Light
while reading its messages.
May the people take pleasure in this book.

AGATE

POWER

The agate gives us power and strengthens our faith in life. It grounds us and connects us with the principle of EARTH.

All gemstones and all beings are connected with God Almighty, but the agate completely commits itself to the planet. No other stone on earth works as quickly as the agate to bring us into harmony with the earth. It passes on to us its power, its endurance, and its strength. Its confidence, it is a good example of faith in the life force our planet.

The agate says: "I give myself completely to the earth; the earth loves and supports me. I give myself completely to humanity; I strengthen them. Simultaneously, I am at one with God because God is *All*."

It gives us confidence. Life becomes easier, and time and again we start anew. The agate is a superb stone for the physical plane.

Agate . . . . POWER—CONFIDENCE—FEELING AT HOME
Composition . . . SiO_2
Hardness 7
Color . . . . gray, brown, tinges of red, black to brown layers
Sources . . . . . . formerly in Idar-Oberstein; primarily in Brazil and Uruguay.
Special note: Agates usually come as slices of a geode—known as a formation with a drusy cavity. This is a hollow rock sphere lined with layers of minerals and crystals. These are found in a multitude of patterns and colors. However, lapidaries frequently dye them exotic colors, such as green, blue, or red. Although we can enjoy such pieces, we should have one that has not been dyed.

Energy class 3

ADAMINE

STRENGTH

This stone aims directly at physical existence. It imparts power and strength to us.

When we wear it next to the heart, we can recover quickly from illness. It helps us to process each experience of illness and integrate this as part of the growth process.

It is important for the coming age.

Adamine . . . . . STRENGTH
Composition . . . $Zn_2[OH/AsO_4]$
Hardness 3.5
Color . . . . mostly green, also white, yellow, pink
Sources . . . . . . France, Greece, Chile, Namibia, Mexico

Energy class 2

ALEXANDRITE

THE JOY OF LIVING

Through alexandrite, joy enters the lives of people with too much self-discipline. The alexandrite reminds us of our origin and our purpose in life—CHEER.

It gives hope to those who despair about life. It strengthens them and constantly reminds them of the Light. It proves that life is not as it seems to be—by changing its color under certain circumstances. It smiles. It is one with God. This is what it radiates—as inconspicuous as it seems.

Alexandrite . . . . HOPE AND CHEERFULNESS
Composition . . . $BeAl_2O_4$
Hardness 8.5
Color . . . . green in daylight, red in artificial light
Sources . . . . . . Ural Mountains, Sri Lanka, Rhodesia, Brazil

Special note: A good alexandrite can be one of the most costly gemstones in the world. Stones for about $130 are very small and inconspicuous in the way they change colors; however, these are adequate for our purposes. Brilliant cut stones are rarely sold these days.

Energy class 1

46

AMAZONITE

FRESHNESS—RELIEF—BREATHING FREELY

The amazonite is a powerful stone for the physical body. It heals pain and infections, but it will refuse to heal whenever this is not appropriate to someone's karma.

The amazonite is very important for modern times, because we are still discovering new goals for ourselves.

Amazonite . . . . REFRESHMENT
Composition . . . $K[AlSi_3O_8]$
Hardness . . . . . 6—6.5
Color . . . . green, blue-green, turquoise
Sources . . . . . . Russia, United States, southwestern Africa, Madagascar, Brazil

Energy class 2

AMETHYST

WISDOM

Amethyst gives rise to belief in the realities of life.

It is a stone of faith. The amethyst clarifies our abilities to visualize and imagine. It enhances our understanding of God.

This stone brings us closer to GOD; we intuitively comprehend who or what God is. Our faith grows stronger when we subconsciously understand the Divine Energy. This is not a simple precious stone. All who open up to it will constantly evolve their sense of responsibility. To obey God means to accept full responsibility for ourselves, our lives, and our actions. This also includes feeling responsible for other people and for the world. Following the inner voice always leads to the solution. Walking the optimal path also uplifts the entire universe. This is not always a path that the ego—the desire nature— would like to follow. Listening to the world is hazardous business. The true wishes and needs (of the world and its inhabitants) require us to make personal sacrifices. The main risk—following the *inner* path—is the best solution for *all*.

The austerely beautiful amethyst challenges our ability and willingness to believe. Only the blue sapphire surpasses its solidity and intensity.

This is a good stone for the physical level.

Amethyst . . . . . PATH TO GOD
Composition . . . SiO_2
Hardness 7
Color . . . . light to dark violet
Sources . . . . . . Brazil, Uruguay, Madagascar

Special note: Some minerals grow crystals inside rock formations called drusy cavities or geodes. In these cases, liquids have collected inside hollow stones; these liquids crystallize. The amethyst is a well-known representative of this occurrence. Amethysts that have experienced extreme heat tend to change color. This is how the yellow citrine, green praseolite, and colorless rock crystal come to being.

The amethyst has a reputation for relieving headaches and healing migraines. This is a generalization. Its influence can ease certain types of headaches. However, this only happens when we give up the inner strife that causes most types of headaches. Such conflict can end under the influence of many different precious stone vibrations.

For example, the amethyst can heal alcoholism, but only if we inwardly understand the fears that cause us to drink; we also must feel eager to make a new life. I find it too dogmatic to maintain that it heals alcoholism, which is its frequent recommendation. This is a wonderful stone for the heart center.

Energy class 1

AMETHYST QUARTZ

SETTING PRIORITIES

The amethyst quartz is a very practical stone. It helps us to set priorities. It knows what is good for us and brings this to our attention.

In power and spiritual ability, it has completely devoted itself to this single task; it would like to help humans use their energies in a more meaningful manner. We waste time, knowledge and abilities, we WASTE ourselves. The stones feel deep sorrow when they observe this. The amethyst quartz has taken over the assignment of reminding us of the essential things so that we can do these essential things in everyday life. This gives us repose and relief and sets energies free for new tasks.

Amethyst quartz . PRIORITIES
Composition . . . SiO_2
Hardness 7
Color . . . . violet with white
Sources . . . . . . Brazil, Madagascar, southwestern Africa, United States

Energy class 2

AMETRINE

FREEDOM—STRIVING FOR PERFECTION

The further we evolve, the simpler we become. This stone has a message for us.

"Connect yourself! Enter into relationships that are ordained by God. Do not depend on your intellect or your desires. Examine your heart; ask what God has waiting for you. There is no greater grace than being able to live in accord with God's will. Do not let yourselves be influenced by those who want to activate your desires. Assume that you can fulfill all your undertakings; you can. Is your choice good for you? God sees farther than you can. Present your desires to Him; ask for His blessing; then ask Him to act for you according to HIS will."

We are most free when we consciously and completely subject our will to God. The ametrine helps us to perceive this. It awakens knowledge about power and the importance of not using it. It teaches peace and understanding for love. It contains the sun and the moon, eros and agape (devotion and affection), and our striving for God. When we wear ametrine, we fulfill a commandment of perception: Love is nothing other than the purity of the heart. Love is the blossom of perfection. It illuminates the heart and shows us vibrations beyond it.
This is a stone for the enlightened.

Ametrine . . . . . ENLIGHTENMENT
Composition . . . SiO_2
Hardness 7
Color . . . . bicolored violet to yellow (half amethyst-half citrine)
Sources . . . . . . Brazil, Bolivia

Energy class 1

A N A L C I M E (Analcite)

FIRE AND TENDERNESS

The analcime is a tenacious, very durable stone. It gives these qualities to human beings. At the same time, it fills us with love for ourselves.

It is a stone of the modern age. When we are despondent, it helps us to move forward and fulfill our tasks. It says, "You can do it. See it through. It is simpler than you think. Trust in your abilities. Connect yourself with God. Love yourself. Everything will go well."

When we use the stone, these sentences are our driving force. The more frequently we use it, the simpler life will become.

Analcime . . . . . FIRE AND TENDERNESS
Composition . . . $Na_2[Al2Si_4O_{12}]\cdot2H_2O$
Hardness 5.5
Color . . . . pale pink, occasional cat's-eye effect, tinges of white or yellow
Sources . . . . . . Harz mountains in Germany, Sicily, South Tyrol, Bohemia, recently in South Africa (with some specimens of the cat's-eye effect)

Energy class 2

ANDALUSITE

FIGHTING FOR PATHWAYS

The person who feels attracted to this stone is a fighter. The wonderful quality of the andalusite is to intensify the desire to combat. This stimulation is so intense that the battler ultimately feels so ill at ease that he or she *must* give thought to the sense of fighting.

Those who give thought to this compulsion will always be able to perceive that conflict is destructive; it invariably reflects on ourselves. We are never born to fight, as we have so often believed. Perhaps we should become familiar with fighting in one incarnation; through such aggressive experiences, we become wise, and we give it up. Our path is the path of love. This ultimately excludes every struggle.

With the andalusite, we perceive that we live contrary to our own nature when we persist in fighting.

Andalusite . . . SENSING OBSTINACY AND STRUGGLE
Composition . . Al[AlSiO$_5$]
Hardness 7.5
Color . . . . . brownish, greenish
Sources . . . . . Brazil, Sri Lanka, Canada, Spain, Ural Mountains, United States

Energy class 3

ANDRADITE (Garnet)

ENDURING STRENGTH—THE FIRE OF LOVE

We gain life anew with this stone. Although it has an inconspicuous appearance, it possesses an enormous power that never depletes itself. It is as if it wants to urge us forward into the Light. It seems to say, "Hurry! I am impatient to see what becomes of your development. Here, use me so that you can grow more quickly!"

In its unconditional love for our path, andradite is an example of true brotherly love. Its selflessness can deeply move us. Great things and changes can develop under its influence. We should place our trust in its example.

Andradite . . . . . ONWARD!
Composition . . . $Ca_3Fe_2^{3+}[SiO_4]_3$
Hardness . . . . . 6.5—7
Color . . . . yellow-green, brown to black
Sources . . . . . . Cechy, Sweden, Russia, United States, Mexico

Energy class 1

APATITE

CENTERING WITHIN OURSELVES

The apatite leads us directly to our inner centers. It provides stillness when we have overextended ourselves; it reveals the ways that we harm ourselves through hectic living.

The energy of the apatite is an important element for healing. In the stillness, we perceive causes and understand correlations. We comprehend how we can heal ourselves and *how we should change our lives.*

This is a stone for courageous people who want to move forward, who have hesitated too long and who are willing to take a big step in life. Apatite is a stone of upheaval. We evoke it by listening within ourselves. Whenever we find the inner center, we will clearly hear the inner voice. Having heard its important message, we would be wise to follow it.

Apatite . . . . . CENTEREDNESS
Composition . . usually $Ca_5[F/(PO_4)_3]$ or $Ca_5[OH/(PO_4)_3]$
Hardness 5
Color . . . . . . colorless, yellow, green, blue, violet
Sources . . . . . Brazil, Madagascar, Burma, India, Kenya, United States, Sri Lanka

Special note: Apatite can appear inconspicuous or display the most magnificent colors. Apatite means deceiver in the Greek language, because one can easily mistake it for other stones such as the beryl or tourmaline. Now and then, apatites are misrepresented as the rare and expensive paraiba tourmaline. Be careful! Necklaces of apatite, previously considered to be almost impossible to cut, have recently become available.

Energy class 1

APPLE CORAL

LIGHTNESS—JOY—CAPRICIOUSNESS

The apple coral brings color into our vibration field. At times it is appropriate for people who take life very seriously. The energy of lightness and joy accompanies a certain flightiness—even moodiness. If you do not know what capriciousness is, you can experience it here in this energy.

People normally light in disposition should avoid this coral. For all others, it can be a teacher and friend at certain times in life. This is a vibration that we should not carry to extremes.

Apple coral . . . . CAPRICIOUSNESS
Composition . . . $Ca[CO_3]$
Hardness 3.5
Color . . . . reminiscent of ripe apples—red with tinges of yellow and brown
Sources . . . . . . Pacific coral reefs

Energy class 3

APOPHYLLITE

JOY FOR OUR HEART

This is a stone that heals the wounds of perception. This is how it introduced itself to my patients and this is how it affected them. It is closely associated with truth; it helps us to perceive it. It also gives comfort at the same time. Truth is only painful when the ego wants to remain ignorant and when the ego is too strong. We can only lose our illusions, not ourselves. Apophyllite relates us to ourselves, since the Divine Essence lies beneath all truth. Truth in itself is liberating and it is our only chance for happiness. What we fear is actually not the truth; we fear the loss of illusions. When people feel ready to give up their illusions, they will always find their truth—their power.

The exact effect of the apophyllite also depends somewhat on its intensity of color.

Apophyllite . . . . CONFIDENCE
Composition . . . usually $KCa_4[(F,OH)/(Si_4O_{10})_2]\cdot 8H_2O$
Hardness . . . . . 4.5—5
Color . . . . colorless with tinges of red, yellow, green, or blue; white
Sources . . . . . . Brazil, India, Europe, United States, Mexico

Energy class 3

A Q U A M A R I N E (Beryl)

VASTNESS—IMMERSED INTO DEPTH

In the aquamarine we have a friend beside us; in a completely selfless manner, it wants the best for us. It examines our path in life in an extraordinary way.

"Human being," it would say, "love with your entire strength; listen to the heavenly choirs; understand that God surrounds you and accompanies you for your entire life. From whenever you come to wherever you go—only God is always at your side. Trust in your judgment; listen to God's loving advice; devote yourself completely to Him. Understand that you are a human being and yet still wholly divine. Show yourself worthy of God." The aquamarine is truly among the great stones; these have a special assignment with human beings. It energetically supports growth; it does this in such a light and empathic manner that we feel deeply touched. We open our hearts very quickly to this precious stone and it can therefore work within our depths. Its vivacity and cheerful aura can sometimes mislead us about its intended purpose: to smooth the path into the Light for human beings and lead them through deep learning processes into liberation—through pain to joy.

As a great friend of mankind, the aquamarine incessantly radiates a vibration of trust—reliance in the Infinite Wisdom of God, in the Almighty Love. It lets us understand that life on earth is a joy. The aquamarine in its loving goodness embraces us, rocks us, smiles, and promises: "I am with you. I guard your growth. Trust me, and I will be able to achieve everything for you."

Aquamarine. . . . CHEERFULNESS AND DEPTH
Composition . . . $Be_3Al_2[Si_6O_{18}]$
Hardness . . . . . 7.5—8
Color . . . . light-blue, blue
Sources . . . . . . Brazil, Madagascar, and worldwide

Special note: Aquamarines should possess the color of the sea—at best blue. Green toned stones should be classified as beryls instead. If they show a lovely light-green, they may even be emeralds. Aquamarines are heated in order to deepen their color. I prefer a lovely, natural blue.

Energy class 1

ARAGONITE

THE ABILITY TO TRANSFORM

The aragonite is versatile. On the one hand, it accelerates the learning process. On the other hand, it reminds us that we should not yet break away from our inner bonds, because the time is not yet ripe. Then it admonishes us to action; yet, it still radiates repose. Aragonite is a very solemn stone; however, a giggle may overcome us when we listen to its message. It does not take itself very seriously and imparts this feeling to us as well.

Aragonite is a strong healing stone that we often underestimate.

Aragonite . . . . . TRANSFORMATION
Composition . . . $Ca[CO_3]$
Hardness . . . . . 3.5—4
Color . . . . various colors
Sources . . . . . . Aragón in Spain, Morocco

Special note: Aragonite stones can differ greatly in appearance. Some stones have wonderful crystalline structures. Others have been broken out of large layers and appear striped. Most necklaces are made from the latter type.

Energy class 3

GREEN AVENTURINE (Quartz)

GLADNESS

The aventurine gives us gladness and success. Why? It connects us to our purpose in life and helps us feel certain that we can fulfill it—if we want to do so. We are only content when we live in harmony with our vocation.

The aventurine is a very determined stone; it leads us to our calling, although we are not always aware of this while working with the stone. It is responsible for the conscious or subconscious perception "I can do it." This is exactly what makes us so happy with the stone. From this energy, we will also become successful.

This is an important stone for physical healing!

Green Aventurine . . GLADNESS AND SUCCESS
Composition . . . . SiO_2
Hardness 7
Color . . . . pale-green to dark-green, a little iridescent
Sources . . . . India, Brazil, Russia

Energy class 3

ORANGE AVENTURINE (Quartz)

RELEASE FROM AMBITION

This aventurine directly influences Inner Knowledge about personal success. We all have times of abundance in our life plans. Whether or not we arrange our lives to experience them is another matter. In any case, this stone helps us to remember our opportunities for success. Furthermore, it gives us the power to thrive; it awakens the desire to live with this victory as well. Afterward, we may require other gemstones to discover what we can achieve, which characteristics we must still develop for this prosperity, and what virtues we need to experience. The orange-colored aventurine gives the impulse and the additional stones help us in the realization.

Orange Aventurine . . . SUCCESS
Composition . . . . . . SiO_2
Hardness 7
Color . . . . golden-brown, orange, slightly iridescent
Sources . . . . Brazil

Energy class 3

AZURITE

HIGHEST PERCEPTION—JOY IN LIVING

The azurite has the rare quality of *complete knowledge*. In this capacity, it helps us attain certain insights into issues that are important for us. Though we may only have partial insight, these perceptions can completely transform us. We are not mature enough for absolute knowledge; however, we can work through certain aspects of it. In its wisdom, the azurite selects the areas that can give us enlightenment; it determines the degree of our ability; sincerely working through these partial aspects, it supports us.

The azurite is connected with the highest wisdom. It should be one of the first stones we choose for ourselves when we are serious about development. It is a gentle teacher, an all-knowing teacher. Yet it will confront us with clear sagacity. At the same time, however, it also teaches that acuteness is our sole opportunity to develop ourselves.

Gently, it makes it plain that we must not lag in our development. Azurite urges us to dive quickly into our *depths*; it teaches us not to hurry along the surface of consciousness. One single moment of depth can give us more perception than one hundred years of shallow life.

Azurite is an important healing stone for modern times.

Azurite . . . . . . HIGHEST PERCEPTION

Composition . . . $Cu_3[OH/CO_3]_2$

Hardness . . . . . 3.5—4

Color . . . . deep blue

Sources . . . . . . Russia, southwestern Africa, United States

Special note: Azurite is very soft. For this reason, pieces of jewelry may become un-sightly in a short time. Necklaces become dull when worn on the skin. I recommend handstones, slices on leather bands, and simple pendants. However, those who love this stone very much can even acquire faceted collectors' pieces.

Energy class 3

AZURITE-MALACHITE

SOLIDARITY

This stone teaches the *meaning* of relationships. It gives us a feeling for working together, for understanding for each other and for friendship among kindred souls. In
addition, a vibration of peace and growth surrounds it. It teaches equality on the basis
of growth, joy on the basis of love, and understanding on the basis of God's unity.

This is a stone for both initiates and beginners. It is also for those who are pugnacious or
disquiet; it gives them the power to be humble.

It naturally also contains the qualities of the azurite and the malachite.

Azurite-malachite . . . SCHOOL
Composition . . . . . Combination of azurite and malachite
Hardness . . . . 3.5—4
Color . . . . mostly blue and green
Sources . . . . California

Energy class 2

BARITE

STRENGTH FROM THE HEART

Barite is a good stone for beginners. It strengthens communication with the heart and therefore with the inner voice. When we wear it for an appropriate period of time, we will better understand what our Inner Knowledge would like to tell us.

Messages from the heart always allow us to think and act holistically. We then feel connected to an inexhaustible source of strength, inexhaustible Light. We feel the heart as our true home. We gain *power* from it.

Barite . . . . . . FAITH IN HAPPINESS
Composition . . . Ba[SO$_4$]
Hardness . . . . . 3—3.5
Color . . . . . . white, gray, black, yellow, brown, pink, tinges of blue or green
Sources . . . . . Germany, England, Czech Republic, United States

Energy class 2

TREE-OPAL

HARMONY WITH NATURE

This stone is the protector of trees. It plants love in our hearts and understanding for symbiosis. Without the plant kingdom, we could not live; we forget this time and again. Whoever works with this opal will find out that life is easier when we open up to other worlds. The plant kingdom, the animal kingdom, the minerals, wind, water—all of nature wants to work together with us. We are part of a *whole*. Everything is one creation. We are so intertwined that we cannot exist if we neglect any part of the whole too much. Our karma with Creation is enormous. The tree-opal shows each person ways to compensate for this karma.

Tree-opal . . . . . ENJOYING NATURE
Composition . . . $SiO_2 \cdot nH_2O$
Hardness 6
Color . . . . tones of brown, beige, red, and yellow with a directional grain
Sources . . . . . . Bohemia; Arizona, United States

Energy class 2

ROCK CRYSTAL

LOVE OF LIFE—CLARITY OF FEELINGS—RESURRECTION

The rock crystal's task is to redeem mankind. It liberates us from compulsions, false love, and rage; its aura incinerates these feelings. Through its clarity, we can precisely recognize ourselves. We learn trust and sense help from the stone kingdom.

Rock crystals can be our best friends—and they want to be! A rock crystal educates tremendously! It is an example for us in the principle of GIVING.

Those who love it will bring clarity into their life and their feelings. The perception of what we really are is then close at hand.

Rock crystals have a special talent; they can reflect the vibrations of other precious stones, even though faintly. They can decide when we need other vibrations than those of the rock crystal; it then refracts these vibrations to us. This is what makes them effective.

Rock crystal . . . . CLARITY—HELP FOR MANKIND
Composition . . . SiO_2
Hardness 7
Color . . . . clear, colorless to white
Sources . . . . . . worldwide

Special note: Some rock crystals are also irradiated, dyed, or changed in some other manner. Here I am speaking of untreated rock crystals, as transparent as possible, raw or cut.

Energy class 1

AMBER

GREAT HEALER! IMPORTANT FOR THE FUTURE

Amber is the blood of the tree, its vital sap. The strength of its tree then transmits to us when we use the stone. Understanding amber means understanding the tree world and that is why this stone will once again become important. Our love of amber is good for the plant world.

Amber intensifies our love for the plant and sun world. It enforces our physical processes and cleanses our bodies. It expands the sun and life potential within us and gives us peace. It symbolizes time and teaches us that time is not significant.

Amber loves us. It suffers endlessly in its own way when we are careless toward nature. It is the guardian of several plant worlds; what we do to nature, we do to the amber as well. To honor it also means to pay homage to nature. The amber would like to teach us. It helps us to understand better the associations between the human world and the plant world.

Amber . . . . NATURE
Composition . . . Amorphous, fossilized tree sap
Hardness . . . . . 2—2.5
Color . . . . light-yellow to golden-yellow to brown, sometimes tinges of white, seldom other colors
Sources . . . . . . Samland coast near Königsberg in Poland, the Baltic Sea, Romania, Sicily, Burma

Special note: Be wary of pressed amber (reconstituted from remnants) and imitations. These require a practiced eye to discern. Inquire and compare between different amber specimens.

Energy class 2

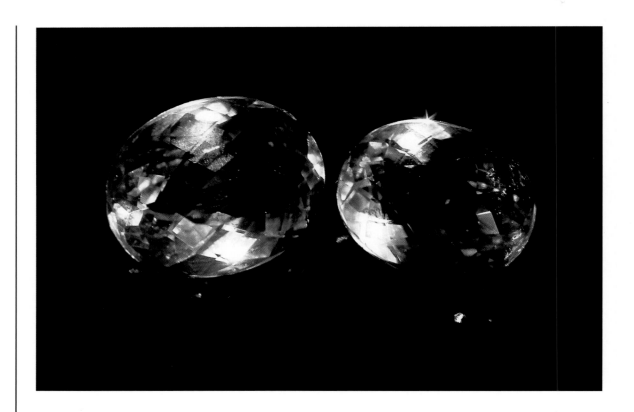

COLORLESS BERYL (GOSHEN)

DEVOTION—SERENITY

"I give this stone to you in memory of Me. Immerse yourself in what is eternal. Merge into Me."

God smiles. Truth is eternal. Love is eternal.

"Find your way to Me. Believe in Me. Trust your heart."

God smiles. His love lies in Absolute Simplicity. The colorless beryl is a symbol of it.

Colorless Beryl . . GOD
Composition . . . $Be_3Al_2[Si_6O_{18}]$
Hardness . . . . . 7.5—8
Color . . . . colorless
Sources . . . . . Brazil, Africa, United States

Energy class 1

B I X B Y I T E (Beryl)

YEARNING AND REDEMPTION

Yearning for love is natural. We all strive for love—to realize love. If our yearning is too strong, we become obsessed and neglect the rest of life. Then we are on the wrong path.

Bixbyite shows where we have gone astray. It reveals our neglect of ourselves through misusing love. It helps us to clarify and understand love. Above all, it heals the excessive yearning for love, which drains away energy for everything else.

Bixbyite . . . . . . LIBERATION
Composition . . . $Be_3Al_2[Si_6O_{18}]$
Hardness . . . . . 7.5—8
Color . . . . strong red to pink
Sources . . . . . . Utah, United States

Special note: A miner named Bixby discovered Bixbyite. Thus comes its name, which has tended to change to a shortened version—Bixbite. It can only be found in the Wasatch Mountains in Utah.

Energy class 1

BLUE QUARTZ

ACKNOWLEDGING OUR FEELINGS

Blue quartz provides another reminder of the laws of life. Its vibrations are very earthy, very close to nature, and yet very profound.

It clarifies the comprehension of life's laws. Life cannot function without rules; we must adhere to them in order to survive. The vastness of the universe, order, interconnection, love, power, and wisdom touch us and enter consciousness; through this *knowledge*, we understand what is truly necessary. In the vibrations of blue quartz, we accept that rules are necessary for survival. At the same time, we question our habitual necessities and receive the power to release all that is superfluous. We can easily overlook this stone by mistake.

Blue quartz . . . . DISCIPLINE AND PERCEPTION
Composition . . . SiO_2
Hardness 7
Color . . . . blue
Sources . . . . . . Virginia, United States

Energy class 3

BOULDER-OPAL

PATH TO ETERNAL LIFE

The boulder-opal is very close to the earth. It possesses all the qualities of the precious opal, yet connects us at the same time with a very direct earth energy. In its cheerful manner, it allows changes to appear more simple than we can imagine. It comforts and encourages us and is like the all-embracing goodness in a somewhat gruff manner. It means well and loves us—and still pushes us benevolently into life. In doing so, it is more direct than the precious opal—heartier in a way. A change occurs in us when we cherish an opal. We become certain of the existence of eternal energies; we connect to them forever.

Cradled in eternal love and in eternal joy, we finally perceive growth to be what it really is—JOY.

Opals have suffered from the reputation of being unlucky stones. Of course they are not. *All* stones trigger learning processes within us with varied intensity—the opal included. Resisting growth can bring us misfortune. Since the opal clearly encourages change, it will attack any resistance. When we pursue evolvement, life does not need to remind us through heavy lessons. Misfortune is only an attempt to wake us up.

If I improve voluntarily, I spare myself from most misfortune.

All opalescent stones are good meditation stones. The gentle to flaming play of their colors range from is reminiscent of life in its complete diversity and beauty. Immersion brings perception. Perception brings peace.

Boulder-opal . . . GROWTH IS JOY
Composition . . . $SiO_2 \cdot nH_2O$
Hardness . . . . . 5.5—6.5
Color . . . . opalescent layer on brown to gray matrix
Sources . . . . . . Brazil, Australia

Special note: Boulder-opals always consist of a thin layer of opal on parent rock. Rock and opal are cut together.

Energy class 3

BRAZILIANITE

PATH TO GOD

A stone to touch—it comforts us.
It says, "Trust in your life. Trust yourself. All difficulties can be mastered if you trust."

The brazilianite refreshes our subconscious *memory* of the time before we incarnated into this physical lifetime. The more clearly we remember our existence *before* physical life, the more contented we can feel while mastering our path. We live can live completely in the moment, and still feel the security of our origin and our goal.

Wear brazilianite for only limited periods of time. Otherwise, we might neglect our responsibilities because we are yearning too much to return to the Higher Worlds. Wherever we come from and wherever we go, the most important time for us is NOW. If we neglect our responsibilities at hand, then we neglect ourselves and our task. We forsake the promise that we have given God.

Brazilianite . . . PATH TO GOD
Composition . . $NaAl_3[(OH)_2/PO_4]_2$
Hardness 5.5
Color . . . . . . pale to strong yellow-green
Sources . . . . . Brazil, United States

Energy class 1

BORNITE

RISK OF LIFE

The bornite reminds us of the risks in everyday life. It helps us overcome the tensions when we are afraid of something new. It says: "Trust life! Try! Take a risk! Everything has a purpose. What you are doing here has its likeness on the spiritual level. Everything you risk remains preserved. Trust in life, TRUST!"

This stone gives despondent people the power to master their lives. It is a great healer on the physical level, since despondency is the basis of many diseases.

Bornite. . . . . . . SURPRISE
Composition . . . Cu_5FeS_4
Hardness 3
Color . . . . between bronze-yellow and copper-red in a fresh fracture, variegated when polished
Sources . . . . . . Germany, United States, Namibia, Peru

Energy class 3

CALCITE

HELP FOR EVERYDAY LIFE

Calcite increases our awareness and empathy. It encourages us to accomplish our goals and find the ways and means of achieving them. It opens our hearts to the troubles and suffering of other people.

The calcite is available in many colors. As a result, its effect expands even more. (See THE CHARACTERISTICS OF GEMSTONES: Colors)

Calcite . . . . SUPPORT
Composition . . . $Ca[CO_3]$
Hardness 3
Color . . . . white, gray, yellow, pink, brown, green, black, tinges of blue
Sources . . . . . . Germany, Romania, Namibia, Mexico

Energy class 2

CASSITERITE

DESIRE FOR GREATNESS

Cassiterite awakens the DESIRE for greatness—for perfection!

The time will come when cassiterite's task is complete; we will want to attain our greatness; we will require other stones and other methods. Sometimes we hesitate, regress, and waste energy. Then we can reach for cassiterite again. After a few days, we are ready to change our ways and make a new attempt.

It is good for all types of addictions.

Cassiterite . . . . . DESIRE FOR GREATNESS
Composition . . . SnO_2
Hardness . . . . . 6—7
Color . . . . brown, colorless
Sources . . . . . . many places

Energy class 2

CHALCEDONY

TRANQUILITY TOUCHES ME

The chalcedony gives us the connection to our Divine Self. It does no more and no less.

For this *reason*, it is often said that it reminds us of the sky. It calms us; it gives us composure; it gives us rest. It leads to intimacy with the Divine Self and every advantage that comes with it. This can open the way for a multitude of blessings.

Chalcedony . . . . QUIETUDE
Composition . . . SiO_2
Hardness 7
Color . . . . light-blue with white stripes or gray-blue
Sources . . . . . . Turkey, South Africa, Australia

Energy class 3

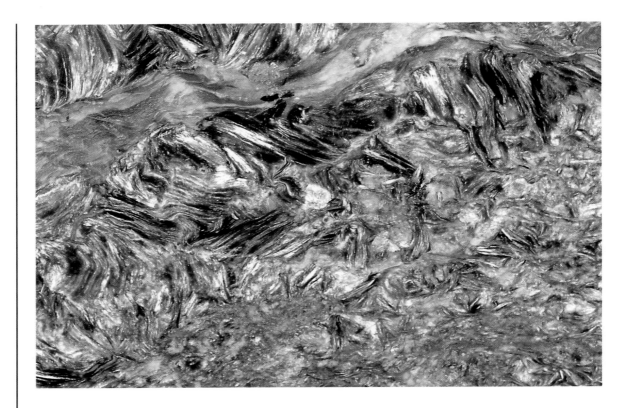

CHAROITE

MERCURIAL AND EGOCENTRIC

Charoite emphasizes these characteristics within us. In a certain sense, it holds a mirror before us to expose these faults. Eventually, we will recognize that these obstruct our progress, and we will need to change.

Charoite is a friend. We should not spend too much time with it; we should simply feel grateful for its assistance.

Charoite . . . . . . EGOISM
Composition . . . $K(Ca,Na)_2[Si_4O_{10}(OH,F)] \cdot H_2O$
Hardness . . . . . 5.5—6
Color . . . . violet with white and black
Sources . . . . . . Charo River in Russia

Special note: Together with pyroxenes, feldspar, and titanium silicate, the charoite forms an interesting rock with a fibrous appearance. Its violet color is mottled. In contrast to sugilite, it makes a restless impression. We could mistake some pieces for sugilite, which has a similar color.

Energy class 3

CHITA

GUARDIAN OF THE WORLDS

As similar as some stones may be in terms of mineral composition, each of them has a very special task.
This stone comes to us with its special message.

I know the guardians of the worlds,
and I say to you that you have not recognized them!
You see them everyday, and you yet do not recognize them!

The Guardian of Mankind is an emerald; it is also the Guardian of Hope.
The Guardian of the Animal World is a ruby; it is the Guardian of All Life.
The Guardian of the Plants is the sapphire; it is the Guardian of All Faith.
The Guardian of the Light is the cut diamond; it is the Guardian of All Splendor.
The Guardian of the Gemstones is the tanzanite; it guards all the treasure of this world.

Go within, and spend the next life to recognize this truth.

Chita. . . . . GUARDIAN OF THE WORLDS
Composition . . . Serpentine with chromite
Hardness . . . . . 3—4
Color . . . . yellow-green serpentine with black, speckled inclusions
Source . . . . United States

Energy class 1

CHLOROMELANITE

REJOICING—HOPE FOR PEACE

This stone gives us a special gift. We feel hope that we will find accomplishment. Chloromelanite gives us insight into the life graph that we planned before we were born.

What a relief! We can end our searching and our agonized mistakes! We feel God guiding us. We feel certain fulfillment according to God's wisdom and in keeping with our choices. We feel permission to focus strength to our live. We no longer have to squander CHI in a consuming search. Repose fills us. We sense peace. The understanding is still new; this has just now reached our hearts. It will take time for the results to become visible in our life, until we really feel them.

The chloromelanite promises us peace. Peace emerges very gradually.

Chloromelanite . . CERTAIN PEACE
Composition . . . A variety of jadeite
Hardness . . . . . 6.5—7
Color . . . . grass-green with little black dots and inclusions
Sources . . . . . . Burma

Energy class 3

CHROMDIOPSIDE

RESPITE FOR TORMENTED HEARTS

The chromdiopside has a very specific effect. It soothes the longing for love.

To wear it means that I no longer have to pine away for love; I can wait. I understand that God gives me everything I need. God gives me richness. When the right time in my life for a partner arrives, then I will meet this person; it is inevitable. This is a law.

The chromdiopside, which has a very specific influence on partnership related love, imparts the confidence to wait for this love. The strength will come to use our time wisely until then, and the knowledge that we are so much more than the wish for a happy love relationship.

The chromdiopside reveals itself to very few people. Be alert for it.

Chromdiopside . . — ! —
Composition . . . $CaMg(Si_2O_6)$ + chromium
Hardness . . . . . 5—6
Color . . . . dark-green
Sources . . . . . Finland, Russia

Energy class 1

CHRYSOBERYL

KEENNESS—CLARITY—DETERMINATION

The chrysoberyl is inconspicuous to many people, but it commands immense powers. It is appropriate for important life decisions. Although we can gain clarity through other gemstones, it fascinates through a keenness of perception that is absolutely astonishing. At the same time, it gives us the strength to master the solution without compromises, when this is necessary. It gives us a certainty for our decision that takes away the negative aspects of integrity and—seen with love—shows it for what it really is: the consistent willingness to walk the path that is right for us.

Good for the physical level. Strong healing stone.

Chrysoberyl . . . . KEENNESS—DETERMINATION
Composition . . . $BeAl_2O_4$
Hardness 8.5
Color . . . . green-yellow, golden-yellow, dark-olive, brown or brown-red tinges
Sources . . . . . . Brazil, Sri Lanka, Burma, Madagascar, Rhodesia, Russia

Energy class 1

THE CAT'S-EYE OCCURRENCE IN GEMSTONES

The cat's-eye teaches differentiation. Whoever is fascinated by these stones seeks the truth. We delight in this occurrence and are thankful for the help.

Some chrysoberyls display a cat's-eye effect. This occurs through microscopic, hollow channels that run through the stone. These refract light through the clear stone and create an interference pattern of light rays.

Other stones can also display this effect. However, it is typical for certain types of chrysoberyl. These types are only found in Sri Lanka and Brazil. When one mentions cat's-eyes to lapidaries, the chrysoberyl is always implied. Other types of cat's-eyes bear the name of the genus stone in front of the term.

CHRYSOCOLLA

RECOGNIZING OUR INNER LAWS

The chrysocolla educates us about order. It connects us with the principles of nature and the laws of life from the perspective of the nature spirits.

We cannot disregard the laws of life without expecting punishment; these laws are always in effect. They act on us, whether or not we are familiar with them. For example, the law of gravity acts on us, even though we are not always thinking about it. We can survive if we ignore spiritual laws, which are much more extensive. When we have no harmony with nature and the nature spirits, we cannot feel happy. We lose a large part of ourselves. The onus is on us to reintegrate. The chrysocolla reminds us of this.

Chrysocolla . . . . ORDER—NATURE
Composition . . . $(Cu,Al)_2H_2[(OH_4/Si_2O_5]nH_2O$
Hardness . . . . . 2—4
Color . . . . green-blue speckled
Sources . . . . . . United States, Peru, Chile, Russia, Zaire

Special note: A chrysocolla stone can crumble very easily. Its place of origin determines whether it will crumble or remain in one piece. Avoid artificially hardened pieces. Chrysocolla is opaque. In Arizona, however, it has been found in a transparent and almost sky-blue form. It also manifests together with chalcedony, malachite, and copper oxide.

Energy class 3

CHRYSOPAL

JOY—EASE—INNOCENCE

The chrysopal brings joy to life; its energy is a light one. It teaches us that nothing is as difficult as it seems. This particularly applies when the stone is almost transparent, when the sensation of lightness is even more evident.

Its blue-green variegation with characteristic inclusions is reminiscent of a wonderful seascape. However, this sea would be from the distant past as the source of life for us all. It would be clear, healthy, and alive—teeming with fish, countless organisms, plants, the ruler of the seas, and all his water beings. We are meant to be friends with the water beings; we are meant to learn from each other. Instead, we have driven them away.

We carry the image of Paradise within our hearts. We would like to recreate it on earth; we have a constant desire for this. This is a continuously bleeding wound; all of us repress it in our subconscious minds. The chrysopal heals this. "It is possible to change one's ways!" This is its is message. "Start forming a bond with the sea and all the invisible beings NOW."

Someday we will be able to accept the invisible beings, and ask them for help. We can still save this earth in time; we should attempt it, despite all foreboding. At Findhorn, human beings and spiritual helpers have harmoniously worked together. This book is also evidence of it. The chrysopal is particularly appropriate for us who long for this working relationship. It gives us lightness and hope. It reassures us that it is not too late for change, and it gives us back a bit of innocence.

Chrysopal . . . . . SPONTANEITY—JOY—CHANGE
Composition . . . $SiO_2 \cdot nH_2O$
Hardness . . . . . 5.5—6
Color . . . . green to blue-green, light-blue, turquoise
Source . . . . . . Peru

Special note: This is a very beautiful opal that does not opalesce. It shows itself in green, blue, and turquoise sea colors. It is sometimes even somewhat transparent and with inclusions of other colors. It is still rather unknown among rock hounds. Do not let yourself be discouraged! It is worth the search.

Energy class 2—3

CHRYSOPRASE

I REST IN MYSELF

This is a stone pleasing to touch. Vibrations of rest, confidence, spiritual refreshment, and well-being immediately begin to reach us. In addition, this is a stone for reflection on our feelings.

Chrysoprase brings relief to the spiritual heart; it is also an important stone for the physical plane.

Chrysoprase. . . . PEACEFULNESS
Composition . . . SiO_2
Hardness 7
Color . . . . apple-green, pale-green, yellowish-green
Sources . . . . . . Australia, South Africa, United States, Brazil, Russia, Silesia in Poland

Energy class 2

COCOXIONITE

ONENESS—SYMPATHY FOR ONESELF

This astonishing stone has many effects. It frees us from pain. It creates order within us. How does it do it?

In an inimitable way it forces us to see ourselves as we really are. Why?

The stone world has observed that we human beings really do not perceive our reality. We live in a cloud of illusions, concepts, wishes, hopes, and compulsions. We realize only a fraction of our divine potential, if at all.

Cocoxionite clears away the misconceptions of being insignificant, dependent on others, limited, and victimized.

The truth is that *we live by our choices*, otherwise we wouldn't be bound by them. We forget this time and again—we can change our lives at any time, *if we wish*.

This stone helps us initiate our cleared perception. In addition, it allows us to feel continuity with our past and with our future. With this gift, we experience a fresh way of viewing ourselves. We gain new self-awareness and self-understanding. *We start to plan life anew.*

Cocoxionite will only be important during a few phases in life, when it will be extremely important! Let us be thankful that it exists. It is a wise being with a great deal of temperament. It has a quick effect.

Cocoxionite . . . . ONENESS
Composition . . . SiO_2 and $FeOOH$
Hardness 7
Color . . . . clear with unique bush-like goethite inclusions
Source . . . . Brazil only

Energy class 2

CELESTINE

BALANCE

Celestine, less commonly called coelstine, balances our moods. It creates an energy within us that enables us to observe everything objectively. Knotty problems of a long duration suddenly seem *different* to us. We discover its hidden causes and our mistaken views about it. This epiphany leads to the optimum solutions for a testing.

"Problems" are learning processes. The celestine teaches us that we do not have to fear any problem; there is always a solution that is good for us as well as all other participants. We merely have to find it. This is the function of this stone.

Celestine. . . . . . BALANCE
Composition . . . $Sr[SO_4]$
Hardness . . . . . 3—3.5
Color . . . . mostly blue; also colorless, white, or with tinges of yellow
Sources . . . . . . Namibia, Madagascar, Germany, England, Sicily, Russia

Special note: Be careful! Some celestines only seem to be solid stones. They disintegrate into smaller crystals out of their matrix when in water. The individual pieces of hard crystal remain intact, but the parent rock becomes sand when in liquid. Remember to cleanse it spiritually!

Energy class 2—3

CONNEMARA

QUARRELSOMENESS

Here we are dealing with a fellow of the most astonishing kind—a fighter.
"Go ahead," it would say, "beat each other!"

However, its true task is to show us the absurdity of squandered energy. Strife creates hatred. It never leads to the loving concord of understanding. Strife hardens those who fight. Our path is the path of love; we should dispense with strife and seek to understand. When we truly understand ourselves, we will also understand what it means to be human and have empathy for other people. When we understand, love works within us. This is why this stone ultimately says—*love each other!*

This is a good companion for all those who love, namely, everyone who participates in the Experiment Earth.

Connemara . . . . HOPE OF SURRENDER
Composition . . . Conglomerate of serpentine with marble
Hardness . . . . . 3—4
Color . . . . tinges of mottled yellow-green and white
Source . . . . Connemara, Ireland

Energy class 3

COROMITE

REMOVING OBSTRUCTIONS

The coromite evaporates all resistance. It acts on our mental blocks and reveals them to us. In this energy of strength and liveliness, we feel prepared to expose any inner obstructions. Feeling its protection, we allow ourselves insight. Reluctance hinders us; we only damage ourselves with it.

When we acknowledge our blockades, we find the determination to overcome them. This requires a different gemstone. However, the coromite is very effective in getting us started on our path to consciousness.

Coromite . . . . . RESISTANCE
Composition . . . SiO_2
Hardness . . . . . 6.5—7
Color . . . . green to gray with red spots and tiny pyrite crystals
Source . . . . India

Energy class 3

COVELLITE

TRUST IN GOD

This stone heals resentment and disrespect for God. We invite a state of Grace when we give up conflict and return to God. Nothing more can happen to us—we are one with Him. Growth causes pain only as long as we resist it. To be allied with God means faithfulness to our self. When we have perceived this, we will again *trust in God* and life will become easier.

Covellite. . . . . . FAITHFULNESS—TRUST
Composition . . . CuS
Hardness . . . . . 1.5—2.5
Color . . . . blue-black, indigo-blue to black
Sources . . . . . . United States, Alaska, New Zealand, Germany, Austria, Italy

Energy class 3

CUPRITE

SELF-RESPECT—DELIVERANCE

Cuprite helps us to thrive. It reminds us of all the deeds in our life that were in harmony with the universe. Many people live more harmoniously with the universe than they suspect; this stone has a very liberating effect on them. It grants unity between the self and the life force. This results in esteem and inner peace.

Cuprite . . . . . . SELF-CONFIDENCE
Composition . . . Cu_2O
Hardness . . . . . 3.5—4
Color . . . . . . dark-red to red-brown
Sources . . . . . United States, Peru, Chile, Russia, France, Namibia

Energy class 1

DANBURITE

REFRESHMENT—SPIRITUALITY

Danburite is a helper in times of need. When we are close to giving up, it gives us strength. It promotes faith and the comprehension of the spiritual laws. It enlivens and encourages.

This stone is very fast acting but its effect is short. After danburite, we need to use other gemstones.

Danburite . . . . . RESCUE
Composition . . . $Ca[B_2Si_2O_8]$
Hardness . . . . . 7—7.5
Color . . . . colorless to golden-yellow
Sources . . . . . . United States, Madagascar, Burma, Mexico

Energy class 1

DEMANTOID (Garnet)

SENTINEL OF OUR GROWTH

Demantoid's role makes it difficult to become friends with this stone.

We often start new cycles in life. The difficulties of change lie in releasing old, familiar habits and possessions. We generally clutch them stubbornly. The more tightly we hang on, the more arduous life becomes. We turn every which way; we invent excuses for ourselves; quite precisely, we tremble with fear.

Lovingly, persistently, demantoid informs us that life is growth and stagnation is death. Its vibrations mature us; we become willing to risk everything—really everything—to fulfill our mission. The power and love of the garnet group combine with the unwavering demantoid; these unite within us. We grow beyond ourselves. This is a stone that we should not select; it will approach us when we become sufficiently mature. It can cause confusion if we are spiritually unprepared.

When we work with demantoid, it overwhelms us with assurance in God, love, and comfort. In addition, it includes the qualities of all great stones of the garnet group. It loves us, helps us and understands us. Radical change becomes easy for demantoid.

Demantoid   . . . .   RADICAL CHANGE AND TURNING POINT
Composition   . . .   Andradite containing chrome (see ANDRADITE, p. 55)
Hardness   . . . . .   6.5—7
Color   . . . .   green, yellow-green
Source . . . .   Ural area

Energy class 1

DENDRITE AGATE

STRENGTH AND DEVELOPMENT

This agate gives us the strength to persist to the end. It supports our spiritual aims and helps us to attain them. It explains the passing seasons of joy and sorrow; its perspective comes from the eternity of God. We can then take our troubles in stride and have stronger trust in God.

The delicate appearance of a dendrite agate reminds us of the wonders of life and our participation in them. Why feel troubled? If we listen to the inner voice and follow it, God will provide for us, always.

Dendrite agate . . STRENGTH AND ENDURANCE
Composition . . . SiO_2
Hardness 7
Color . . . . white to yellow with dark-brown to black dendrites
Sources . . . . . . India, United States, Brazil

Energy class 2

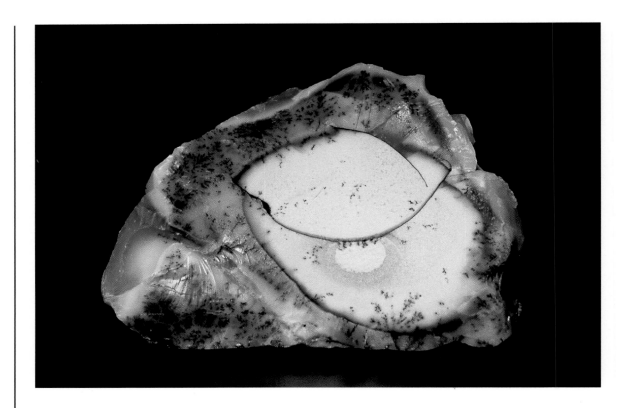

DENDRITE OPAL

OVERCOMING EASE

When someday our perspective of life's difficulties will relax, when we finally lean back and draw a deep breath, this stone enters our lives.

Its message is, "Go ahead and rest. However, there is still much to learn. Do not fall victim to the delusion there might be stagnation anywhere. Do not expect a holiday from improvement; it would mean the end of your growth. While enjoying your spiritual harvest, consider what to plant next. Sow your next crop as you reach for today's ripe fruit."

Do away with this fallacy: "When I finally reach my goal, then I'll be happy and I can take it easy." We need to learn to rest independent of what we are doing, may it be during our active times, during our growing pains or during the phases when we have finished a project.

This is a friend for times of dissatisfaction and fear.

Dendrite opal . . . TREMBLING WITH DELIGHT
Composition . . . $SiO_2 nH_2O$
Hardness . . . . . 5.5—6
Color . . . . various tinges of color, with dendrites
Sources . . . . . . Mexico, Peru, Brazil, Silesia

Energy class 1

BRILLIANT CUT WHITE DIAMOND

LIGHT OF PERFECTION—HIGHEST BLESSING

"Whoever wears me has found the grace of God."
With this simple sentence, the diamond enters our lives. It may take decades to comprehend this remark. All humans are equal; we all live in God's mercy. However, diamond would like to reveal the secret behind the mystery—the reality behind the facts.
"Search for these truths!" It calls to us and provides further explanations.

The brilliant cut, faceted white diamond is the symbol of absolute perfection—the Light within us—the blessings of God. I like to call it a "brilliant."

Those who wear it will remember their future perfection; they will feel affiliated to God; they will understand their task in life. The brilliant cut diamond protects and safeguards. It strives for and achieves absolute perfection. In its radiance, we can sometimes grasp a sense of perfection. It encourages our path to perfection.

Feel receptive to the fire of a brilliant. Immerse yourself completely in its rays. Here you will find the speediest opportunity for opening your heart.

Brilliant magnifies everything within us. In this manner, it reinforces our virtues. However, it also brings out our difficult natures, to direct our deliverance. Daily cleansing is even more important than for the other stones. Never wear it when ill; the patterns of illness sink into the stone and affect us later.

With the exception of tanzanite, brilliant stands above all other stones. The pure of heart or those who strive for a pure heart will find their strongest friend in it. Brilliant has no limitations.

Brilliant . . . . . . ABSOLUTE PERFECTION

Composition . . . C—crystallized carbon (apply to all diamonds)

Hardness . . . . . 10 (apply to all diamonds)

Color . . . . crystal white to slight tinges of yellow

Sources . . . . . . foremostly Jägersfontein, Wesselton & River mines, Africa; India; South America; less in Australia & United States; fragments also found in meteorites.

Special note: In this book, brilliant means every white diamond that can develop its perfect beauty and its resplendent sparkle through a professional cut. The whiter a brilliant is, the higher is its price. Brilliants are also classified according to the degree of clarity. This determines their price, brilliance, beauty, radiance, and (possibly) their effectiveness. A brilliant is a diamond that has been faceted into a brilliant cut design. Diamonds can also be faceted as baguettes, trapezoids, fantasy cuts, and other artistic creations. A brilliant cut has fifty-eight facets, evaluated by cut quality and proportion. The thin surface layer of a white diamond may be permanently tinted green, yellow, or amber by radiation of deuterons or alpha particles in a cyclotron. White diamonds become green when exposed to radium. Neutron irradiation in a cyclotron or an atomic pile will drive the new colors deeper throughout the diamond. A spectroscope will detect irradiation in a colored diamond. I do not recommend irradiated diamonds for spiritual work. In the United States, natural colored diamonds usually come with GIA verity certificates.

Energy class ABSOLUTE PERFECTION

BROWN DIAMOND

DEVELOPMENT OF MY LIFE

Brown diamonds fortify us. They reflect the desire for happiness. They undergird our confidence in happiness to come. They buoy our feelings; in this way, we accustom ourselves to contentment and living with a cheerful heart.

They are majestic—cut, or faceted, or radiant; therefore, they embody the quintessence of heaven and perfection. In addition, their brown tones remind us of the earth and—by this association—of our purpose in earthly life.

Brown diamonds especially suit people who have difficulty adjusting to earthly existence. The brown diamonds remind us of our vows; these are to master all the experiences on earth and to evolve. At the same time, these stones remind us of our power, potential, and inner splendor.

We come from God and return to God. Why should we not enjoy earthly life? It is an unequaled opportunity for growth. We have consented to this experiment of life. We create our own reality. We make the decision to improve our lives; we can change anything that is no longer relevant to us.

Brown diamond . . REST
Composition . . . C—crystallized carbon
Hardness 10
Color . . . . beige to brown
Sources . . . . . . primarily India, Africa, South America

Energy class 1

YELLOW DIAMOND

PLEASURE IN BEAUTY

The cut yellow diamond shines like the sun. In its majestic beauty, it reminds us of the immortality of all life and the eternal link with God.

Those who wear it feel poignant about their existence before this life on earth. The yellow diamond teaches us with the same directness as all diamonds. Its effect is strong.

Yellow diamond. . . BREAKTHROUGH OF THE LIGHT
Composition . . . . C—crystallized carbon
Hardness 10
Color . . . . light to deep canary yellow
Sources . . . . Silver Cape & Bywater mines in Africa, also India & South America

Special note: The yellow diamond, along with the brown diamond, is the most plentiful. A rich yellow color commands a high price. The surface of a yellow diamond turns green when exposed to radium.

Energy class 1

PALE-BLUE DIAMOND

OPENING THE HEAVEN WITHIN US

What a friend! With this child of God, we enter into a pale-blue kingdom of heaven. Like all faceted diamonds, this one also radiates and glistens so that the heart fills with joy and thankfulness. We should enjoy this friend when permitted to see it. Those who acquire it will see the Light of God in it in a special way. A personal love of this stone will create a great deal of growth.

Pale-blue diamond . . . JOVIALITY—SIGHT OF HEAVEN WITHIN US
Composition . . . . . . C—crystallized carbon
Hardness 10
Color . . . . pale to deep blue
Sources . . . . Wesselton mine in Africa, India, South America

Special note: Blue diamonds are extremely rare. Blue diamonds are usually very small and frequently tinted by radiation. White diamonds bombarded with high-energy electrons become pale-blue in color. It is better to have three tiny, natural blue diamonds than one that is larger but irradiated.

Energy class 1

PINK DIAMOND

ALL-EMBRACING LOVE

The angel of this stone stands before us in radiant beauty. It is the purest vibration of all-embracing love. It does not tolerate ego; a life with it must explore the deepest learning processes. We should be careful when we want to select such a stone: Are we mature enough for this? Is the time right for us to open to it? We should gradually acclimate to it, and only wear it when God has expressly recommended it.

Pink diamond . . . LIVING UNCONDITIONAL LOVE
Composition . . . C—crystallized carbon
Hardness 10
Color . . . . pale to deep pink
Sources . . . . . . Africa, India, South America

Special note: Pink-colored diamonds are traded for a high price. Pink is rare, but not as scarce as red, deep blue, or deep green.

Energy class 1

RED DIAMOND

(no photograph)

FIRE

This stone catapults us to God. It accommodates uncommonly few people. However, these people experience a multiple transformation when they wear it. These people review their long lives with many mistakes; they call out to God in deepest remorse. They receive the grace of changing their ways. However, their lives will completely change after a few years. Nothing—absolutely nothing—in their milieux will be the same.

Do not seek this stone. Development should take place gradually. Those who find their way to red diamond stand in a desperate position. Inwardly, nothing is more important to them except reconciling with God. It is a stone for the truly heroic. The red diamond burns us. Out of our ashes, the purified self seeks the arms of God.

Red diamond . . . . INCINERATING THE PERSONALITY
Composition . . . . C—crystallized carbon
Hardness 10
Color . . . . pale to deep red
Sources . . . . Africa; India; South America

Special note: This color of diamond is among the most rare and the most expensive. Shortly before publication of this book, I saw a red diamond in a jewelry store. The stone had been removed from an antique setting. This diamond had a black appearance. On the reverse side, I could see red through the light reflections. It reminded me of a deep-red garnet with a black effect. We decided not to use a photo.
Some black and dark brown diamonds take on a red tint when they are bombarded with radiation. We can detect radiation in some diamonds with a spectroscope. Some unscrupulous gem merchants may coat dark colored diamonds in a red film that can only be removed with sulfuric acid.

Energy class 1

BLACK DIAMOND

DEEP PROCESSES—BREAKTHROUGH

The black diamond stirs our unimagined depths. Our repressed emotions and deepest fears rise to the surface of our minds—hate, envy, malevolence, revenge, and other nether responses. Why are we afraid? Beneath all this aggression hides love; our fearsome aspects are also nothing but love—injured love, frustrated love, wishful love.

Black diamond give us the power to confront them and adjust them. It shows us a new path; it protects us. Not everyone should try a black diamond. It is too harsh for some people. We can soften the response of a black diamond; we use it with other stones—those that vibrate with holistic love, trust, or healing. Pink, green, and warm-colored stones work best. Black diamond works like a scalpel. Sometimes we need a deep incision for healing. We should approach black diamond with caution but we do not need to fear it!

Black diamond . . . PROFUNDITY AND BREAKTHROUGH
Hardness 10
Composition . . . . C—crystallized carbon
Color . . . . steel gray to black
Sources . . . . India, Africa, South America

Energy class 1

DIOPSIDE

A GIFT TO OURSELVES

Diopside is a lively stone for lively days. It can be used to replace a number of gemstone qualities, which makes it an ideal stone for traveling with limited luggage.

When we ask it for help, diopside will connect us with whichever gemstone qualities we need at the moment. Its effect is quick but not long lasting. It is not a replacement for other stones. Its actual function is to momentarily connect us to the vibrations of other gemstones.

As a mediator between mankind and other stones, diopside has unique facility. Its calling in the world is to be an intercessor *par excellence*.

Diopside. . . . . . MEDIATOR
Composition . . . $CaMg(Si_2O_6)$
Hardness . . . . . 5—6
Color . . . . green, also brown to green, seldom colorless
Sources . . . . . . the Alps, Sri Lanka, Burma, Kenya, Tanzania, Brazil, Canada, United States, Russia

Special note: Diopside has an effect when we make a request.
We could say, "Please connect me with the energy of the aquamarine. Thank you!"
Another request could be, "Please connect me with the stone energy that is most important for me at the moment. I thank you!"
The universal law of prayer or petition binds request and gratitude together without fail.

Energy class 3

DIOPTASE

REFLECTION—HEALING OLD WOUNDS

A peaceful heart is the effect of the dioptase. It helps us to retreat within. It reminds us of the prime idea: We are on this earth to be. All lessons are about being. Mastering the art of being is one of the greatest lessons.

Live entirely in the moment. Be at one with eternity. The ultimate truth, the ultimate perception is found in BEING. *Those who love—are.*

Dioptase. . . . . . HEALING
Composition . . . $Cu_6[Si_6O_{18}]\cdot6H_2O$
Hardness 5
Color . . . . dark, luminescent emerald green with tinges of blue
Sources . . . . . . Zaire, Namibia, Russia, Chile, United States

Energy class 1

DOLOMITE

MATERNAL LIVING

Here is a greatly underestimated stone. Delightful experiences of oneness await us with it.

Dolomite helps both men and women who avoid the topic of motherhood. Humanity could not continue without the maternal instinct. This principle gives birth to great things. No other stone teaches that motherhood requires the balance of fatherhood to develop. Woman and man, mother and father belong inseparably united in God.

Dolomite helps us to accept this need for balance. When we acknowledge this, we can walk the path of everlasting rebirth. Dolomite is a stone for the heart center.

Dolomite . . . . . INNER RENASCENCE
Composition . . . $CaMg[CO_3]_2$
Hardness . . . . . 3.5—4
Color . . . . white, yellow tinges, gray, brown, red-brown, seldom colorless or clear
Sources . . . . . . throughout the world

Energy class 2

DUMORTIERITE

ENJOYING LIFE

Often, we forget laughter on the spiritual paths.

Dumortierite does not discriminate between important or insignificant experiences. It would like us to recognize the humor behind everything. Nothing is as solemn as it seems. We live in illusion; nothing is as it appears. Look behind the curtain of pain— behind the suffering! Joy and laughter wait for us there. We just have to recognize it.

Some gemstones help us achieve comprehension. Dumortierite amuses us without teaching us.

Dumortierite . . . LAUGHTER
Composition . . . $Al_7[O_3/BO_3/(Si/_4)_3]$
Hardness 7
Color: . . . . violet-blue, deep blue, also blue-green to tinges of brown and red
Sources . . . . . . Sri Lanka, Brazil, United States, India, Namibia, France, Madagascar, Russia

Energy class 2

PRECIOUS OPAL

JUBILATION

The precious opal expresses the principle of JOY. It makes life easier through an energy of constancy.

As our feelings merge with an opal in progressive depths, as this intimacy develops, we realize that satisfaction can only be found within us. Love nourishes it.

We often do not feel safe enough to relax into joy; we are afraid to be happy. Often we are wrenched away from what we cherish most. After many disappointments, it becomes difficult to trust good news. This defensive stance prevents any happiness that we could enjoy.

Life means change; *life is consistent in change.*

The opal encourages us to accept our lot. Life's lessons and testings are iridescent like a precious opal. Those who cannot adjust to continual change become lost. We must change ourselves in order to grow. Those who do not change cannot mature to perfection. Those who do not change cannot come to God.

The opal then helps us to say yes to unrelenting change. We can then experience deep joy and solidarity. We discover that life is dependable; it has rules and laws. In continual change lies the potential for growth, reliability, and joy.

Life does not want to be measured by our expectations. *It teaches us to watch and hear.* Everything is good; everything is right—including everything painful and unpleasant. Let us open up to life. The opal helps us in the process.

Precious opal . . . UNFOLDMENT—GLADNESS
Composition . . . $SiO_2 \cdot nH_2O$
Hardness . . . . . 5.5—6
Color . . . . white, gray, dark, or transparent, with pale to bright moire effects creating opalesce.
Sources . . . . . . Australia, Brazil, Guatemala, Honduras, Japan, United States

Special note: Precious opals are expensive. However, there are wonderful necklaces made of small fragments that are quite inexpensive. My white opal necklace, for example, shows little color play. I use it to meditate; I hold in my hand and slowly search for the opalescent colors. Its shifting flickers of color are more subtle than with flaming, intensely opalescent pieces. This applies to all opals with delicate color play. They are good forerunners for the more intense opals.
Every opal loves moisture. It can crack if it dries out too much. We should put our opals into water now and then or keep them in moist towels of cotton for a time. They are also sensitive to shock.

Energy class 3

EILAT STONE

REDEMPTION FOR OURSELVES

There is no stone greater than the eilat. It is absolutely free from the vibration of pain, melancholy, contempt, or other negative feelings that stones can absorb and reflect. A gemstone in its highest vibration is still receptive to the vibrations of people. This one is not.

It illustrates that unity is possible; *growing together is good*; peace is achievable; our goals are attainable.

The eilat stone comes only from Israel. It is a fusion of chrysocolla, turquoise, and malachite. It vibrates with the virtues of growth, union, creativity, and healing. It teaches that the greatest human goal possible is to *live in love and peace*.

In its infinite wisdom, eilat bides its time. Someday we—the diverse people of this earth—will unite. It waits for us; someday we will recognize that we are the Light of the LIGHT and that we are reborn in God.

Eilat stone . . . . . PEACE
Composition . . . Fusion of chrysocolla with turquoise and malachite
Hardness . . . . . ranging from 2—6
Color . . . . blue tones with turquoise and green
Source . . . . Eilat, Israel

Energy class 1

IVORY

PARDON

Mankind has used ivory as jewelry material since ancient times. The first pieces of ivory were made from the tusks of elephants that had died a natural death—that is, not harmed by human hands. When humans began to hunt and kill elephants for their tusks, ivory lost value for those who consider animals to be their brothers and sisters.

We avoid ivory today. Sometimes, a piece will choose an owner, who will be surprised to find that the ivory vibrates with the quality of forgiveness—even though the animal died in the cruelest manner. With humility, we can learn great lessons from any animal. When we become aware of our karma with animals, we should ask God for help in filtering our empathic feelings; we wish to help the rights of animals but we do not unconsciously wish to experience the suffering of tortured animals.

127

ENSTATITE

FREEDOM

We will feel free when we can discern what is essential in life. This stone makes it happen. Holding or wearing it, we develop an instinct for necessities; we commune with God; we understand our assignments in this incarnation; choosing these tasks requires the assistance of other stones. We feel calm. Used alone, enstatite connects the subconscious with the higher knowledge. It does not bring this inner wisdom into consciousness.

Enstatite . . . . . . RELIEF
Composition . . . $Mg_2[Si_2O_6]$
Hardness . . . . . 5—6
Color . . . . green to green-brown or dark-brown
Sources . . . . . . Tanzania, Sri Lanka, South Africa, Kenya, Burma, Brazil, Mexico, United States

Energy class 2

EOSITE

EXUBERANCE

Love embraces us; rapture touches us. And then we have to trudge off to work to pay the rent!

Eosite counsels us; it teaches us that we can lead our mundane lives with cheerfulness and love. This is why, under eosite's influence, we can react with good humor where we formerly would have felt resentful.

It helps us to take life with a light heart.

Eosite . . . . JOY IN DAILY LIFE
Composition . . . SiO_2 and some $Pb[Mo,VO_4]$
Hardness 7
Color . . . . pale-pink to coral to apricot
Sources . . . . . . Tibet, Italy

Energy class 3

EPIDOTE

STRUCTURE AND STABILITY

Epidote centers our thoughts. It stabilizes us so that we can organize ourselves. It helps us to master consistency and routine.

This is also useful in defeating fears about communication. Others can understand us only when we declare ourselves. With the help of epidote, we give form to the thoughts and feelings that we had not put into words; the reason for our inability to express our ideas would be because we had not completely understood ourselves.

Epidote . . . . . . STABILITY
Composition . . . $Ca_2(Fe^{3+},Al)Al_2[O/OH/SiO_4/Si_2O_7]$
Hardness . . . . . 6—7
Color . . . . green, red-brown to dark-red to violet-black
Sources . . . . . . Austria, Mozambique, Brazil, Sri Lanka, Burma

Special note: Please also refer to UNAKITE (Epidote), p. 361.

Energy class 2

EUCLASE

PEACE

Euclase, a form of datolite, is a rare stone and worth seeking. It gives us peace, because it is associated with the principle of justice. It teaches that *life is justice* despite appearances to the contrary.

Our deeds during this life and past lives give rise to our circumstances. Our *behavior* has an *effect*. Our words, thoughts, and emotions also create reactions. Everything that we send out will returns to us—*absolutely everything!*

Healing my spiritual wounds brings me good things. As I become less encumbered and more selfless, the more simple my life will be. Life wants to give us gifts; it can only bestow on us what is just, according to the law.

Euclase . . . . . . PEACE
Composition . . . BeAl[OH/SiO$_4$]
Hardness 7.5
Color . . . . colorless, chartreuse, green-blue, pale-blue to sapphire-blue
Sources . . . . . . Ural area, Brazil, Zaire, Tanzania, Zimbabwe, Austria

Energy class 1

FALCON'S EYE

PROMISE

This stone promises us that we can make real our greatness; it encourages us in this way. Be careful; it also has a very material nature. We should only use it for a short period of time so that it does not make us greedy.

When its promise has inspired us, we should move on to another gemstone (by asking what is right for us). Above all, we should seek the path that will lead us to inner greatness. What do we need to heal, learn, understand, and experience? There are other many stones that can help in this process.

Falcon's eye . . . . AMASSING ENERGY
Composition . . . SiO_2
Hardness 7
Color . . . . dark-blue, green-blue
Source . . . . . . South Africa

Energy class 3

FIRE OPAL

JOY OF THE HEART

Strength flows through us. The will becomes strong.

The fire opal is a good stone for timid people. Its fire rouses them; its energy gives them confidence.

Fire opals crack easily and then show fissures. This is a metaphor for us; even during times of obsessive devotion we should remember our own needs. Spirit and love can only develop in a body that obeys the laws of health and nature.

Which of us lives this way all the time? The fire opal reminds us that there is a high price for squandering our vital energy. Disregarding the laws of life attracts punishment. One day the body will break. It is like a fire opal that has exhausted itself, been overused, or been deprived of the necessities for survival (moisture, good care, and respect).

We have certain requirements for a healthy life. If we do not provide these things for ourselves, we ruin our well-being. If we provide these conditions, then we will enjoy strength, beauty, and love!

Fire opal . . . . . . STRENGTH—DELIGHT—VITAL ENERGY
Composition . . . $SiO_2 nH_2O$
Hardness . . . . . 5.5—6
Color . . . . from yellow to orange to red
Sources . . . . . . Mexico

Energy class 1

FLUORITE

REMOVES BLOCKADES

The fluorite dissolves blockades and permits us to recognize our limitations. It soothes pain and heals emotional wounds. It is a stone for demanding times.

Fluorite approaches our limits with determination. With its help, we can distinguish between necessary boundaries and obstructions. It encourages us to overcome our mental blocks. It brings Light into our darkness and sparks belief in ourselves.

This is a wonderful stone for healing. Its rainbows of colors complement its essential vibration qualities.

Fluorite . . . . . . REMOVES BLOCKADES
Composition . . . CaF_2
Hardness 4
Color . . . . the entire color spectrum, often striped in several colors
Sources . . . . . . worldwide

Special note: Some fluorites from China bear pyrite crystals on the surface. These are very beautiful! Also marvelous are fluorites that have tiny quartz crystals on them; they glitter here and there with pyrite.

Energy class 2

F O S S I L

HEAVINESS—MEMORIES OF DEATH AND TRANSITORINESS

Here we experience a wonder; what was alive millions of years ago is now imprinted in stone, completely preserved in its energy. People who are open to subtle vibrations will feel the history of this living creature. We should contemplate these stones with a respect for life; they do not bring us joy.

In their direct manner, fossils remind us of death and transience. They usually also contain a vibration of fear. In certain life situations, they can be good teachers. When we have learned their lesson, we should reach for pink-colored stones. In their energy of Light and love, we release the vibration of fossils to all-embracing love.

Fossil . . . . DURABILITY
Composition . . . Rock, carbon, nitrogen, and calcium carbonate
Hardness . . . . . corresponding
Color . . . . usually beige, gray, brown to black
Sources . . . . . . worldwide

Energy class 3

JET

GRIEVING

Jet dissipates sorrow and regret. It helps us to process the past and does not allow avoidance. With this stone, we reach a deep level of sorrow that even sincere, truth-loving people repress. We reexperience and accumulate this sorrow over *many* lifetimes; for lack of emotional strength and maturity, we deny the existence of these feelings.

Invoke jet at certain moments, to heal these deepest wounds. It is worth the trouble.

We should limit its use from a few hours to a few days. At the same time, we should wear stones that comfort us, such as all the sunny and pink-colored gemstones; these we should wear before, during, and after using jet.

Jet . . . . SELF PARDON
Composition . . . Brown coal
Hardness . . . . . 2.5—4
Color . . . . . . black, dark-brown
Sources . . . . . England, Spain, France, United States

Energy class 3

FOUND OBJECTS

JOY

Everything radiates vibrations. Sometimes we like something at the sea, in the forest, in the mountains, or on the street. Everything has a soul. Perhaps it evokes a memory; perhaps it feels good to touch; perhaps we love the sight of it.

A piece of plastic once said to me, "Observe God's creation in everything. Love me, do not discriminate by worth, do not lose yourself in judgment. Love life, and love me."

Found objects . . . RESPECT FOR LIFE
Composition . . . Organic, synthetic, or mineral

Energy class 3 (usually)

ROCK

Every material has spirit in it. Even very ordinary stones have personalities. They, too, influence us. Four examples are basalt, firestone, granite, and marble. What is there to say about them?

BASALT

Hard and enduring, it helps us to understand ourselves and prepares us for peace.

FIRESTONE

Solid and very tough, it channels the knowledge of humanity; it wants nothing for itself; it serves humanity.

GRANITE

Durable, rugged, and competent, it makes a connection; it forms a sense of community; it radiates a certain unrest.

MARBLE

Lighthearted and joyful, it stimulates a willingness to love; it encourages merriment.

BEACH ROCK / WATER ROCK

The many types of water rock know the history of their oceans, seas, lakes, rivers, or streams, which they have shared for countless years. They contain all the information about the element water. Through all of this, they maintain their individuality, their mineral energy, and their vibrations.

Each stone records the history of its environment, the planet, and humanity. All information is stored within it. It shares its experiences with other stones, and has access to their history. All stones are part of the Whole.

GIRASOL QUARTZ

DELIGHT—REST—COMPOSURE

Wear girasol quartz and feel an inner lightness. How lovely: This stone reflects our best attributes and augments them. We delight in our virtues and abilities; we can perceive them objectively and we are happy with ourselves.
We understand that we are better than we feared. Tranquillity and equanimity infuse us. We relax and enjoy the moment. This is a stone for pleasant hours with ourselves.

Girasol quartz. . . SELF-KNOWLEDGE
Composition . . . SiO_2
Hardness 7
Color . . . . translucent milky-white
Sources . . . . . . Brazil

Special note: Girasol quartz is sometimes called milk quartz. However, the chalk-white quartz that is usually termed milk quartz is not meant here. The difference between the two is their translucence and opacity.

Energy class 2

GLASS

FIRE—STRENGTH—LIGHTNESS

Glass gives us strength. It awakens awareness of human potential.

When we cherish a piece of glass, we cherish ourselves. Glass symbolizes our creativity, audacity, harmony with the earth, daring, and *affection*.

We can discover ourselves in a chunk of glass. Contemplating it, we can recognize our merit and we honor God as the elemental force in mankind—the elemental force in matter. Glass leads us to ourselves. Our cheer, lightness, confidence, and dignity grow. This is a friend for times when we doubt ourselves.

Glass. . . . . . . WONDER
Composition . . . quartz, lime, soda, heat; lead and trace minerals for color
Hardness . . . . . 5—6
Color . . . . all colors and opacities
Sources . . . . . . man-made and naturally occurring

Special note: The effect of glass depends on its color, although the vibrations remain the same. A large piece of turquoise-colored glass—or a small but intensely red or green piece—on an acupuncture point produces a reverberation in addition to the glass vibration.

Energy class 1

MICA

CONSENT TO LIFE

Today we need nothing more urgently than this choice. Sometimes when our world seems to fall apart, when nothing world seems to matter, mica leads us to a consciousness that may be unfamiliar. We feel intrigued about the unknown and we start to muse about experiences we would like to try. We ponder the existence of God and God's manifestation in every form of matter. Divine Energy ensouls even man-made things that we often label as "dead".

Mica is for people who have just begun their spiritual path and who want to continue ascending the steps of enlightenment. This is also for great souls who are in danger of losing their relationship to the simple things.

Mica . . . . SIMPLE PERCEPTION
Composition . . . Various minerals
Hardness . . . . . 2.5—3
Color . . . . colorless, white, brown, raspberry, pink, violet, dark-green, black
Sources . . . . . . worldwide

Energy class 3

GOLDEN BERYL

EYE OF LIFE—GUARDIAN OF THE SUN

This is a golden stone in the best sense.

It says, "Respect life, and remember the sun in your heart."

Following the yellow sapphire, the golden beryl is the most powerful among the yellow stones. Its energy is very clear but it does not focus as strictly as the yellow sapphire. A gentle and kind air surrounds us when we are receptive to this stone. It effects are intense and rapid. It emanates a radiance that makes us want to surrender ourselves. It vibrates with clarity and truth; it channels Light and love. The golden beryl signifies a homecoming to many of us. This feeling affects the holistic being; we understand divine Light energy; we awake to a deeper bond with God. This is for all who love God and would like to be closer to Divinity. The golden beryl creates a direct connection.

Golden beryl . . . GUARDIAN OF THE SUN
Composition . . . $Be_3Al_2[Si_6O_{18}]$
Hardness . . . . . 7.5—8
Color . . . . bright-yellow to golden-yellow
Sources . . . . . . Brazil, Sri Lanka, Namibia

Energy class 1

GOLDSTONE (AVENTURINE GLASS)

HUMOR

Changing Delight. Laughing Joy. The Fun of Living.

Little Star in My Hand. Lightness of life. Illusion

Goldstone conquers a serious nature. It teaches, "Laugh about yourself. Laugh about your judgment. Laugh about your shyness to enjoy life in its entire splendor."

Good for people with strong prejudices.

Goldstone . . . . . CAPRICIOUSNESS
Composition . . . man-made glass with flecks of glitter
Hardness . . . . . 5—5.5
Color . . . . usually red-brown or dark-blue with sparkles

Energy class 1

COLORLESS GARNET (LEUCO GARNET)

JOY—UNEXPECTED SOLUTIONS

All garnets are associated with the principles of LOVE and STRENGTH. Under the influence of this stone, we learn to believe in miracles. We feel permitted to hope for a marvel when we have done everything we could. We have the right to expect one.

In God's teaching there are specific laws. When I devote everything in my life for a spiritual goal, God will do His part. What is logical, a matter of course, and lawful to God, astonishes us as truly unhoped for and blessed.

Colorless garnet tells us, "When you have done everything that God has requested of you, then open your arms and receive your miracle. God loves you."

Garnet . . . . EXPECTING MIRACLES
Composition . . . $Ca_3Al_2[SiO_4]_3$ (leuco grossularite)
Hardness . . . . . 6.5—7.5
Color . . . . colorless
Source . . . . Tanzania

Special note: Our understanding of the effects of gemstones is very important here. This garnet does not cause wonders. Yet, it channels the impulse to end our tasks. The characteristics for this purpose (such as strength, courage, patience, endurance, effort, etc.) can be given to us by other stones. When we have ended our tasks, our wonders can occur.

Energy class 1

YELLOW GARNET

RISING UP TO THE LIGHT

The yellow garnet gives strength and fulfillment. It connects the principle of LOVE with that of the sun. In its vibration field, we experience heartfelt joy, because we believe in ourselves; we know that we are created for love and happiness; we may experience both. This stone promises us that life is a *joy*; we have the strength to live in joy. When we turn to it, love flows through us; the sun streams through us. No other stone so strongly influences self-confidence like this one. We trust in ourselves. We live our strength. We are one with ourselves, our life, and our tasks.

We should possess a yellow garnet—it is of inestimable value.

Yellow garnet . . . FULFILLMENT—JOY
Composition . . . $Ca_3Al_2[SiO_4]_3$ hessonite—$(Mg, Mn)3Al_2[SiO_4]_3$ umba garnet
Hardness . . . . . 6.5—7.5
Color . . . . lemon-yellow to golden-yellow
Sources . . . . . . mainly Sri Lanka and Tanzania

Special note: Deeply pigmented yellow stones without a deviation into cinnamon or golden-brown are meant here. Their pale and yellow coloring increases with less iron. The actual hessonite color ranges between orange and brown tones.

Energy class 1

RED ALMANDINE GARNET

REFLECTION OF LIFE

"A reflection of all life lives in distant worlds," speaks the stone. "You have created energy on this earth that continues in a lively manner. Every thought and every word are waves that reach unimaginably distant horizons. These are preserved in time and space until the person who has thought or spoken them lets them go.

"Free yourself and heal this world. Then you will be able to heal other worlds. You are important with every expression of your being. Pain and happiness lie in your hands. Release your suffering and your desires to God; experience the state of faith beyond them. In your meditations, visualize your future self. Create a space within your life that you can enter and expand.

"There is more to the universe than you can comprehend. The key to the very highest energies waits within you until you can use it. Request it to nestle first in your hand and promise to use it for the blessing of all.

"God has asked you to be *magnificent*. Overcome every challenge. Recognize the magnificence of God looking back at you from the mirror. Search for the God of the gods in the expanses of the resurrection."

Red almandine garnet . . . RESURRECTION
Composition . . . . Fe$_3^{2+}$Al$_2$[SiO$_4$]$_3$
Hardness . . . . 7—7.5
Color . . . . red with a violet or blue tinge
Sources. . . . . Austria, Sweden, United States, Zimbabwe, Brazil, Sri Lanka, Madagascar

Special note: A woman client wore a necklace of almandine for one week. She told me that her menstrual flow had increased; she was convinced that this necklace had some-how caused it. I explained to her that the message (energy) of the almandine had caused a relaxation within her. Her subconscious mind had felt at home and metaphorically discharged a big sigh of relief. Letting go of our expectations in life can have a wide range of physical and emotional reactions. For her, it was this physical emancipation of feminine energy.

Energy class 1

RED PYROPE GARNET

LOVE—COURAGE TO LIVE—STAMINA

This garnet is a power stone. Symbolically, it goes at everything head first. It connects us with the symbol of LOVE—a very earthy and energetic caring—a *holistic agape*. It challenges us to take actions based in love. No stone connects us more with the principle of persevering love. The true *passion for everything* is selfless and unconditional. Garnet gives us enough strength and courage to fulfill this love. Through its vibrations, we also find forgiveness easier to express.

This is an ideal stone for married couples who have lost affection for each other. It is also an excellent stone for all those who want to express their ideal of love into action. Only in love are we creators in this universe. Only in devotion are we truly divine. Divine agape is the requirement. This lives in our hearts, so every action is divine that arises from our hearts.

Sometimes we feel so injured emotionally that some acts of true ardor exact a great cost. Only by *realizing* our *love* can we save the earth and survive as humanity. The garnet helps.

Red pyrope garnet . . . LOVE—VALOR—STRENGTH
Composition . . . . . . $Mg_3Al_2[SiO_4]_3$
Hardness . . . . 7—7.5
Color . . . . blood-red, often with a brown tinge
Sources . . . . Africa, India, Bohemia

Special note: During the Middle Ages, garnet and other red stones were called carbuncles. The inexpensive garnet necklaces, which we can buy anywhere gemstone beads are sold, are either pyrope or almandine.

Energy class 1

GROSSULARITE (Garnet)

PERCEIVING OUR STRENGTH

Grossularite brings us to the limits of our strength. At the same time, it shows us our potential strength. This is always much greater than we believed.

We live on this earth in order to test our strength, strengthen our wisdom and live our love. This stone contains all three vibrations but it emphasizes our STRENGTH. We can achieve much with its help. Since it channels wisdom and love, we will wisely use our strength with grossularite.

Grossularite . . . . PEACE WITHIN ME
Composition . . . $Ca_3Al_2[SiO_4]_3$
Hardness . . . . . 6.5—7.5
Color . . . . green, pink, yellow, copper-brown (often tiny black inclusions)
Sources . . . . . Sri Lanka, Canada, Pakistan, South Africa, Tanzania, Russia, United States
Energy class 1

HEMATITE

COURAGE—COURAGE—COURAGE

We should use this stone wherever we can. Those who wear much hematite will often experience surprises. Life becomes more colorful. Its vibration of courage passes to us; our behavior changes. We take more risks; naturally, this alters our lives.

Those who love hematite will gain a friend forever. It strengthens and heartens us.

Hematite . . . . . COURAGE
Composition . . . Fe_2O_3
Hardness . . . . . 5.5—6.5
Color . . . . . . anthracite-grey, black, brown-red
Sources . . . . . England, Germany, United States, Norway, Sweden, Taiwan, Spain, Brazil, New Zealand, Elba

Special note: Polished hematite has a metallic look and a silvery-dark-gray glow. During its polishing, the grinding water turns to blood-red, which is why it is also called "bloodstone". Hematite and magnetite are nearly identical, except for their color overtones. Hematite is red-brown; magnetite is more black. I test these stones by rubbing them on unglazed porcelain (such as the reverse side of a plate or tile) to check their markings.

H A Ü Y N I T E (Haüyne)

JOY—LAUGHTER—RESURRECTION

Haüynite is exceptional among the stones.

It is connected with The Madonna—her energies of love and absolute devotion.

The Holy Mother embodies femininity, womanliness, faithfulness to God, and complete devotion. This devotion symbolizes mankind's attempt to give itself. It is always difficult to give up the ego and just be. Mary has exemplified this for us.

The feminine aspect is equally important for both men and women. The principles of life require that we first must GIVE when we want to receive something. As long as we have not given, we will not receive.

Giving is misunderstood. We usually mistake giving for sacrifice. Giving is a joy. As long as we have not recognized this, we are not human.

Haüynite teaches that we can give with a free heart. We are perpetually receiving blessings. Giving and taking is a cycle; the one is dependent on the other.

Redemption and resurrection free our hearts. When we can give *more than feels comfortable or safe*, we will experience redemption and inner resurrection.

God is with us. Let us release what is in our hearts—joy, sadness, sympathy, pain, passion, rage, daring, fear, forgiveness, anger, happiness, injury, resurrection, discouragement, love, hopelessness, beauty, purity, sincerity, affection, and caring.

We have much to give. Let us begin anew in every moment.

Haüynite . . . . . RESURRECTION
Composition . . . $Na_5Ca_2[(SO_4Cl)_2/Al_6Si_6O_{24}]$
Hardness . . . . . 5—6
Color . . . . Madonna-blue (color of her mantle in old paintings), also gray
Sources . . . . . . Eifel in Germany

Special note: Very small pieces appear in volcanic basalt rocks. However, even in tiny chips it shows its magnificent blue color!

Energy class 1

HELIODOR (Beryl)

STONE OF THE GODS—GATEWAY TO LIGHT

This stone is the closest to our hearts. No other stone is as deliberate and consistent as it succeeds in breaking through to the Light, to us, our strength, and our purpose.

We must, however, recognize the right time to use it. In many phases of our lives, heliodor is meaningless to us, and we will not notice it. At the right moment, it opens the gateway to Divine Love, and we open our eyes. No other stone is as helpful in making us feel responsible for our lives.

At the ripened moment, we stand in the Light and sheltered in the love of God. We become knowledgeable about the laws of life. Perception after perception comes to us.

We develop maturity. We rise to our potential greatness. We feel prepared for *everything*.

The heliodor calls people who are conscious of the Divine Greatness within and their human duties. They choose new responsibilities. They remain always in the Light and always in communion with Divinity. This is the stone for rebirth and beginning new cycles. The principles of the SUN (yellow) and HEALING (green) connect through this stone with the keen, clear sight of the beryls.

Heliodor reveals itself to very few people. Blessed be those to whom it comes!

It says, "I am the guardian of life. God is in me. Whoever wears me will recognize his own Divinity."

Heliodor. . . . . . GATEWAY TO LIGHT
Composition . . . $Be_3Al_2[Si_6O_{18}]$
Hardness . . . . . 7.5—8
Color . . . . . . green-yellow
Sources . . . . . . Brazil, Madagascar, United States, South Africa

Energy class 1

HELIOTROPE (Blood Jasper)

DEVELOPMENT OF THE PHYSICAL LEVEL

Heliotrope is an important stone for the physical level. It gives us strength and courage to examine our physical natures. It aids us in being sensitive to our physical needs.

It stimulates cleansing processes and can draw poisons from the body. However, we need several stones for these special purposes. They must always be fresh (cleansed). Other conditions should also be arranged to be successful.

With the help of gemstones and minerals, we can influence physical illness; this requires a large quantity of stones—even if they are only a few varieties. During certain healing sessions, single stones are enough, but they usually must be of a special size and quality. Afterward, we must return them to the earth to regenerate themselves.

We should always wear a heliotrope when we need support and help for our body. This point is important for us. It sets the impulses in motion for healing.

Heliotrope. . . . . PHYSICAL BODY
Composition . . . SiO_2
Hardness 7
Color . . . . dark-green with red inclusions
Sources . . . . . . India, Siberia, North Africa, United States, China, Australia

Special note: Heliotrope is very important for the physical body. Wear it in the usual manner. One might also connect two necklaces to wear them around the waist.

Energy class 3

HERKIMER QUARTZ

TRAUMA

The herkimer quartz unequivocally reveals our level of development. It allows us to be honest with ourselves. It gives us the courage to change. It illumines our limitations; we realize that we cannot surpass our blind spots without guidance or help.

This is a good stone for those who do not want to accept help from others.

Herkimer quartz . . . SHOCK
Composition . . . . . SiO_2
Hardness 7
Color . . . . colorless
Source . . . . North America

Special note: The herkimer quartz is a form of rock crystal; what makes it special is its crystal growth habit of points at both ends. It used to be called herkimer diamond. It radiates more intensely than the typical rock crystal and is even more powerful. In this perfected form it is unique—like many gemstones and minerals.

Energy class 1

HESSONITE (Garnet)

SELF-ASSURANCE—ELEMENTAL POWER

Confidence flows through me. I reflect on my personal strengths and on myself. I have lived many lives; I have died many deaths. I am rich in experiences and ability. There is always a solution. There is always a goal that I can reach. I am the creator of my circumstances in life. I can change them. I listen inwardly, and I find my path.

I am a child of God and I live immortally. The path through matter is only an assignment for me. I can walk it with serenity and composure.

The hessonite loves all humans. It is similar to them. By invoking the above affirmations, it aids the human race. It likes to serve.

Hessonite . . . . . SELF-ASSURANCE
Composition . . . $Ca_3Al_2[SiO_4]_3$
Hardness . . . . . 6.5—7.5
Color. . . . . brown-orange, golden-brown to brown, translucent cinnamon, very
delicate cognac-brown (pale brown-gold)
Sources . . . . . . mainly Sri Lanka

Special note: Rich brown necklaces and stones are available. Especially look out for the subtly cinnamon-colored faceted hessonite.

Energy class 1

HIDDENITE (Spodumene)

FAITHFULNESS TO GOD

Hiddenite deals with personal rights. It clarifies complicated situations and encourages the patience to wait for a solution. It vibrates with exact directness and gentle healing energy. It opens the heart to problems that must be solved.

It connects us with God and the laws of life. It causes us to want to align with them. This is how it shows us the solutions to our problems. Listen to God. Move within these laws. We will certainly receive help. It comes as an intuition—as a feeling.

The special gift of this stone is the following. When we feel injured from without, when our freedoms face censure, when someone misunderstands our rights, it helps to understand the viewpoint of the opposing person. In this way, we avoid new karma.

We can stand up for our rights without feeling animosity. Resentment creates more resentment; strife creates more strife. Observing these feelings without participation releases us from the karma of this situation.

I react appropriately to my problem and I continue my development.

Hiddenite . . . . . FAITHFULNESS TO GOD
Composition . . . LiAl[Si$_2$O$_6$]
Hardness . . . . . 6 -7
Color . . . . yellow-green, sometimes emerald-green
Sources . . . . . . United States, Brazil, Afghanistan

Energy class 1

HONEY CALCITE

WARMTH—CONTENTMENT—CONFIDENCE

Sun of Life—this stone symbolizes it. It warms us *immediately*; it delights us in a moment and it augments us. Greatly differing results can occur with these vibrations! It's wonderful! All of them will appeal to us! SUN is the energy we all yearn for; honey calcite gives it to us. It is a first-aid stone for many types of injuries.

This also has a strong influence on the body.

Honey calcite . . . WARMTH
Composition . . . $Ca[CO_3]$
Hardness 3
Color . . . . honey to golden-yellow, sometimes delicate yellow with white
Sources . . . . . . Romania, Mexico, United States

Special note: Honey calcite is the term for opaque, heavily pigmented, yellow calcite. The transparent, more brown-gold calcite (see CALCITE, p. 81) is usually called golden calcite. The honey calcite is one of the quickest acting of all gemstones. We feel comfort and warmth under its influence.

Energy class 2

HONEY OPALITE

CONNECTION WITH NATURE

Honey opalite soothes the soul. It clears up misunderstandings and gives us the resolve for a new beginning. It solves problems in an unusual manner; its vibrations awaken our spirit of defiance. We reflect on our own strengths and no longer feel like victims.

This is how it promotes creativity and growth. It relieves tension, because we can find solutions to our problems. It is a good stone for children.

Honey opalite . . . RECOLLECTION
Composition . . . $SiO_2 nH_2O$
Hardness . . . . . 5.5—6.5
Color . . . . yellow-brown, dark veined banding
Sources . . . . . . Brazil

Energy class 3

HOWLITE

DISRUPTION OF OUR STRUCTURES

Howlite's concentrated energies symbolize the human struggle for Light. It is very receptive and it vibrates with trust. Use it to examine the limits of faith.

Rose quartz also stimulates trust, lightness, and joy, but howlite reveals our resistance and fear. It is aids self-actualization. Say yes during this struggle, where many of us have shut down our feelings. Our fears deprive us of new experiences and limit the quality of life.

After Howlite shows us our lack of trust and lack of faith in God's kindness, the rose quartz will be able to help us further. It will in turn lead us to another stone. Our development is a *path*, as is the use of gemstones.

Howlite . . . . . . TRUST—GROWTH
Composition . . . $Ca_7[B_3O_4(OH)_2/Si_2B_4O_{10}(OH)_6]_2$
Hardness . . . . . 3.5—4.5
Color . . . . snowy-white, white, with black, gray, and brown veins
Sources . . . . . . United States, Canada

Special note: Howlite is a porous stone and takes dye well. It is often colored blue and misrepresented as turquoise.

IOLITE

RENUNCIATION OF LOVE ROBS ME OF MY ROOTS

Iolite awakens our hunger for the love of the whole self.

When will I finally accept myself? When will I respect and honor myself? When shall I be able to say, "I love myself," with a pure heart?

Iolite exposes the poverty of the self-image. We come to understand that our level of self-acceptance reflects in our relationships with others. My lack of sympathy for my needs and feelings has limited my ability to empathize with others. My lack of self-regard harms my life choices. My desire for a higher quality of life awakens this longing for a better relationship with myself.

When I sincerely love myself unconditionally, then I am better able to love others and to love God. Pure love of the soul, body, inner child, and adult self has nothing to do with selfishness; it has more to do with venerating God's creation.

When I finally love myself, I have understood that God loves me. I have understood that I am Divine, even within the restricting earthbound world. The love of myself includes forgiving my mistakes; it means understanding my potential and my imperfection. Love of myself makes me free. Love of myself liberates my path.

It enables me to feel generous. Love of myself gives me the right to be one with God.

Iolite demonstrates the spiritual necessity of self-esteem; it brings on the first halting steps toward loving myself. When this desire completely awakens, I will need other stones in order to connect me with my feelings of love.

Iolite . . . . DESIRE FOR LOVE
Composition . . . $Mg_2Al_3[AlSi_5O_{18}]$
Hardness . . . . . 7—7.5
Color . . . . blue tones
Sources . . . . . . Burma, Brazil, Sri Lanka, India, Madagascar

Energy class 2

JADE/JADEITE

PERFECTION—LOVE

Jade's vibrations permeate the heart. Healing occurs through inner peace. The jade gives us this peace when we are mature enough to accept it.

When we are still immature, it reassures us and reminds us of perfection. Jade calms the heart; it promotes faith in God; it imparts *knowledge* for healing. Those who feel attracted to jade, long for healing. This healing encompasses the entire essence of *being*. This is where the memory of the paradise within us continues to live. Here waits the knowledge that can create a paradise on earth. Timidity and depression have overcome mankind. We believe that we cannot change the earth. We forget at the same time that we have created the earth as we now see it. War and hardship are *our* achievements. Falsehood, destruction, and exploitation are the results of *our* decisions. Suffering and death are *our* responsibility. We should create an earth where people can live in peace. We are capable of creating abundance for all. We can free the spirit of each individual.

We have confused richness of life with material greed; we have mistaken freedom for power over others. We have to change our values in order to change the world. The jade in its gentle vibration reminds us of the perfection within ourselves; we can exist and choose on the basis of this perfection, which is our birthright. Every choice made from the Divine Fire Within is good for all and is good for the world. Jade is a great healer. It channels the vibration of perfection and therefore ABSOLUTE LOVE, which can heal all of us.

Many stones are misrepresented as jade. It is important to be knowledgeable and to be discerning—two requirements on the path to perfection.

Jade/jadeite . . . . PERFECTION
Composition . . . $NaAl[Si_2O_6]$
Hardness . . . . . 5.5—7
Color . . . . green, also other colors
Sources . . . . . . China, New Zealand, Russia, Burma, Mexico, Canada, Poland, United States

Special note: Many green stones, most frequently serpentine and nephrite, are offered as jade (see NEPHRITE, p. 222 and SERPENTINE, p. 286). All inexpensive articles in a light green are produced from serpentine or other materials. Serpentine is a mineral in its own right, sometimes also with black inclusions (see CHITA, p. 85). It often appears identical to jade. However, serpentine is a much softer stone; it has a different vibration from jadeite and nephrite, which are very similar. Both jadeite and nephrite are usually called jade in their countries of origin.

Energy class 2

JASPER

STRENGTH AND ENDURANCE

The jasper is a dynamic stone. It gives us the courage to survive. It imparts endurance and toughness. It conveys its fire to us. Jasper always associates with the principle of POWER. It grounds us.

In its presence, we feel powerful and secure. It strengthens our self-confidence. It gives us the peace of accomplishment.

Jasper . . . . STRENGTH—ENDURANCE
Composition . . . SiO_2
Hardness 7
Color . . . . earth-red, red-brown, variegated, often striped or speckled
Sources . . . . . . worldwide

Special note: Many varieties of jasper exist. However, here we chiefly mean the reddish stone. Because of its greatly differing formations, jasper has many fantasy names. Every type possesses its own vibration. Try out the various stones and you will find additional friends as a result!

Energy class 3

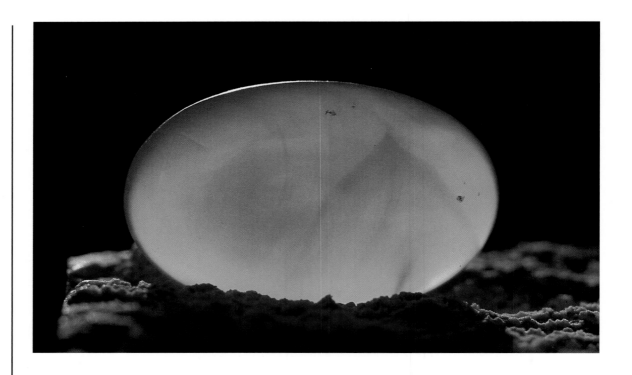

CARNELIAN

VITALITY—STAMINA—SEXUALITY

Fire in the stone kindles fire within us. The carnelian warms intensely. It can increase a fever. We normally use it to feel more active. It enhances our own vital energy and it protects us from lethargy.

Carnelian can stimulate erotic desire. It enhances pleasure during sex play and releases our inhibitions. It encourages our intimacy with a lover; it increases our sense of well-being when we are with them. It inspires us to feel happy, innocent, and playful.

The carnelian is an earnest stone. It bursts with strength and vitality and it can also be gentle. It invites us to participate in its qualities.

Through carnelian's companionship, we can experience a life of wellness—full of *joie de vivre*, humor, laughter, and strength. It bolsters our courage to risk loving and to live life to the fullest. The carnelian shows us the way.

Carnelian . . . . . VITAL ENERGY
Composition . . . SiO_2
Hardness 7
Color . . . . pale-red to reddish-brown
Sources . . . . . . mainly India, also Brazil, Uruguay

Special note: The typical carnelian comes from India. The loveliest red tones come from there. Dyed agate or chalcedony is often sold as carnelian. The sard belongs to this family but has a brownish appearance. I look for the genuine carnelian from India and buy the dyed ones by their feeling.

Energy class 3

BLUE CORAL

FAITH IN LIFE—HOPE FOR SALVATION BY MEN

The blue coral admonishes, "Change your ways! Move in the direction of life; stop working against life and its laws." It exhorts and scolds us.

A person who wears coral understands that life is love but has yet to learn how to achieve love for the good of all.

A tiny piece of the coral is sufficient to put us in a thoughtful mood. It connects us to our responsibility, which is the *preservation of life*.

Blue Coral . . . . . PRESERVING LIFE
Composition . . . $Ca[CO_3]$ (apply this to all coral)
Hardness . . . . . 3—4
Color . . . . gray-blue to lavender
Sources . . . . . . coral reefs in tropical and subtropical latitudes

Energy class 2

GOLD CORAL

DELIVERANCE

Accepting my path in life has meant foregoing many of my desires. Later, I perceived that those aspirations were insignificant. The issues of life are much more important than any personal design.

When I have laid aside most of my fantasies, this coral embraces me. If we find it, gold coral will remind us of God's promise of redemption. Golden coral is God's messenger during a critical time. We regard it as an indication of the everlastingness of God and of life.

Gold coral . . . . . TRUST IN DELIVERANCE
Composition . . . $Ca[CO_3]$
Hardness . . . . . 3—4
Color . . . . bronze to brown with a gold reflective surface
Sources . . . . . . coral reefs & near bodies of land in tropical and subtropical latitudes

Energy class 1

PINK CORAL

TRUST IN LIFE—TENDER LOVE

The gentle energy of this coral attracts us. Tenderness and gentleness envelop us when we hold it. It teaches the principle of giving. It teaches that giving makes us happy.

This coral awakens the most beautiful thing within us—truth in our love.

Children especially love it.

Pink coral . . . . . LOVE—TENDERNESS—JOY
Composition . . . $Ca[CO_3]$
Hardness . . . . . 3—4
Color . . . . . . pale-pink (angel skin) to coral to salmon
Sources . . . . . coral reefs in tropical and subtropical latitudes

Energy class 1

A SPECIAL COMMENT ABOUT THE HARVESTING OF CORAL

Coral forms itself from individual little animals (polyps) that join in colonies by secreting lime substances. In time, they form plantlike coral beds and then vast reefs, which teem with other marine life. These underwater continents are crucial to our planet's ecological balance.

Through irresponsible harvesting, humans have reduced the coral in the world to a dangerous minimum within a few decades. This is a further example of how we have mistakenly "enriched" ourselves without any respect for the consequences to us, to nature, and to her growth processes.

Within a few decades—or even sooner—when coral harvesting becomes illegal, we will discover precious stones. These will vibrate with the energy of coral and the oceans of the world. They will tell us about coral and their spiritual relation to the human race.

It is always good to apologize for what we have unscrupulously eradicated. We should also tell God how sorry we are for this.

Even if we find gemstones that are similar to this energy, coral will eventually vanish to humanity, unless we vigilantly establish protected areas. The spirit and immortality of coral will remain preserved on the Divine level.

If we would succumb to the pain that we really feel over what we have destroyed and eradicated on this earth—if we sincerely risk the emotional distress—this would shake our foundations; the only thing we would want to do would be to go home to God. As long as our lot is on this earth, we will still feel this empathic pain subconsciously; it is as if we were killing ourselves bit by bit. There is nothing left for us to do but heal the planet of this horrible pain. This healing is the path to God.

RED CORAL

LAUGHTER—LIVELINESS—WARMTH

Red coral warms the body and the heart. It understands itself to be a bridge between the body and the spirit. It was a gift from the ocean beings to the human race. We have not treated this gift in a deserving manner.

We have exploited these organisms that have grown in the ocean since prehistoric times. The pain about our mistreatment of the earth is endlessly torturing every one of us subconsciously. No wonder we suppress it so vehemently! However, nothing can be suppressed forever. Those individuals who are conscious of this pain will change their behavior.

In its devotion to humanity, red coral gives rise within us to laughter, liveliness, warmth, and joy in life. One day, it will no longer be there for us. Other stones will have to replace it with the same characteristics. It still reminds us of our inadequacy and mistakes as it completes its last message.

"Do not get lost in melancholy; *always make a new start*—under any circumstance."

The coral will remain preserved on the spiritual level.

Red coral . . . . . VITALITY
Composition . . . $Ca[CO_3]$
Hardness . . . . . 3—4
Color . . . . medium (Sardinia) to dark-red (morion, ox blood)
Sources . . . . . . coral reefs in tropical and subtropical latitudes

Special note: Inferior coral is porous and shows holes and tears. These faults are filled with red wax that melts with heat and discolors clothing. There are also other ways to dye coral, but this coloration often fades.

Reconstructed coral imitation is made from coral dust mixed with a binding substance. This is molded into beads or other shapes. It is also important to be sure that we acquire a genuine, untreated piece of coral. The label "coral" on a necklace does not at all mean that this is natural coral.

Certain types of coral are now protected by law. For example, the sale of red Mediterranean coral is illegal in Germany.

Energy class 2

BLACK CORAL

STURDINESS AND JOY

With the black coral we have a good helper for overcoming fears. It possesses all the qualities of red coral (strength, vitality, etc.) but still lets us participate in the knowledge of death and transition. This helps us to amass strength and to hope for resurrection.

Black coral is perfect for times of crisis when we feel too exhausted or discouraged to pray or attune to the Light.

Black coral. . . . . CONQUERING FEARS
Composition . . . $Ca[CO_3]$
Hardness . . . . . 3—4
Color . . . . black to blackish-brown
Sources . . . . . . coral reefs in tropical and subtropical latitudes

Special note: In Germany, it is prohibited to sell black coral.

Energy class 2

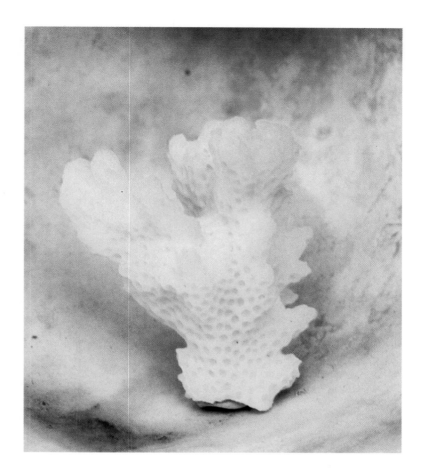

WHITE CORAL

SIMPLICITY

This coral enlivens us. In its presence we feel the hope for happiness. Its direct message is that simplicity belongs to happiness. A simple heart is the best condition for happiness.

Live simply. Feel the liberation. Go into the Light.

White coral . . . . SIMPLICITY
Composition . . . $Ca[CO_3]$
Hardness . . . . . 3—4
Color . . . . pure white to white with angel skin tones

Special note: Coral, pearls, and amber dissolve in body acids. Perfume, makeup, lotion, suntan oil, or perspiration can diminish their beauty. Always dab them with a soft towel after wearing them on bare skin. Cleanse their energy with clear water, or even better, with spiritual means.
White coral is inexpensive. To wear it for physical well being, buy a thin necklace and do not worry about body acids harming it. Then, return it to the water with thanks.

Energy class 2

BRANCHING CORAL

MERCY—RENEWAL OF THE BODY

This coral teaches us an important lesson: Even inferior gemstones can contain a great energy.

Branching coral grows with jewelry quality coral. They form a whole organism on the reef. For this reason, the branching contains the same energy as the coral itself. However, its vibrations are coarser and less distinct—like a blurred reflection or like an unclear print.

When we become conscious of coral's essential role and our karmic debt to them, we should also thankfully make use of its help.

Branching coral . . BEING ONE WITH THE TOTALITY
Composition . . . $Ca[CO_3]$
Hardness . . . . . 3—4
Color . . . . all colors
Sources . . . . . . coral reefs in tropical and subtropical latitudes

Energy class 3

CHIASTOLITE (Andalusite)

SOLEMNITY—REMINDER OF DEATH

This stone strengthens our serious natures. It accompanies us in the search for the meaning of life and death. It teaches us respect for ourselves and our inner struggles. Grappling with truth leads us through many deaths. This stone assures us that every death brings redemption closer.

Chiastolite. . . . . DEATH
Composition . . . $Al[AlSiO_5]$
Hardness 7.5
Color . . . . gray-beige-brownish with a cross sign
Sources . . . . . . Southern Australia, Bolivia, Chile, France, Spain, Russia, United States

Energy class 3

K U N Z I T E (Spodumene)

BLISS—JOY OF LIFE

Kunzite is a gift of the gods to us! It promises feelings of bliss and it keeps its pact. The radiance of pure love through this stone warms us very much; it demands nothing from us. On the contrary—it vows to uplift us!

It speaks of God's love and the gift of heaven to the human race, "LOVE! LOVE! LOVE!" Those who feel dispirited about love and who believe that they have failed, will find new courage here. They understand that love is much different from what we always expect it will be—it is quite simple! They risk opening their hearts and devoting themselves to happiness and rapture.

Kunzite . . . . . . ECSTASY
Composition . . . $LiAl[Si_2O_6]$
Hardness . . . . . 6.5—7
Color . . . . pink, violet-pink
Sources . . . . . . Brazil, Madagascar, Afghanistan, Pakistan, United States

Special note: Be careful when having such a stone set. Try to find a ready-made ring or pendant or have the stone treated and set where you bought it. The trio of spodumene-kunzite-hiddenite is very easy to split and very sensitive to pressure. Some stones are so brittle that they break even after being faceted. Before it is treated, ask the jeweler if he will replace the stone if it breaks. If you buy it where it is also treated and the company is large and respected, they might take responsibility for possible damage. On the other hand, remember that there are no coincidences. It is your responsibility to decide whether or not your stones are preserved.

Energy class 1

K Y A N I T E

SUPPORT—ENDURANCE—HAPPINESS

Kyanite give us an understanding for love. It encourages us to risk love. It awakens hope for love and promises success.

It is a good helper where endurance is necessary in order to walk the path of love. This stone wants to be loved. Its nature is to reciprocate. It has consecrated its life to love.

Kyanite . . . . . . LOVE AND PATIENCE
Composition . . . $Al_2[O/SiO_4]$
Hardness . . . . . Longitudinal axis 4.5, vertical 6.5
Color . . . . blue-white to blue, seldom green, yellow, brown
Sources . . . . . . India, Russia, Brazil, United States, Africa, the Alps

Energy class 1

LABRADORITE

TRUTH—TRUTH—TRUTH

The labradorite advances our growth through truth and honesty. It conveys to us that there is no other path; there is nothing more beautiful than *reality*. Candor is always good. We may fear it because we do not understand it. We do not understand that inner greatness lies beneath every painful fact. Labradorite loves human beings very much. It wants to help us understand the meaning of uprightness.

We must search within ourselves. Beneath our own masks and illusions is the negative self. To recognize and accept the negative self causes maturity. The key to the Higher Self, to our Divine quality, lies in saying *yes* to the side that we do not want to see. We are children of God. When we recognize and accept our dark sides—when we embrace them—we will understand.

When I strive for integrity—when I am willing to perceive my entire reality—then gifts (the greatest gifts) will always come to me.

God is great. God is veracity and honesty. We can also be this way. Cradled in the love of the labradorite, we perceive and enjoy our entire truth.

Labradorite . . . . . TRUTH AND HONESTY
Composition . . . . $(Ca,Na)[(Al,Si)_2Si_2O_8]$
Hardness . . . . . . 6—6.5
Color . . . . gray with strong blue shimmer, also turquoise and green-golden sheen
Sources . . . . Canada, Madagascar, Mexico, Russia, United States, India

Special note: Labradorites can be both opaque and transparent. They are iridescent in quite astonishing colors but mostly in a bright blue. There are very fine stones, with a shimmer of pink, violet, yellow, orange, green, blue, and turquoise. They have delicate inclusions and often appear dull, until the light strikes at the right angle; then, a blue or turquoise practically blinds us.
Dealers sometimes offer labradorites as moonstones. Both come from the feldspar family.

Energy class 2

PINK LABRADORITE

ENLIGHTENMENT AND GROWTH

These stones occur very rarely. They enter our lives with a special task. They would like to serve humanity in a very practical way; they absorb the human vibrations of our age and relay its messages to the kingdom of gemstones. There, nature angels select undiscovered minerals; we will discover them in the near future. After we discover these new stones, these gemstones and minerals will help us to evolve further.

The pink labradorite also directs information about us to Those who plan our destiny. It can only do this when we wear it and come into contact with other people. For this reason, its gift to us is enjoyment of life!

Pink labradorite . . TRUST IN HUMAN BEINGS
Composition   . . . $(Ca,Na)[(Al,Si)_2Si_2O_8]$
Hardness . . . . . 6—6.5
Color . . . . distinctly pink-colored shimmer
Sources . . . . . Canada, Madagascar, Mexico, Russia, United States, India

Energy class 1

LAPIS LAZULI

POWER—POWER—POWER

The force of the lapis lazuli is a gift of God. Very few people can wear lapis; it challenges the entire being. Those who do wear it should know that they will experience intense situations.

The lapis brings up many old issues. This can be painful. Yet, it also gives us the strength for transformation and insight. We can perceive and learn many things—usually about ourselves—when we wear it. It gives us intimate knowledge of our deepest psyche. Visionaries will understand its advice. For others, the cognition will occur subconsciously. They might manifest as physical symptoms, unrest, and nervousness. If we have already done a great deal of work on ourselves, we can wear this stone in the consciousness of our inner strength and truly adorn ourselves with it.

The lapis lazuli wants to be loved. When it is of the best quality, we will have many reasons to enjoy it.

Be careful with children: the stone might be too powerful and frighten them. If possible, do not wear it at night.

Lapis lazuli . . . . STRENGTH AND INSIGHT
Composition . . . Main component lasurite: $Na_6Ca_2[(S,SO_4,Cl_2)_2/(Al^6Si_6O_{24})_2]$
Hardness . . . . . 5—6
Color . . . . luminous royal-blue, pale-blue to dark azure-blue with sparkles
Sources . . . . . . Afghanistan, Russia, Chile

Special note: Genuine lapis is characterized by flecks of pyrite. Lapis lazuli is often imitated. The most common practice is to dye lesser stone qualities. The dyed Nunkirk jasper is sold under the name of German lapis or Swiss lapis but also misrepresented as lapis. In this case, reliable gem dealers (or dealers who regularly sell at well known gemstone exchanges and cannot afford to lose their good reputation) can give good advice.

Energy class 2

LAVENDER JASPER

ENJOYING LIFE

Repose surrounds us when we breathe in deeply. Then strength fills us and the world looks completely different once again.

This is how the effect of lavender jasper takes place. This type of jasper not only gives us strength and endurance but also tranquillity and reassurance. I highly recommend it for times of agitation. It is also good when we feel frenzied and fear losing composure. When we want to accomplish something that is beyond our strength, lavender jasper can boost us. This is a stone that loves us very much.

Lavender jasper . . . . REPOSE AND STRENGTH
Composition . . . . . SiO_2
Hardness 7
Color . . . . pale-violet
Source . . . . United States

Energy class 3

LAZULITE

STILLNESS—PEACE

Lazulite calms our nerves. It dissolves tensions and gives us serenity.

It creates a continually reflective mood. This is a good stone for people suffering from heart disease. It leads us to know the importance of connecting with God; as a result, strength and harmony blossom within us. We become willing to love and learn. We feel willing to ascend our destined path. In order to continue in this direction, we will require other stones.

Lazulite . . . . . . YEARNING FOR GOD
Composition . . . $(Mg,Fe^{2+})Al_2[OH/PO_4]_2$
Hardness . . . . . 5—6
Color . . . . sky-blue, indigo-blue, blue-white to white
Sources . . . . . . Canada, Brazil, India, Madagascar, Switzerland, Austria

Energy class 3

LEOPARD JASPER

MERCY AS SELF-EVIDENT TRUTH

Sometimes, apparently insignificant stones are the ones that begin important feelings in our hearts.

"God sees your efforts. God knows that you follow Him. Why despair when God is so close to you? Those who obey God and want to comply to what is right have achieved the highest thing: the right to every mercy. However, God is more than mercy. God is the striving upward in the Light behind the Light; you are the same. Take your little steps. They are giant steps, outside of time and space.

"Comfort your heart, knowing that you are one with everything. You *are*. Enjoy it!"

Leopard jasper . . ENJOY THE GIFT OF MERCY
Composition . . . SiO_2
Hardness 7
Color . . . . beige, black-brown-gray-yellow-white spots
Source . . . . Brazil

Energy class 1

LEPIDOLITE

INNER STRENGTH

Lepidolite reveals our inherent strength. This stone limits itself to the qualities of the heart but it ensures that the mind recognizes these qualities. It heeds the rest of our personality to give the heart a chance to develop. The voice of the heart is often timid and easily suppressed. Here is a stone that gives support to emotions. It places the defense behaviors and insecurities in the background.

Lepidolite . . . . . STRENGTH
Composition . . . $K(Li,Al)_3[(F,OH)_2/(Si,Al)_4O_{10}]$
Hardness . . . . . 2.5—3
Color . . . . pink to pink-violet, pale-violet, red-gray, white
Sources . . . . . . Europe, California, Mozambique

Energy class 3

MAGNESITE

A STONE FOR THE FUTURE

The magnesite forces us to be still. It presents us messages that we do not yet understand. In one or two years it will reveal itself to us.

It is good for people with heart disease.

Magnesite . . . . . STILLNESS
Composition . . . $Mg[CO_3]$
Hardness . . . . . 4—4.5
Color . . . . . . white, yellow-white, yellow, brown, gray-white
Sources . . . . . . worldwide

Special note: Magnesite is frequently dyed blue and sold as turquoise. We use unprocessed stones.

Energy class 1

MAGNETITE

DISSOLVES HARDNESS

This stone will be very important for the future. It dissolves hardness within us caused by a lack of love. When we are hard, we do not love enough.

The magnetite makes us aware of this hardness. At the same time, it dissolves it. This happens by it putting us in a state in which we are able to accept our mistakes. It is not a simple stone. Yet, because it strengthens and encourages us, we still feel good in its vibration.

Magnetite . . . . . RECONCILIATION AND JOY
Composition . . . $Fe^{2+}Fe_2^{3+}O_4$
Hardness . . . . . 5.5—6
Color . . . . anthracite gray, glows when polished
Sources . . . . . . Brazil, the Alps, Norway, Sweden

Energy class 2

MALACHITE

HELP FOR HUMANITY

The malachite is a great helper. It has an enormously quick effect on the physical level. From the spiritual viewpoint, it creates the connection between God and humanity in a very material manner. It heals wherever it can. This is its nature.

Apart from its greatest tasks—an impact on the physical plane—the malachite is a stone that reconnects us with the essence of nature. This is how it gives us strength and power, understanding and knowledge, repose and security. All of this lies in nature. In nature, we can discover everything that we should know about God. The path to God also leads through nature and through the simplicity of the heart. Losing everything is always a sign that we should start over and become more simple. Malachite helps us in this process; it encourages us to separate voluntarily from inappropriate people, ideas, or belongings—whatever no longer fits us.

Life is change. Only when I can let go of one thing or the other can something new come to me.

The malachite is a teacher. It shows us how everything important can come to us—and many more good things!

Malachite . . . . . WARMTH—HEALING
Composition . . . $Cu_2[(OH)2/CO_3]$
Hardness . . . . . 3.5—4
Color . . . . green, usually striped
Sources . . . . . . the Ural Mountains, Zaire, Australia, Chile, Zambia, Zimbabwe, Namibia, United States

Special note: The malachite is a very soft stone. It is beautiful when polished. However it can also easily become dull. Malachite necklaces can be repolished but this sometimes costs almost as much as a new necklace. I therefore recommend pendants and hand-stones instead.

Energy class 3

MARCASITE

FORGETTING A GRUDGE

Resentment is a bitter lesson. In a variety of hurtful situations, it always returns to us until we learn to release it. There are no victims; there are only histrionic people who create certain problems for themselves. Some have continued this behavior for many lifetimes. Their grudging, strife, hatred, and emotional scarring remain unhealed.

Resentment drains an immense amount of energy! If we do not heal it, it will destroy us. Marcasite does not heal resentment; it allows us to forget our feelings of umbrage for a short time. We have permission to imagine a life without animosity. For once, we feel free to recognize the difference.

Understanding how much resentment drains strength from us, we should request that life show us our paths to healing. Then we should quickly make use of them.

Marcasite . . . . . FORGIVE AND FORGET
Composition . . . FeS$_2$
Hardness . . . . . 6—6.5
Color . . . . pale-brass with a tinge of green or greenish
Sources . . . . . . worldwide

Special note: Well-known marcasite jewelry sometimes consists of pyrite, a mineral similar to marcasite. The true marcasite gradually deteriorates because of the effect of air. We should preferably use inexpensive handstones.
The so-called "gold dollar" (radiating pattern of marcasite aggregate) often appear under the name of pyrite.

Energy class 3

MELANITE (Garnet)

REGRET—MEANING OF LIFE

Those who love a melanite feel death in their hearts.

There are many deaths. We die every day. However we also free ourselves from the pain of the past everyday. Melanite works in this sense. It shows where we have neglected life. It also draws our attention to squandered energies. It promotes a balance—the balance of our life. With it, we understand the life that we have already lived.

However, to the same degree it also opens up the heavens for us for a new beginning. It promises us a happier life.

"Everything will be all right. You are on the right path. Hold me to your heart and understand that God loves you. No one sees the Eternal Life with a broken heart. All of your wounds will heal in the Light of Eternal Life. All pain vanishes before God. You will rise again and be a bride—the bride of God. Rise before God. Stand at His side and be His friend, His brother, His helper, His love. Understand that you are ETERNAL. Pause in your everyday life; connect yourself with this feeling. God is within you.

"There is only reason for joy."

Melanite . . . . . . COMPASSION—NEW LIFE
THE GATEWAY BEHIND THE GATEWAY
Composition . . . Andradite containing titanium (see ANDRADITE, p. 55)
Hardness . . . . . 6.5—7
Color . . . . appears black, then flashes brown-orange in sunlight
Sources . . . . . . Chile; Vesuvius, Italy; Albanian Mountains, Kaiserstuhl, Germany

Energy class 1

METEORITE

RESTLESSNESS—DISTANT WORLDS

Countless peoples have lived before the earth people. Countless peoples live with them on distant planets. To be a human being means greatness. However, we do not live our greatness. The disregard for other beings and manifestations is proof of this.

When we disregard life, just because it seems unreachable to us, we deny life. We also deny it through our behavior towards animals, plants, minerals, and spiritual beings. Ultimately, we vehemently deny life in view of ourselves. Does anyone really live his or her vital energy? We are but faded reflections of ourselves.

The energy from meteorite pieces always draws our attention to expansion, to the necessity of going beyond our habits in life and our prejudices. There is no growth unless we give up our old ways. There is no development without courageously moving forward. We are so much more than we think—why are we hesitating?

Meteorite . . . . . BEING HUMAN AND RESPONSIBILITY
Composition . . . Iron meteorite—approximately 90% iron
Hardness 6
Color . . . . dark or shiny silver tones
Sources . . . . . . worldwide

Special note: The photographed piece of meteorite was etched in order to enhance the unusual metallic pattern, which does not exist in earthly iron. The name of this weave-like structure is the "Widmannstätten structure."

Energy class 2

MILK OPAL

JOY IN MY LIFE

The simple opals have a wonderful quality of lightness. With this, they take our hearts by storm. The milk opal imparts to us a very quiet joy in life. This is a type of modesty that we have forgotten and a silent joy that allows our heart to blossom in a wondrous way. It shows that the gentle and quiet things within us have great power. It is a gemstone angel with a silent vibration of happiness.

Milk opal . . . . . SILENCE IN THE HEART
Composition . . . $SiO_2 \cdot nH_2O$
Hardness . . . . . 5.5—6
Color . . . . milk-white
Sources . . . . . . Bohemia, Fichtel Mountains in Germany

Energy class 1

MOLDAVITE

PRAYER—GRAPPLING WITH GOD

If we listen within ourselves, we will always find God. As long as we do not want to hear this voice, our life is difficult. It is up to us to change it.

The moldavite shows us how senseless a struggle with God is. Recalcitrance is coquetry and a squandering of vital energies. We perceive this with the help of this stone and turn anew to God.

The moldavite can neutralize radioactivity.

Moldavite . . . . . PRAYER
Composition . . . $SiO_2(+Al_2O_3)$
Hardness 5.5
Color . . . . green
Source . . . . Bohemia

Special note: Moldavites are also called glass meteorites (tektite). Theoretically, the falling meteorites struck sand containing quartz; this melted and solidified as glass. The tektite shower fell across hundreds of kilometers; they hurdled this far from the impact.

Energy class 1

MOONSTONE

UTTER DEVOTION

When we find this stone, something new enters our lives. Many superstitious people fear this stone. Moonstone calls for dedication, surrender, and sacrifice.

Some people wish to achieve a disciple's temperament; they will wear small moonstones with the this goal in mind. However, when inner resistance is too great, the stone can have no effect.

Rebirth of the heart will come to those prepared (by life or by other stones) to accept the moonstone experience. What used to appear difficult to us will become insignificant under its influence.

However, it teaches the principle of absolute femininity, which is pure devotion. This is normally arduous for us to follow unconditionally. We would like to do so, but the apparent necessity of giving up one's self very much prevents us from doing this—until we have understood that we have gained much more in this way when we follow its call. It teaches femininity in its true strength.

With the help of pink-colored stones, we can overcome our fears of it.

212

Moonstone . . . FEMININITY
Composition . . $K[AlSi_3O_8]$
Hardness . . . . 6—6.5
Color . . . . . . gray, milky, preferred: translucent, best: blue shimmer
Sources . . . . . Sri Lanka, India, United States, Tanzania

Special note: Good moonstones with a strong blue shimmer have become rare and expensive. A less expensively priced moonstone with a blue glow can be a labradorite.

Energy class 1

APRICOT MOONSTONE

OPENING OF THE HEART—FEMININITY

The qualities of the transparent to gray moonstone vibrate with *reassurance*. People often misunderstand the principle of femininity. Where devotion and sacrifice would be necessary, we are often content with letting go and supporting. This wonderful stone helps us to understand dedication without withdrawing from it. It allows femininity to blossom gradually. Our understanding grows. Our fears disappear. It promises maturity and perfection, *encouraging* our devotion. We will feel intuitively whether we can then live these qualities with the help of the little moonstone or under the influence of another stone when we have grown beyond the apricot-colored moonstone and only wear it out of love.

All moonstones are naturally also important for men!

Apricot moonstone . . . HOPE FOR FEMININITY
Composition . . . . . . $K[AlSi_3O_8]$
Hardness . . . . 6—6.5
Color . . . . apricot, sometimes near beige
Sources . . . . Sri Lanka, India, United States, Tanzania

MOUKAITE

HELPS JOYFULLY FULFILL EVERYDAY DUTIES

This type of jasper has a very purposeful effect on those of us who use it. After two or three days, we suddenly dedicate ourselves to long-neglected work. If we are open enough, we will also feel that we do this joyfully. If not, we simply take care of the work.

Moukaite . . . . . SERVING JOYFULLY
Composition . . . SiO_2
Hardness 7
Color . . . . variegated white-yellow-brown-red-violet
Source . . . . . . Australia

Special note: The moukaite amazes time and again with its prompt effect!

Energy class 3

MOSS AGATE

RESPECT FOR LIFE

The green moss agate protects us from succumbing to feelings of disrespect. It makes sure that we respect life. It reminds us of the needs of nature and our own needs.

This is a good stone for collecting our thoughts. Its vibrations bring repose; it helps to insure safety; it encourages us to act more reliably; through our improved behavior, it opens the way for good luck. We feel good in its presence. We once again know who we are.

Both green moss agate and white moss agate are wonderful helpers for all those who write.

The white moss agate strengthens the principle of purity of thoughts and goodwill towards life.

Moss agate . . . . REVERENCE FOR LIFE
Composition . . . SiO_2
Hardness 7
Color . . . . colorless, translucent, with green inclusions
Sources . . . . . . China, United States

Special note: The typical moss agate has inclusions that look like moss. These are made of hornblende, a complex silicate mineral. The white moss agate has very few green inclusions.

Energy class 3

MOSS OPAL

JOYFUL MOMENTS

The moss opal is the rascal among the gemstones. It is roguish and loves to play jokes on us human beings. It raises our spirits for the moment when we wear it! We really "feel our oats;" it invigorates us. This is why it is an especially good stone for times of need.

It reminds us that we are more than what we feel at the moment. Every pain, every affliction, every crisis, every death is a step towards perfection. We only feel these conditions as painful when we defend ourselves against growth.

Our original state is happiness. All life and all life situations are only stations in our return home to happiness, our return home to GOD. So this stone is a friend that enables us to recognize our happiness. The energy enters our consciousness; we feel exuberant. This euphoric state is a gift from the moss opal; it gives us the subliminal perception that there is nothing worth worrying about.

Seen from this perspective, each of us should possess a stone and a necklace and wear them accordingly.

Moss opal . . . . . STRUCTURE—HIGH SPIRITS
Composition . . . $SiO_2 nH_2O$
Hardness . . . . . 5.5—6
Color . . . . colorless to yellow with dendrites, preferred translucent
Source . . . . Brazil

Energy class 2

MORGANITE (Beryl)

ANGEL OF WISDOM

The morganite is the angel of wisdom united with love. True wisdom comes from the heart; it communes with the heart. Symbolized by the delicate pink, the highest vibration of *holistic love* surrounds the morganite. This is the highest vibration of *holistic love* we know and for which we aspire.

We therefore feel secure and loved within its energy—although it shows us our fear of love with the highest degree of clarity. Yet, at the same time, it helps us overcome this fear of love because a part of its wisdom transmits us. This reminds us that there is no reason to be afraid of love.

Our fear of love developed through past-life experiences. People we have loved hurt and abandoned us. Someday, we will perceive that life and death are one. We will realize that we cannot lose anyone or anything. We will feel our immortality. We will know security in absolute love, then we risk loving without any conditions—then there is nothing more that can hurt us.

We human beings are capable of unconditional love. We only have to try it.

Morganite . . . . . LOVE—WISDOM
Composition . . . $Be_3A_{12}[Si_6O_{18}]$
Hardness . . . . . 7.5—8
Color . . . . pale to dark-pink, apricot
Sources . . . . . . Madagascar, Brazil, United States, South Africa

Energy class 1

NEPHRITE

REPOSE—COMPOSURE

The nephrite is a reflective stone, very similar to the jade energy. We experience inner peace when we use it long enough—and in this respect it is "our" stone for inner peace!

With it we simply see the world a bit more serenely. We delight in little things. We feel more in harmony with ourselves.

This is a good stone for meditation. It is important for the physical level. In the coming years, it will be a very important stone for all of humanity.

Nephrite. . . . . . REPOSE
Composition . . . $Ca_2(Mg,Fe^{2+})_5[OH/Si_4O_{11}]_2$
Hardness . . . . . 6—6.5
Color . . . . green, also other colors
Sources . . . . . . China, Russia, Australia, Burma, Brazil, Canada, Mexico,
New Guinea, Europe, Taiwan

Special note: Dark-green stone, usually sold as jade, is the primary subject here. The jade-type stones have been reclassified as jadeite and nephrite since 1863. Both can be pale-green or dark-green and it is very difficult to differentiate between them. Early jade carvings are always nephrite. Only in recent times has jade been exported from Burma to China and has been processed there.

This is important to know; dealers use the term "jade" very carelessly. In Idar-Oberstein, I bought an aragonite necklace as yellow jade. This was in a reputable retail store where the boss himself cut stones. I assume that he had purchased this material as jade. Large gemstone companies process nearly every type of gemstone on their premises. Their clerks are the most learned in this matter. So are those lapidaries who love stones from the depths of their hearts. However, dealers generally do not investigate the differences, since they rarely care about the energies of the stones. This is an exercise in perseverance for us.

Energy class 2

OBSIDIAN

CHANGING ONE'S WAY—TRANSFORMATION—BREAKTHROUGH

Use the powerful obsidian in doses. Its enormous energy can set up situations that are too much for us.

This stone cuts short chaos and calls for order. It admonishes us to observe the laws of life. It lives uncompromising austerity. When we subject ourselves to the vibrations of this stone, we must feel prepared to go through our depths. We are certain to have Light— but after the purification!

We can soften its massive movement forward with pink stones. Austerity paired with love brings us just as quickly forward and is not as painful.

This stone also channels the Light; it radiates the highest qualities. We should never forget that the painful processes within us only occur because we do not know how to appreciate certain qualities and prefer to cling to our illusions. The more we press forward to our own Light being, the more we will value the gemstones that are of great truth and austerity. What seems austere or strict to us is a swift, consistent striding towards the Light.

Obsidian. . . . . . CHANGING ONE'S WAYS
Composition . . . primarily SiO_2
Hardness . . . . . 5—5.5
Color . . . . black, gray, brown, green
Sources . . . . . . United States, Mexico, Europe, South America, Iceland, Russia

Special note: Obsidian is a mineral similar to rhyolite. It primarily consists of silicic acid hydrate in the form of glass. It forms during volcanic eruptions.

Energy class 3

ONYX

STRENGTH AND ENDURANCE

The black onyx imparts repose to us. It strengthens our trust in our own strength. In contrast to other black stones, it possesses a certain lightness. It shows that seriousness does not have a heavy feeling to it. It imparts repose to us through the feeling of sincerity, seriousness, and the significance in our life. It helps us understand that joy rests in seriousness.

Onyx. . . . . . . SIGNIFICANCE
Composition . . . SiO_2
Hardness 7
Color . . . . black or white on black
Sources . . . . . . Brazil

Energy class 3

O N Y X — M A R B L E

MUCH LIGHTNESS

Jewelry of onyx marble brings us joy. It is a pleasure to touch objects made of this material. Calcite or aragonite artifacts can falsely pass for onyx. Onyx marble has a beautiful vibration. If we know of which stones our Light objects are made, we can read about them under their proper names.

In this case, this onyx—better called onyx-marble—delights our heart.

Onyx. . . . . ELATION
Composition . . . . Calcite and/or aragonite (see CALCITE, p. 81 & ARAGONITE, p. 62)
Hardness . . . . . 3—4
Color . . . . . . light, pale-green, yellow, brown
Sources . . . . . marble caves of Romania, Namibia, Mexico, Spain, Morocco

Energy class 3

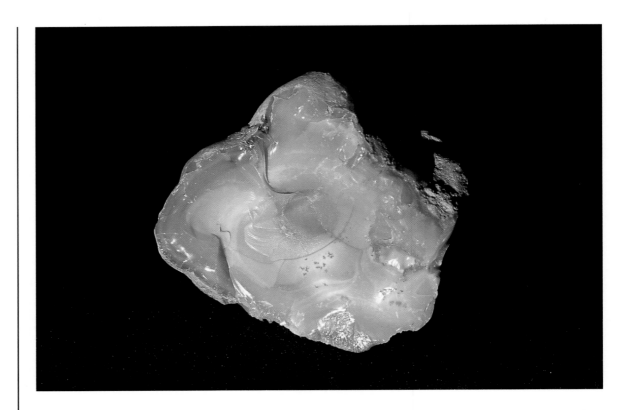

YELLOW OPAL

GIVING UP REGRET

The yellow opal is a cheerful stone. It is self-confident and happy and it imparts these qualities to the wearer.

It also says: "Enjoy life. Do your duty. Delight in God; and be thankful that YOU exist."

It helps a great deal on the path to perfection.

Yellow opal . . . . . JOY IN LIFE
Composition . . . . $SiO_2 nH_2O$
Hardness 6
Color . . . . yellow to ochre
Sources . . . . Hungary, United States, Mexico, Brazil

Energy class 1

GREEN OPAL

PLEASURE—ABSOLUTE PLEASURE!

This stone is a joy to hold in the hand! It has an immediate effect! Joy, happiness, and delight flow through us. We have a wonderful revelation—the utter, divine delight of *being alive*. Briefly, we harmonize with everything. Delicious pleasure fills us. We want to embrace God and the world right then and there. We love ourselves unconditionally.

With this stone, we have permission to experience how this state feels. In order to live it, we require a long path and the help of many stones.

Green opal. . . . . MARVELOUS PLEASURE
Composition . . . $SiO_2 \cdot nH_2O$
Hardness 6
Color . . . . ocean green
Sources . . . . . . Hungary, United States, Mexico, Brazil

Special note: While writing this, the green opal surprised me with an overwhelming vibration of joy. I immediately rushed to a dealer. I bought an even larger one but its effect disappointed me. I placed it over my heart; my mood worsened! This time, it showed me exactly which energy (worry in mental circles) obstructed my joy! This is the effect that stones can have! If this is not your reaction, simply devote yourself to them longer.

Energy class 1

VIOLET OPAL

HOPE FOR A NEW LIFE

No opal is as fond of human beings as this one. Its quality is life, namely the awakening of *new life*.

When we use this stone, a hope for peace germinates within us. This peace is a result of the surrender of the inner struggle. This conflict is against God and the material world. After a great deal of examination, we can perceive our difficulties. All of them originate in the reluctance to subject completely ourselves to the will of God. This stone reveals how our lives could improve when we take a risk, recognizing God as our absolute guide.

We simply need to speak our plights to God.

"I love you, God, I love you so much that I even fulfill this task for you—to be a human being. I love you for giving me this task. I know that it is important. This is why I make every effort to fulfill this small task that you have entrusted to me among so many others. I welcome the assignment be a human being with all the torments, all the joys, and all the trials.

"Let me forget that it is only one task among many; let me fulfill this task with my entire respect, dignity, and love, as if it were the most important one that you have given me.

"Let me understand; being human means to feel separate from you. Someday I will see that this separation has never and does not exist. Hold me in your arms, God. Allow me the pain and insecurities that I want to suffer. Afterward, let me understand why I needed these illusions."

The violet opal gives us the hope that this knowledge will become accessible for us. It comforts us on all paths. Its strength is so great that we can pray to it as the love of God itself.

Violet opal . . . . . PEACE THROUGH OURSELVES
Composition . . . $SiO_2 nH_2 0$
Hardness 6
Color . . . . lavender to violet
Sources . . . . . . Hungary, United States, Mexico, Brazil

Energy class 1

OPAL MATRIX

ABUNDANCE OF LIFE—PERCEPTION OF THE EARTH

The earth is like a good mother. She gives unconditionally. This stone symbolizes life, wealth in simplicity, the power in naturalness, and sincerity.

Those who love the opal matrix have returned to simplicity, modesty, and inner abundance.

It is a good teacher for the ambitious.

Opal matrix . . . . ABUNDANCE
Composition . . . $SiO_2 \cdot nH_2O$ in a rock base
Hardness . . . . . 5.5—6.5 (opal) and rock conglomerate
Color . . . . rainbow opalescence
Sources . . . . . Brazil, Australia, Guatemala, Honduras, Japan, United States

Special note: Opal matrix is opal in a parent rock with a small number of precious-opal inclusions. The whole rock is cut into spheres or pieces.

Energy class 3

ORTHOCLASE

EARNESTNESS FROM THE HEART

The orthoclase gives our hearts repose because it instantaneously reaches the entire body with its vibrations. It spreads the message "I need time and reflection; I can give myself space for this. I have *permission* to do so."

In life, nothing is as important as walking our spiritual path. When we give first importance to the exercises required for this purpose in our daily routine, we will receive every type of help and experience with complete surprise how easily the things that we saw as problems take care of themselves. The Spiritual Life is our actual life. Those who have perceived this and act accordingly will always have an easier time of it than other people.

Orthoclase. . . . . PERCEIVING THE ESSENTIAL
Composition . . . $K[AlSi_3O_8]$
Hardness . . . . . 6—6.5
Color . . . . translucent yellow
Sources . . . . . . Madagascar, United States, India

Energy class 1

PADPARADSCHA (Corundum)

JOY IN LIFE—VITAL ENERGY—FORESIGHT

The Padparadscha is a very gentle stone with enormous energy. No other stone achieves as much within such a short period of time.

What does it achieve? It helps us to attain a far-reaching change and a completely different way of dealing with vital energies. The Padparadscha enables us to have a type of connection to our *original being*. Waves become calm, mysteries understood, trust flows through us and gentleness frees us.

This stone is a gift of the gods to great souls. Those who wear a padparadscha understand God. They have heard His call and are unequivocally responsive.

As usual, this stone first removes all resistance that we have. This can cause a difficult time. However that soul who unconditionally wants to obey God is not willing to do this? After the purification process, it gives us a clarity of the mind and heart that is without equal.

The Padparadscha is also a powerful stone for the physical level. Stones with strong colors are suitable for this. The apricot-colored stone also reveals a special secret to us.

"Whoever loves it belongs to God and becomes His successor."

In earthly terms this means that those who wear it have dedicated themselves to God because they believe in God, know Him, and know where His paths lead them—into the absolute *Light*. Jesus has exemplified this for us, "God and I are one."

Padparadscha . . . CLOSENESS TO GOD
Composition . . . Al_2O_3
Hardness 9
Color . . . . red-orange to apricot to peach
Sources . . . . . Sri Lanka, Tanzania

Special note: Padparadscha is a member of the sapphire family. The sapphire and the ruby belong to the corundum group. Colors define the names of each gemstone in its group. A corundum that does not match any gemstone color is a "discolored sapphire." For our purposes, there are neither discolorations nor limitations—only divine gifts. This applies to the sapphire as well as all gemstones. Apricot-colored sapphires are Padparadscha; how could such a treasure be considered a discoloration?

Energy class 1

PALLASITE (Meteorite)

MERCY—PERCEPTION OF OTHER WORLDS

With this "stone" we hold something special in the hand—a piece of another world. There is more to the universe than we see, hear, or know.

The pallasite lets us give consideration to where we stand. We take such a tiny space in the universe with our planet that seems to be the only important one to us. Let us listen to its message and its voice.

"Distant worlds want to be discovered. However before you deal with other planets, you should first take care of yourselves. Many people are more distant from each other than they are from the moon or the sun. What use is it to explore the moon when you do not know yourselves? How do you want to encounter the beings of other planets in love when you do not love each other or your earth and its residents in their diversity? You have not yet even perceived that animals are great souls, so how do you want to recognize that extraterrestrial beings are great souls, in whatever physical form they may happen to be at the moment? Guard yourselves against self-righteousness! Guard yourselves against the damage that you do to each other! Perceive God in *everything!* God may appear to you in the form of a flower, a stone, or an animal—will you recognize Him or will you let Him suffer and later say: "I am sorry. I did not know that it was YOU!"

236

The message of this meteorite is, "Perceive yourselves so that you can perceive God! Live your life on this earth with complete dedication and in all the love that you are capable of. Do not long for distant worlds. Discover the worlds within yourselves."

Pallasite . . . . . . MERCY—PERCEPTION OF TRANSIENCE
Composition . . . rock-iron: peridot; 90% iron, 8% nickel, & 2% foreign matter
Hardness . . . . . corresponding to each mineral
Color . . . . shiny silver-colored metal; peridot is brown, yellow, & olive
Source . . . . Esquel, Argentina

Special note: Iron meteorites are very rare. The peridots enclosed in these meteorites are NOT different in their physical and chemical qualities from those from earth. There are slight differences existing in the inclusions. Some of the stones are removed and cut. However, sizes of more than one carat are rare.

Energy class 1

PARROT-WING

CHILDREN OF GOD

"Humans, recognize me as a child of God," says the stone. "Recognize me as what I truly am—a part of you! You connect to everything that lives. Risk looking into your hearts; and perceive the pain that you have caused when you behaved irreverently to all life. This pain rages in each of you. Take me in your hand; feel what I still have to say to you

"Mankind is destined for great things; these cannot happen until you risk opening your hearts. We, as children of God like you, show you paths and support you. Trust in your strength so that you can fulfill your destiny. We wait."

Parrot-wing . . . . RECOGNIZING THE ENERGY OF GOD WITHIN ONESELF
Composition . . . Fusion of quartz (SiO_2) with copper minerals
Hardness . . . . . 6—6.5
Color . . . . green and blue-green patterned
Source . . . . . . Mexico

Energy class 1

PARAIBA TOURMALINE

ANGEL OF MODERN TIMES

This is a gift to us in a difficult time—the time of upheaval. It flows with chaos. We can no longer do without upheaval and chaos; the situation that we have created for ourselves demands them.

Particularly the sensitive among us, those who long for paradise and want to be close to God, those who fall into the temptation of wanting to leave the earth despite knowing better—the tourmaline is a gift for them.

They give us power and strength, and they achieve a direct connection to God. It reminds us of the promise that God gave us.

"I am in you. You are in me. Whoever obeys me will live eternally."

God is our strength. God is our source. We may give God the name of life, of spirit, of Light, as the source of all strength, and more—this creative energy abides in our *hearts*; it waits for us to express it. Those who obey God obey themselves. Their hearts originate in God. They see in advance the consequences of their actions. Those who love God have found their source. Our task is to live this devotion—energetically, without sentiment or illusion.

The Paraiba tourmaline strengthens us in a unique way on our path. It imparts so much courage and knowledge to us that we do not need any other stones—if there was not such a diversity to admire and try to train knowledge and collect experiences. God comes to us on many paths. Through this tourmaline, He expresses Himself perfectly.

The green Paraiba tourmaline is for people who work as healers. With the protection of this stone, the negative vibrations of the patients have a difficult time reaching us. When we wear a ring with a stone that has at least three carats, we create a vibration that resists most of the influences in our immediate vicinity. It also comforts healers who always think they cannot give enough and should work more in order to help many people. When we have given too much, without creating a compensation for it, we become ill, we harden ourselves, we create disturbances that are difficult to change. Healers should never forget that we are *all* in the process of learning. Learning, desire, and joy are a part of my development. When I neglect my needs, I cannot give help to other people.

When we are healers, these green tourmalines help us to create a refreshing compensation in our life.

Paraiba tourmaline . . . ANGEL OF MODERN TIMES
Composition . . . . . . XY[(OH)$_4$/(BO$_3$)$_3$/Si$_6$O$_{18}$]
Hardness 7
Color . . . . unusual tones of green, blue, lilac, turquoise, gray
Source . . . . Paraiba, Brazil

Special note: The Paraiba green is a medium emerald-green, sometimes in the direction of mint. Under artificial light it has an almost unnatural effect. The luminous blue has not existed in tourmalines up to now since it changes into a strong turquoise when heated. The entire color palette is absolutely unusual for tourmaline. A very high copper content creates their special colors. There are also red stones in these tourmaline deposits but these are not sold. Mankind discovered Paraiba tourmaline only a few years ago.
Be careful when selecting a Paraiba tourmaline. Apatites are sometimes mislabeled as Paraiba tourmalines. Here we can depend on a hardness test. Apatite can be scratched by a knife; in contrast, the tourmaline scratches window glass. Of course, a salesperson would not like this! Buy the stone with reservations; be sure that you have the right to exchange it. Or, buy it from a well-known company. Patient salespeople there might even permit you to witness a secondary examination. Some stores buy stones in large quantities and randomly test only a few. If you know this, you can request an examination with a clear conscious (this is called the designation of gemstones).

Energy class ANGEL OF MODERN TIMES

BLUE PARAIBA TOURMALINE

ANGEL OF GREATEST HAPPINESS

We invite a guest into our house; it is this angel. It comes when we review the long path of our lives or when we say, "I have given much; I do not know how to go on, now I need *Your* help, God—only Yours—so that I do not lose heart."

At this point, we already know our deep connection to God; we will have long felt His intimate Presence. We will even be mindful of this during moments of doubt or unrest. As humans (bound and influenced by the material world), we feel moments of separation.

Blue Paraiba comes to those who attain oneness with God, yet constantly examine and judge their doubt. God especially loves these people. He would always like to comfort them but they have chosen the path of doubt in order to protect themselves. God also knows that His comfort can only touch them at certain times. He embraces them; He knows that they seldom notice. He feels their consuming longing for His love and accepts that they can feel His love only rarely. He loves them infinitely and cannot relieve the pain of their suffering even through mercy. He accompanies and protects their lives. He observes their unloved and lost feelings. They want to return home to Him; they do not know that they have already arrived. God gives these people the blue Paraiba for company so that they can feel secure on earth, although they must take the path that they have chosen.

Blue Paraiba tourmaline . . .   ANGEL OF GREATEST HAPPINESS

Energy class 1

GRAY PARAIBA TOURMALINE

ANGEL OF SIMPLICITY

It is a gift of grace when we can live in simplicity and are happy at the same time. This angel purposefully leads us into dimensions of simplicity, repose, and objectivity. It explains, "Trust your path. If your path is a path of silence and simplicity, then include me in your heart and I will reward you for it.

"Go in peace. Do not look at what awakens the desire within you but look instead at the Light and perceive God's grace. Be simple, live in modesty and joy. Lift up your heart in the peace of God and return home."

This is a stone for great souls who have found their path.

Gray Paraiba tourmaline . . . ANGEL OF SIMPLICITY

Energy class 1

GREEN PARAIBA TOURMALINE

ANGEL OF GROWTH

The green Paraiba comes to those who beg for help. It finds people who accomplish great tasks and yet always feel inadequate. It goes to those who always seek God (who await discovery in their hearts). It answers those who ask God for help (and cannot imagine the extent to which God upholds them). Green Paraiba approaches those who constantly hunger for the Light (without perceiving that they radiate the Highest Light). These people need comforting; the green Paraiba does this.

However by comforting them in that it surrounds them with healing, it fulfills their greatest wish—the wish for further, uninterrupted growth. "Go with me," it says, "I will guide you. Trust in my tasks of guiding you through the doors of Light that are still unfamiliar to you. Trust in my possibilities of initiating you into immense growth. Trust in yourself and in me that I am God."

To wear these stones means the highest grace.

Green Paraiba tourmaline . . . ANGEL OF GROWTH

Energy class 1

TURQUOISE PARAIBA TOURMALINE

PERCEPTION OF MY TASKS

The turquoise-colored Paraiba tourmaline is an avatar for the Angel of Joy. It strengthens us on our path and allows us to perceive that our true joy lies in the fulfillment of our tasks. To do so, it gives us strength, inspiration, perception, and patience—whatever we may require on our path there.

It also appeals to our sense of justice. The turquoise Paraiba reminds us that we fulfill our task on earth only when *all* people have found their path and their goal. It awakens the desire within us to support others who need help on the path. It therefore opens the heart to the joy of giving, supporting, and helping. Since it exemplifies these levels for us, it could well be that it does not want to stay with us for long. When we acquire it, we should keep in mind that giving is greater than wanting to possess. We should love it from the very beginning as if life had only loaned it to us for a short period of time.

Turquoise Paraiba tourmaline . . . . ANGEL OF JOY

Energy class 1

VIOLET PARAIBA TOURMALINE

CONCRETE HELP

The violet Paraiba tourmaline connects with the Angel of Aspiring Love. This angel protects our spiritual development.

It helps us understand that helping and protecting energies surround us. Its unique task is placing angels at our side. There are angels who want to convey a special message to us. Other angels help us for a special, short-term assignment.

With this intercession, impulses of the manifold types of help penetrate through to us. Everything is possible. Help is unlimited and so is grace. The violet Paraiba finds very few people. It has an apparently inconspicuous effect. Only a few people recognize its greatness. We should honor it with our love.

Violet Paraiba tourmaline . . . . ANGEL OF ASPIRING LOVE

Energy class 1

P E R I D O T (Olivine)

SUN—SUN—SUN

The peridot shines in the depths of our being. It illuminates our questions and needs; it comforts and lets us hope. Its special quality is a vibration that enables us to differentiate the essential from the irrelevant. Hope is born from the perception of our safety in God. The original source of all being is love. The peridot reminds us of this; we feel relieved, safe, and secure. All divine qualities can flow through us anew. A portion of these vibrations reaches our consciousness—we feel like a new person.

This is the *nature* of the peridot, which is why it has the reputation of a calming and joyful effect. However it can naturally do more. Everything is possible through the connection with our original source. This is a very important stone for healing.

Peridot. . . . . . . HOPE—JOY
Composition . . . $(Mg,Fe)_2SiO_4$
Hardness . . . . . 6.5—7
Color . . . . olive-green, yellow-green
Sources . . . . . . St. John's Island, Dahlak Archipelago in the Red Sea, Burma, Mexico, Sri Lanka, Australia, Brazil, Norway, United States, Lanzarote in the Canary Islands
Energy class 1

PEARL

SORROW—BEAUTY—PERFECTION

The pearl is the only "stone" that a living creature has paid for with its death. The pearl is born through the death of a mussel, an oyster. Human beings put an object of resistance into the living being, and the being tries to overcome this pain. The animal layers skin after skin around the painful core, creating a pearl. It is therefore no surprise that every pearl contains this energy of pain and suffering.

When we decorate ourselves with normal pearls, their energy transfers to us. If we have largely overcome pain and suffering, we will be able to enjoy the beauty of the pearls. If this is not the case, the sorrow within us will intensify. This can have the effect that we finally feel it; it can be that we are able to cry it out. If we again repress it, it can change itself into illness or bitterness.

In this way, the pearl helps us to work through our sadness, see our despair, and heal our pain. Those who are familiar with deepest pain will appreciate the beauty of the pearl.

Only through the transformation of pain do we reach the Light. We become more beautiful and perfect. Those who love pearls know why.

Pearl . . . . PAIN
Composition . . . 84—92% CaCO$_3$; 4—13% organic; 3—4 % H$_2$O
Hardness . . . . . 3—4
Color . . . . iridescent white to cream
Sources . . . . . . oceanic and shoreline oyster beds

Special note: In natural pearls, the colors differ according to their places of origin. There are also color deviations in cultured pearls (96% of the world market) but these are usually bleached or dyed. Here we are speaking about the pale-pearls, whitish-cream with a mother-of-pearl shimmer. When we see rows of pearls lying next to each other, we recognize the differences—one has a chalk-white effect, another grayish, and another has a cream to pale-beige color. The pearls with a hint of a delicate-pink shimmer are the most popular. The glow of the pearls is called "luster."
Pearl farmers implanted foreign objects into oysters. The animal attempts to compensate for the pain by producing mother-of-pearl (encasing the foreign object). The oysters die during the harvest of the pearls. In the cultivation areas there is an atrocious stench of death and putrefaction. Pearls fulfill a task and contribute their part in serving humanity. Whenever we wear pearls, we should always give thanks to the being that gave its life in order to help us.

Energy class 1

PINK PEARL

OVERCOMING HATRED

This pearl suffers. With it, we get a feeling for what tortured beings truly endure. It reminds people who have lost their way *that they have strayed*. It spreads a feeling of hopelessness that nearly lames us if we are sensitive people.

With this pearl, the animal kingdom points out to us that we have forgotten the agreement that we have made with God—to protect all living beings and especially those that are subordinate to our development.

We should be on guard that we must not experience the pain of our breach of promise without help—it can kill us. If we continue to kill animals, we will continue to kill human beings. We are more interconnected than we know.

Pink pearl . . . . . PREMONITION OF DEATH
Composition . . . 84—92% $CaCO_3$; 4—13% organic; 3—4 % H_2O
Hardness . . . . . 3—4
Color . . . . iridescent coral to red
Sources . . . . . . oceanic and shoreline oyster beds

Special note: The color is clear red. The so-called pink pearl is very rare, very small, and decidedly inconspicuous. We will hardly want to wear it. However, with this pearl it becomes clear that there are no coincidences in nature, only special cases.

This rare pearl radiates a unique energy, namely its task. Even if we continue to disregard it, *it fulfills its calling*. It exemplifies for us that no single bit of energy goes to waste, even when this seems to be the case to us. If we live our true task in opposition to our entire surroundings, this always has large results, even if we cannot imagine this. Its divine gift is to notice, guide, direct, and find us.

Nothing occurs without God's consent, without His accompaniment. Our environment seems painfully foreign and ignorant to us. We often feel hopeless; we may feel tempted to run away from our task. During such dark times, we may forget that approval from people is not at all important; our essential partner is God. This is where the contact, concrete answer, and security are. With God's help, we achieve everything. We are naturally thankful when we find friends and understanding among people. However GOD is our source of strength, comfort, and true joy!

This is why everything that we accomplish to fulfill our true tasks has a very great effect on the spiritual level and therefore on all of humanity and the other realms. The animal kingdom, for example, can receive much healing from the sincere love and regret of a single person. Everything is energy! Everything that we feel, think, say, and do has a far-reaching effect. This is the first thing that we learn once we start on our spiritual path. The pink pearl influences us through its existence—even if none of us will wear it. Every stone and every mineral, concealed in the earth or ignored in warehouses, fulfills its task and affects us. Although we put gemstones on us or wear them so that they influence us, we should never lose sight of this other perspective. *Everything is energy.* Every mountain, valley, or drop of water possesses an individual aura and obeys a task. Everything that lives influences us indirectly. We must deeply understand the laws of life to comprehend this truth. We need to be great in relation to this truth; we must live our lives accordingly. Until each of us has achieved this goal, we will not find peace.

Energy class 1

BLACK PEARL

LETHE

The black pearl does mourning work. With it, we look into our own heart. About what are we still in mourning? What have we not yet gotten over? The pearl goes into the depths.

Its comfort is the message of transition. Everything is transitory. Joy is as temporary as pain. Everything is also renewed. The only thing that is not transitory is the Great Light, GOD. The pearl—itself transient—knows this. It shares it with us. The comfort lies in the perception of eternity.

Black pearl . . . . PERCEPTION OF TRANSIENCE
Composition . . . 84—92% $CaCO_3$; 4—13% organic; 3—4 % H_2O
Hardness . . . . . 3—4
Color . . . . iridescent dark gray to black
Sources . . . . . . oceanic and shoreline oyster beds

Special note: Naturally black pearls are very few. Nearly all of them are dyed.

Energy class 2

MOTHER-OF-PEARL

LIGHTNESS—LAUGHTER—RESPECT FOR LIFE

Mother-of-pearl possesses a gentle energy. It reminds us of the joy in life but does not demand that we open up to it. It permits us the position of a spectator. This may please us—but it hardly will change us. Since life is *change* and we only grow through change, we will only use the mother-of-pearl for pleasure but not to help us grow.

Joy enhances our life. Change and growth make us happy.

Mother-of-pearl . . CHEERFULNESS
Composition . . . 84—92% $CaCO_3$; 4—13% organic; 3—4 % H_2O
Hardness . . . . . 3—4
Color . . . . iridescent dark gray to black
Sources . . . . . . oceanic and shoreline oyster beds

Special note: This is the inner side of a mollusk shell; therefore, it is the same substance as pearls.

Energy class 3

PHENACITE

JOY IN OUR PROCESS

This is a good stone for people with allergies caused by despair. This stone shows us what we have *missed* in life. At the same time, it demonstrates what paths we now can go in order to achieve happiness. In this way, it heals despair and regret.

Despair always gives rise to allergies. Additional reasons can be further despair, denial, subconscious conflicts, desire for revenge, a death wish, and much more. Allergies always indicate a struggle within us. We discover the reason behind a certain allergy when we focus on its solution. We do not heal an allergy by removing the allergen; only through *illuminating* the background reasons for lowered immunity. This closely connects with *change*. Everything else is an illusion. I can bolster my body by avoiding allergens. I can gain strength by working on the psychosomatic reasons. However, avoidance is never a solution. The opposite is the case.

Many great souls (who are still small children at this time) are currently helping their parents recognize the senselessness of our unethical "progress." Many of them have allergies; their reaction to the damaged environment shows how badly we have abused nature. The dead-end street we have landed on is a result of our life-style. Unfortunately, very few of us recognize this sacrifice. We should thank them and ask, "What can I (as an adult) contribute to the preservation of life? How can I have a second chance at

LIFE?" However, a part of this is first perceiving my own life-negating forms of behavior and ways of life. The truth hurts—and so does change. When we have gone through both, we will feel free and happy.

Allergies are great teachers. *We* create the stimulus; we create our immuno-sensitivity. We want to change ourselves—but our egos do not. When we perceive, with the help of the phenacite, where our failures lie, then we are already on the path to healing—*if that is what we want.*

Phenacite . . . . . BLISS
Composition . . . $Be_2[SiO_4]$
Hardness . . . . . 7.5—8
Color . . . . colorless, pale-yellow, pink
Sources . . . . . Brazil, Sri Lanka, Mexico, Zimbabwe, United States, Switzerland, Namibia

Energy class 1

PHOSGENITE

GRACE—RETURN HOME TO THE TRINITY

Listening within—this is what this stone allows. What it gives us is inestimable. It is a mediator on our path back to our home. It shortens all the learning processes.

For those among us who no longer misuse strength and have made the agreement with life that they only want to live what is best for them, who have put aside their individualism for the good of the Light, humanity, and themselves, for these people it means active *Grace*. For these people, and really only for these people, it is a guide with a very special quality: it predicts the future.

Nothing tempts us as much as the topic of the future. Many people have failed on their path because they have misused their knowledge about future events, because they have believed inner allegories to be pictures from the future and no longer put enough effort into the here and now and because they could not deal with the rare gift of knowledge about the future.

The phosgenite is a friend to all souls who have struggled with pictures of the future, who have foreseen death and failure, who have turned away from God because of this gift. This stone gives them happiness. Their past suffering will now be rewarded. Those who saw people dying in the visions and helplessly had to experience how everything they saw also occurred, also bear pain within themselves that is greater than a person can endure. These people do not need to be afraid of anything more. However they do not know it. They still believe that things depend on their help, that they have the tasks of rescue ahead of them.

The phosgenite says to them, "Everything is planned. *God has planned everything from the beginning.* People only believe that they have the will to decide. This is an illusion." Before time began, Those Who Guide Us decided what will happen today. Before time, we made the decision of how we live today, how we grow and what we want to experience. Despite this, it is important to understand that we have the choice in what we do every day. We choose every moment between what we inwardly comprehend and what is incomprehensible for us. However, every choice that seems new to us in every moment, of which we believe that it is happening now, happened before the very beginning of time.

The phosgenite does not command us to understand this. Instead, it says: *"Trust.* Let yourself be guided; accept the karmic task of your life. You can never really leave your path, even when you think that you have."

"Guard this stone well!" says God. "Believe in life. Everything that exists can help you. The breath of Grace is in everything. Those who know this make use of this wisdom and they return home to the path."

Phosgenite . . . . PERCEIVING LIFE
Composition . . . $Pb_2[Cl_2/CO_3]$
Hardness . . . . . 2—3
Color . . . . colorless, white, gray, yellow
Sources . . . . . Sardenia, Poland, Greece, Argentina, and Namibia

Special note: The phosgenite is very rare. It finds its way to people who need its help.

Energy class 1

PINK OPAL

SATISFACTION

The pink opal shows us where we have had success. It makes sure that we acknowledge our efforts just as much as we acknowledge what we have accomplished. It speaks to us of joy and holistic love, reminding us that life only has a purpose when we take enough time for our inner life.

This opal works purposefully on our satisfaction. When I do not acknowledge myself, I cannot live my love. The pink opal creates the preconditions for this purpose.

Pink opal . . . . . SATISFACTION
Composition . . . $SiO_2 \cdot nH_2O$
Hardness 6
Color . . . . pink with inclusions
Sources . . . . . . Mexico, Peru

Special note: The pink opal also has the name Andes-opal. Occasionally it is misnamed as chrysopal.

Energy class 2

PRASEOLITE

GRACE—FULFILLMENT OF A LIFETIME DREAM

This stone does not occur naturally. These are amethysts and other quartz stones that have been heated until they turn green.

This makes their task even more astonishing. They inspire people to feel able to realize a fantasy—the wish of a lifetime. Praseolite helps to purify this ideal. We can abandon our illusions; this will help to develop strength and foresight. We gain the courage to realize our daydreams. The vision becomes reality. When we have erroneous fancies, praseolite awakens God's potential within us. We see our real potentials and how to use them. What we learn is often greater than the dream we had at the beginning. We grow with the belief in ourselves. We grow with this stone.

Once again it is shown how the Highest Power can lie within the apparently inconspicuous. Blessed are those who have found themselves.

Praseolite . . . . . JOY IN LIFE—GIFT
Composition . . . SiO_2
Hardness 7
Color . . . . . . celery-green, pale-green

Energy class 1

PREHNITE

JOYFUL HELPER

This stone cheers us up. It is good for colds and strengthens our immune system. Although it is not a great helper, it has a quick effect on the small problems in life. For a short time, it encourages us that we will make it. Afterwards, we need other stones.

Its quality is the quickness with which it works and the encouragement it gives us in a light and easy manner. This is why we may experience it as more pleasant than the hematite, which stands for COURAGE but energetically pushes us forward at the same time.

Prehnite . . . . . . ENCOURAGEMENT
Composition . . . $Ca_2Al[(OH)_2/AlSi_3O_{10}]$
Hardness . . . . . 6—6.5
Color . . . . yellow-green, brown-yellow
Sources . . . . . . Australia, China, Scotland, South Africa, United States

Special note: This stone has an extraordinarily healing effect in stress situations. It changes our perception of issues that consume us; it makes them seem unimportant. Prehnite reminds us to prioritize what is more significant over our current distractions. This is how it calms us. We then relax and have a sense of well-being.

Energy class 2

PURPURITE

ENJOYMENT OF LIFE

What a helper! When I cannot make a decision, I hold a purpurite in my hand. Within a few hours, *I have* decided what to do—even if it may take a while for this decision to penetrate in my consciousness!

Purpurite . . . . . DECISION
Composition . . . $Mn^{3+}[PO_4]$
Hardness . . . . . 4—4.5
Color . . . . . . purple, lilac, deep-pink, dark-brown
Sources . . . . . Namibia, Europe, United States

Energy class 2

PYRITE

BREAKTHROUGH

The pyrite is an extremely powerful stone. It provides the breakthrough to our feelings.

We should only use the pyrite when we feel attracted to it. It is a wonderful helper that we cannot thank enough.

Pyrite . . . . BREAKTHROUGH
Composition . . . FeS_2
Hardness . . . . . 6—6.5
Color . . . . shiny & brass-like with tones of yellow, brown, gray; sometimes variegated
Sources . . . . . . worldwide

Special note: Pyrite can develop rust spots. These can stain fabric and spread on the pyrite. We should only use water to cleanse stones that we use on the body. Clean particularly delicate pieces of jewelry or stones in a spiritual manner (for example, necklaces or fluorite with chips of quartz and flecks of pyrite).

Energy class 3

SMOKY QUARTZ

CONNECTION—ORDER—INTERMEDIATE WORLDS

The smoky quartz connects us with our Higher Self. It encourages us to take up contact with this Higher Self. It also encourages us to pray.

In addition, it wants to tell us that we can trust because we bear all knowledge within us. When we have learned to take up contact with our inner knowledge, we can move more freely. We do not have to puzzle constantly over a problem, but listen within and receive the optimal answer for a situation.

The smoky quartz is an excellent stone for those who are unaccustomed to the contact to their inner self.

Smoky quartz . . . LISTENING WITHIN
Composition . . . SiO_2
Hardness 7
Color . . . . brown to smoke-gray to black (morion)
Sources . . . . . . worldwide

Special note: Some smoky quartzes are very dark in color and have the name morion. Some of them are artificially darkened by radiation, so shop carefully.

Energy class 2

RHODOCHROSITE

BEAUTY OF FEELINGS

The rhodochrosite awakens tender feelings within us. It speaks to us when our hearts become hardened through many lives of unhappiness. "Take a new risk," it says.

Gradually, rhodochrosite prepares us to love again, to open our hearts, and to receive love. In its gentle manner it lets us participate in the feelings of love that it radiates. We again sense that it is worthwhile to love and that we need love to remain spirited.

It is a stone for the initial willingness to love. In the process, it has dedicated itself to earthly love.

Rhodochrosite. . . DELICATE LOVE—BEGINNING
Composition . . . $Mn[CO_3]$
Hardness . . . . . 3.5—4
Color . . . . pink tones striped with white, rarely translucent
Sources . . . . . . Argentina, United States, Russia, Peru, South Africa

Special note: Rhodochrosite usually has a pink and white striped appearance; it also grows as crystals of breathtaking beauty that are intensely pink and transparent.

Energy class 2

RHODOLITE (Garnet)

WORKING THROUGH THE PAST

This powerful stone reconciles us with our past. It mantles us in the vibrations of love. It opens subconscious insight into past-life experiences. This is how it teaches us. It points out where, because of our ignorance, we have not forgiven and where we quarrel or hate. It permits us to see these events with the eye of love and to understand them. At the same time, it supports us in the process of forgiveness with its power. It shows us that forgiveness is the only way to healing and peace.

The rhodolite is perfect for those who keep their heart closed because they are afraid of love in that it gives them trust.

Rhodolite . . . . . COMING TO TERMS WITH THE PAST
Composition . . . $Mg_3Al_2[SiO_4]_3$
Hardness . . . . . 7—7.5
Color . . . . red with a distinct tinge of violet
Source . . . . Tanzania

Special note: The rhodolite is also called Cape garnet.

Energy class 2

264

RHODONITE

HEART OPENER

Rhodonite brings serenity. It can bring us healing if we use it with enough frequency. It is a very earthy stone. Its vibrations of caring are fairly practical.

The people who like to wear it hold no illusions about love; they know what they are doing when they open themselves to early love. These people are willing to sacrifice something for the good of the community.

This robust stone is a good helper.

Rhodonite . . . . . HEART OPENER
Composition . . . $(Ca,Mg)(Mn^{2+},Fe^{2+})_4[Si_5O_{15}]$
Hardness . . . . . 5.5—6
Color . . . . mostly a dark rose-color with black inclusions
Sources . . . . . . United States, Australia, Russia, India, Madagascar

Energy class 2

RHYOLITE

SHARING PLEASURE

Rhyolite has great respect for us. This is the reason for its message.

"You are capable of giving a great deal; believe this. We value your potential. Do not try to force yourselves to be perfect—whatever you may understand this to be. We love you as you are. We constantly learn from each of you.

"The human realm is an example to us. There is much we do not understand but we are trying to learn. In gratitude we give you our strength, our beauty, and our understanding. Use the energies that we have saved for you.

"Stones are living beings. Do not ignore us—love us! We will surely thank you.

"As you develop yourselves, many other kingdoms of life are developing beside you and through you. Do not underestimate your power! We are all parts of a totality.

"We look forward to seeing you in a brighter sphere."

Rhyolite . . . . . . HOPE FOR DEVELOPMENT OF THE HUMAN BEING
Composition . . . SiO_2
Hardness 7
Color . . . . green with yellow and beige, patterned
Source . . . . Australia

Energy class 1

ROSE QUARTZ

TRUST—JOY—CONFIDENCE

The rose quartz builds up our trust. We usually do not remember that we are trust and usually think we have to acquire trust and develop it within ourselves.

With this stone, we are successful in linking with our primordial trust. The external effect shows itself in feelings of trust, joy, and confidence. This is why we also perceive it to be calming and protecting.

It is a good stone for people who no longer want to change. There is certainly a good reason for elderly ladies wearing it frequently. It has a soothing effect with its delicate vibration because it makes no demands. It enhances the evening of life (for men as well)!

Those who do want to change need it even more! When we find our development to be too strenuous, when things do not move quickly enough for us or when we are despondent, it helps us in a gentle but emphatic manner. Every development is more difficult without it. In its own way, it gives us courage to love life. Despite its delicate aura, the rose quartz is a very powerful stone! (Even children love it very much.)

Rose quartz . . . . COURAGE TO LIVE
Composition . . . SiO_2
Hardness 7
Color . . . . pink to pale-pink
Sources . . . . . . Brazil, South Africa, Madagascar

Special note: Rose quartz very rarely comes as a crystal or in an almost transparent form. These pieces then possess an infinitely beautiful vibration but are correspondingly more expensive.

Energy class 2

R U B Y (Corundum)

THE VIBRATION OF ABSOLUTE LOVE SURROUNDS US WITH THE RUBY

The ruby emanates itself into the world. It loves us human beings very much and it shows us what love is—unconditional effusing.

This stone gives us the possibility of recognizing our potential for love and loving it. It teaches that LOVE is above everything else. Love alone leads to God. Love alone leads to people. *Those who love, live.* Those who do not love are dead.

The ruby makes us aware that we *are* love. This is not a matter of working for or acquiring love. It is a matter of the perception that we are love and only need this love to live.

The ruby helps us open our heart so that we can exude. Its message is, "God and love are one. As you entrust love with your development, you also entrust your path to God."

Created in millions of years, the ruby also contains the knowledge of all the events on this planet. In keeping with its tasks, it knows about all the obstacles that human beings can put in the way in order to avoid the love in their hearts. It guards our growth and heals our fear of love.

Ruby. . . . . ABSOLUTE LOVE
Composition . . . Al_2O_3
Hardness 9
Color . . . . red, quality: "dove-blood" color (trace of violet)
Sources . . . . . . Burma, Thailand, Sri Lanka, Kenya, United States, Tanzania

Special note: The ruby is one of the expensive gemstones. The purer and more transparent it is, the more expensive. The opaque stones are also good enough for us. There are dealers who extricate pieces of ruby out of zoisite material and sell them. This is where I have discovered the most beautiful pieces, as large as a small chicken egg and strong in color, with a wonderful energy. They are powerful and lively as well as inexpensively priced.

Energy class EXPRESSION OF PERFECTION

RUTILE QUARTZ

ENDURANCE AS QUALITY OF LIFE

We should wear rutile quartz as often as possible. It gives us a stable view when appropriate. It helps us to walk our path with integrity. It connects us to the Light potential as it makes our steps easier.

The rutile quartz is a very great healer. It can take away our pain because it changes our views when this is necessary. Pain is holding on tightly to wanting, and wanting is not good for us. The rutile quartz makes it easier to let go and change one's way of thinking. It is a personable friend of the human race.

Rutile quartz . . . CONSISTENCY
Composition . . . Rock crystal or smoky quartz (SiO_2) with needlelike or fibrous inclusions of rutile (TiO_2)
Hardness 7
Color . . . . colorless or brown, gold-yellow to red rutile needlelike inclusions
Source . . . . Brazil

Energy class 2

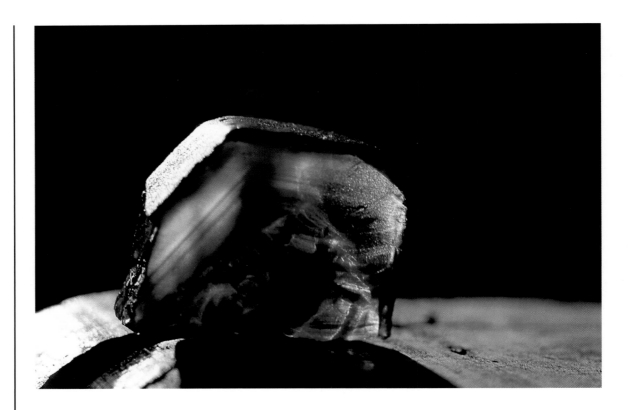

BLUE SAPPHIRE (Corundum)

FAITH OPENS OUR HEARTS

The blue sapphire leads us to God. It vibrates with the principle of faith. To feel attracted to this sapphire is to feel attracted to God.

It cleanses us of the thought that GOD is a father figure. It teaches that God is an energy of love and wisdom, of justice and kindness. God is a vibration of pure Light, an expression of power and strength. The sapphire heals us of all the images of God and makes room for the Creation of all life.

It calls on us to recognize God within us. This sets in motion a (probably painful) purification process. We will receive rewards as we deeply trust in the Creation.

The sapphires in all colors cause the most straightforward learning processes. The blue provides clarity and truth and this in the quickest manner. In its absolute connection with God, we learn that clarity and truth are always healing. This sapphire is an extraordinary stone. We should honor it accordingly.

Blue sapphire . . . FAITH
Composition . . . Al_2O_3
Hardness 9
Color . . . . blue
Sources. . . . . . Burma, Sri Lanka, Thailand; Cashmere, Cambodia, Nigeria, Montana, United States, Australia, Tanzania

Energy class EXPRESSION OF PERFECTION

COLORLESS SAPPHIRE (Corundum)

A PLEASANT TIME

This sapphire makes us laugh. It assumes that we human beings *enjoy* our diverse lives!

At the same time, it is a fact that we have usually tormented ourselves in our earthly lives. Only now, as the totality of humanity, do we recognize that this wasn't necessary. We had to experience certain lessons but we could have chosen another way. Now this stone comes and says, "Pain? What's that? Your life is pleasant. Why do you not sense this?" Other stones can reveal the secrets of life to us but colorless sapphire gives us the *vision* of how we could live. In order to have a pleasant life, it is only necessary to give up the struggling, the ego, and the wanting. "So what," says the sapphire, "that's only a trifle!"

Be receptive to this sapphire's obvious approach; request that it affects you. Life could become amusing.

Colorless sapphire . . PLEASANT LIFE
Composition . . . . . Al_2O_3
Hardness 9
Color . . . . colorless
Sources . . . . Burma, Sri Lanka, Thailand, Australia, Tanzania, Cashmere, Cambodia, Nigeria, Montana in the United States

Energy class 1

YELLOW SAPPHIRE (Corundum)

WILLINGNESS TO LOVE

Love is our highest objective. Without love there would be no life and no happiness. Most people do not know that they are afraid of love. They only desire it.

Love demands everything from us—and this is exactly where our fear lies! Since the yellow sapphire connects us with the Highest Sun, the Highest Light, we become *willing to love* in its presence.

Yellow sapphires change our lives very much. They also want to be loved—very much. Their influence can then be very strong. This sapphire heals all wounds that prevent us from throwing ourselves into the arms of love.

Yellow sapphire . . WILLINGNESS TO LOVE
Composition . . . Al_2O_3
Hardness 9
Color . . . . yellow
Sources . . . . . . Burma, Sri Lanka, Thailand, Australia, Tanzania, Cashmere, Cambodia, Nigeria, Montana in the United States

Energy class 1

GREEN SAPPHIRE (Corundum)

Photograph on page 274

TRANSITION—TIME FOR PARTING

People who have lived many decades would like to separate themselves from this world, whether they are aware of this or not. However habit is strong. Although we did not even want to immerse ourselves in this world at the beginning, now we do not want to leave it—against our better judgment.

This is where the green sapphire helps. It prepares us for God's eternity, for the kindness and love to which we will glide and the joy that is waiting for us. It gives us courage to take leave from everything that could delay our parting. It makes it easier for us to let go. It lets us sense where we are going. We will gradually become more tranquil, put our affairs in order, and perceive this as our last task in life. This task includes more than just putting things in order externally—much more important is the inner creation of order—*forgiveness*.

The transition becomes easy with this sapphire.

Green sapphire . . TRANSITION
Composition . . . Al_2O_3
Hardness 9
Color . . . . green
Sources . . . . . Burma, Sri Lanka, Thailand, Australia, Tanzania, Cashmere, Cambodia, Nigeria, Montana in the United States

Energy class 1

PINK SAPPHIRE (Corundum)

Photograph on page 274

PRIME OF LIFE

This sapphire has a very delicate pink-color, which is very different from the color of rubies.

It is a friend of *children*. This naturally applies to all stones. However this is their special guardian, companion, and teacher. It makes it possible for children to find their way more easily in this world.

Just after birth, we are still close to the higher worlds. The rude plunging into earthly life hurts; the shock is usually great. The newborn's soul has just left the arms of God; now it has to struggle for air, while it misses love, warmth, care, and understanding. The new mother's love is still unfamiliar to the soul at the moment. It apparently has difficulty separating itself from the obvious contact to God's helpers. Although the soul has prepared for this life on earth (in the best way possible), it first feels forsaken and expelled into the emptiness. Coldness surrounds it. It is foreign here.

The pale-pink sapphire makes it easier to become accustomed to life here. It is like God's ray of Light in this cold new world, which is how the child experiences the transition from all-embracing love to life on earth.

If you want to do something good for a child, the vibration of the pink sapphire makes it possible.

Pink sapphire . . . GUARDIAN OF THE CHILDREN
Composition . . . Al_2O_3
Hardness 9
Color . . . . rose-pink
Sources . . . . . . Burma, Sri Lanka, Thailand, Australia, Tanzania, Cashmere, Cambodia, Nigeria, Montana in the United States

Energy class 1

BLACK SAPPHIRE (Corundum)

Photograph on page 274

DARKNESS SURROUNDS ME

Thank you for this stone! The black sapphire lets us dive into the emptiness—an emptiness that we always fear, the infamous nothing, the suppressed darkness.

In the company of the sapphire we perceive that there is no emptiness. There is only BEING and where there was nothing, there is Light and sun. Darkness is the brother of the Light, the radiant brightness.

"Release your fear. I will lead you through darkness to the fire. Enjoy the darkness. Be a human being." This is what the black sapphire says. It does not help us transform our darkness. It takes away our fear of it. It shows it to be a self-evident form of being.

Black sapphire . . RELEASING DARKNESS
Composition . . . Al_2O_3
Hardness 9
Color . . . . black
Sources . . . . . . worldwide

Energy class 1

VIOLET SAPPHIRE (Corundum)

Photograph on page 274

COMPANION

The violet sapphire is the companion of sick children. When a soul chooses to enter the world in a certain condition that we call illness, it clears away karma. This particular sapphire helps here. These souls sense their own truth within its vibrations out of the love of their developmental process they have chosen the possibility of being ill—out of the love for themselves and other people. The sapphire transforms the energy of a defect into perception and understanding. The children and young people remain connected with the knowledge of their greatness and their choice. They will more calmly master their task and live more in peace with themselves and the circumstances that they have chosen.

This is a good stone for adults who feel dissatisfied with life. It also reminds them of their choice. I wanted to live like this in order to learn this and that or to release this and that. I can have satisfaction in my life. All possibilities are open to me, *if I only wish them.* The violet sapphire creates this certainty but it does not show the possibilities.

Violet sapphire . . COMPANION OF THE CHILDREN
Composition . . . Al_2O_3
Hardness 9
Color . . . . violet
Sources . . . . . . Burma, Sri Lanka, Thailand, Australia, Tanzania, Cashmere, Cambodia, Nigeria, Montana in the United States

Energy class 1

SARD

SHOWING REMORSE

With the sard, we dive into our depths. This is where all treasures lie. However, one should note—there is no work on ourselves, no understanding, without the confrontation with the dark side in us.

To see the dark side in us always means remorse. To be able to say "I'm sorry" is one of the most important prerequisites for our path into the Light. This stone helps to recognize the remorse within us. It also enables us to *acknowledge* it. In relation to remorse in particular, which is a key for every development process, the sard gives us clarity and strength.

Sard . . . . REPENTANCE
Composition . . . SiO_2
Hardness 7
Color . . . . brown
Sources . . . . . . mainly in Brazil

Special note: The sard is—like some other stones—already mentioned in the Bible. It is of significance for us because it has a task of its own. Chemically, it differs from the carnelian only by some trace minerals. While the carnelian has a red to reddish-brown appearance, the sard shows us a brown with a tendency toward red. Both are chalcedony from the large family of quartz. When they are dyed, which is frequently the case, we have acquired chalcedony. This is why we make the effort to find a natural sard or carnelian. We can only consider the stone in the photograph as a color pattern because a striped chalcedony is called agate. However the brown in the picture is the typical brown of the sard.

Energy class 3

SNOWFLAKE OBSIDIAN

A STERN STONE—AND YET CHEERFUL

Those who wear snowflake obsidian must prepare for certain processes. They must let go of the old; they should examine their relationships; they must brave the unknown and explore their own depths.

How does it work? It strengthens the belief in ourselves and therefore allows us to examine our life and our life situation. Under its protection, we question our life. It is sufficient to carry a larger stone with oneself for a week in order to set the foundation for a new life.

The impulse begins. Until this impulse has moved into our consciousness, until we have created the preconditions for it and until our life situation has changed—until that time, many other stones will accompany us with their healing vibrations.

Snowflake obsidian . . EXAMINATION
Composition . . . . . primarily SiO_2
Hardness . . . . 5—5.5
Color . . . . black with pale-gray spots
Sources . . . . mainly United States and Mexico

Special note: Obsidian is a rock primarily made of silica acid in the form of glass. It occurs in volcanic eruptions. As gas escapes from the obsidian, radial white spots sometimes form. Called spherolites, they are the characteristic markings of snowflake obsidian.

Energy class 3

S E L E N I T E   (GYPSUM)

LIGHT—TRANSIENCE

Those who like selenite have not yet found themselves, but long to do so. It promises us a wonderful development when we learn to listen to our inner voice. It strengthens this wish and purifies our perceptivity. In addition, it strengthens our willingness to turn within. It gives us the feeling that we have certain accompaniment on this path. Its effect intensifies with rose quartz.

Selenite . . . . . . LIGHT
Composition . . . $Ca[SO_4]·2H_2O$
Hardness . . . . . 1.5—2
Color . . . . transparent colorless, tinges of white
Sources . . . . . . worldwide

Special note: Selenite is another term for gypsum. This is almost transparent gypsum, which is usually called selenite. Opaque gypsum, which often has another color, possesses a different vibration.

Energy class 2

SEPTARIAN NODULE

RESPONSIBILITY FOR ONE'S LIFE

This stone stores memories that are important for certain people. The clairvoyant with this stone in his hand will perceive their weak points. At the same time, this stone reminds us of events that are long past but still influence us today to the point that we do not want to fulfill our current task (because we have not forgiven) because of the experience. We are afraid of the drama from that time. In addition, we are also afraid of failure and ruin. Every nugget conceals a mystery and various messages for different people.

However since this stone not only lets memories come to life again, but primarily gives us the strength to pursue our current life, it leads us to more responsibility for our life. It allows us to mature.

Septarian nodule . . . MYSTERY AND GROWTH
Sources . . . . worldwide, mainly in Utah in the United States

Special note: This is a large limestone or clay ironstone nugget, which houses within it calcite, pyrite, some types of quartz, or similar minerals.
The characteristic patterns form in this way; liquid mineral solutions collect through fissures in clay containing lime. This later becomes hard stone.
Composition, colors, and hardness vary according to mineral content.

Energy class 1

SERPENTINE

LIGHTNESS IN MATTERS OF THE HEART

The serpentine in its best quality radiates gentleness. It flatters our feelings and allows us to become tender with ourselves.

This gentle vibration of attention, tenderness, and love can have a stronger effect on some people than a powerful stone with keenness and absolute clarity. When there have been greater injuries in the past, some of us respond better to gentle energies than to powerful ones.

Gentleness is strength. Without gentleness there is no love. We should enjoy this energy that we lose touch with so often in this age. This stone gives repose and gentleness to us.

Serpentine . . . . . TENDERNESS
Composition . . . $H_4Mg_3Si_2O$, also mineral groups, often $(Mg,Fe^{2+})_6[(OH)_8/Si_4O_{10}]$ (antigorite: brownish green lamellar) or $Mg_6[(OH)_8/Si_4O_{10}]$ (clinochrysotile: green with a cleaving habit)
Hardness . . . . . 2—3, sometimes harder
Color . . . . translucent to semi-translucent, pale to dark yellow-green, also white, brown, black
Sources . . . . . . worldwide, antigorite from Valle d'Antigorio in Piedmont

Special note: The serpentine has a wonderful vibration aura. Despite this, we must be certain whether we are buying jade, serpentine, or a variation of serpentine; each of these minerals has its unique vibration. Serpentine is plentiful. It is exported in Eastern Asia as New jade. Because of this, many dealers will tell you that you are buying jade when you are holding serpentine in your hand. Ask the specialist! Labels can also be deceiving!

Energy class 3

SIDERITE

MASTERING EVERYDAY LIFE

Great things have a great effect. What is great? Living my task. Living it in peace with myself is a gift.

We often underestimate the greatness of everyday life. Everyday life trains the consciousness for stability, patience, and greatness. Unusual events have the reverse effect; for a short time, we rise above our self-imposed limitations.

Training through the Light, life, always leads us to the most essential thing—to love. Those who live love will find a different lifetime with each new day; they will explore their capacity for greatness within it.

This is a good stone for the heart center.

Siderite . . . . . . STABILITY
Composition . . . $Fe[CO_3]$
Hardness . . . . . 4—4.5
Color . . . . yellow to brown-yellow to yellow-gray
Sources . . . . . . Brazil, Germany, Austria, England, Russia

Energy class 3

SILLIMANITE

GREATNESS—CONCLUDING TASKS

The sillimanite is a good stone for concluding large tasks in a just manner. When we work on a project that has inspired us, there inevitably comes the time when we become tired of the work. We suddenly believe that we are no longer a match for the task. We are afraid of being cheated and receiving no thanks for our efforts. At the same time, we forget completely that we take every effort on ourselves for ourselves. We never accomplish anything for other people but we always fulfill tasks only for ourselves and our growth and never for others, even when this seems to be the case.

In the deepest sense we fulfill tasks because this is an agreement we have made with the Almighty Energy and because we want to obey God. We should always see a task independent of the criticism and reaction of other people. The sillimanite helps us to understand this. It connects us with God and the moment in which we have taken on a task before the face of God. If we ask our heart, it will always know when this was and what it was about. To ask our mind is less successful because it will orient itself on external standards.

When we wear a sillimanite, we will remember what we have promised God. We will immerse ourselves in the joy that accompanies our task and we will happily stretch out our hand to receive God's reward for us.

Sillimanite. . . . . GREATNESS
Composition . . . $Al_2[O/SiO_4]$
Hardness . . . . . 6—7
Color . . . . white with yellow, brown, green, or blue
Sources . . . . . . Germany, Austria, India, Burma

Energy class 1

SINHALITE

JOY IN EVERYDAY LIFE

This stone obligates us to something new. It creates the consolidation of individuals into a whole, which means that its strength lies in connection and unification.

It is ideal for couples who want to get to know each other better (to be used alternately by each of them), for groups that are working together on a project, and for people who have large spiritual tasks to fulfill.

It obligates us to faithfulness to these tasks, to seriousness, and to consideration for other groups with common interests. It is a stone for the future.

Sinhalite . . . . . . UNION
Composition . . . $MgAl[BO_4]$
Hardness . . . . . 6.5—7
Color . . . . pale-brown, green-brown, dark-brown to black
Sources . . . . . . Sri Lanka, Burma, China, Tanzania, Russia

Energy class 1

SCAPOLITE

PEACE THROUGH FAITHFULNESS TO ONESELF

The scapolite reminds us of our task. It has the effect of following our spiritual time-table. With its help, we become more willing to approach our duties and to fulfill them.

This is an important stone for the future.

Scapolite. . . . . . FULFILLMENT
Composition . . . $(Ca,Na)_4[(CO_3Cl)/(Si,Al)_6Si_6O_{24}]$
Hardness . . . . . 5.5—6
Color . . . . colorless, yellow, pink, violet
Sources . . . . . . Burma, Madagascar, Brazil, Tanzania, Mozambique

Energy class 1

EMERALD (Beryl)

AN EMERALD LIES IN THE DEPTHS OF THE HEART

The emerald renews us. It connects us with our origin and our promise to be human beings.

When the emerald was born, it vowed to help the human beings. "I lead them into their own DEPTHS so that they perceive who they are," it said. Within this promise are its gift and its help. Whatever we have perceived and understood about ourselves—there is more to learn. Whatever we may learn about God, there is always more to learn.

The depth within us conceals all mysteries and all treasures. It enables us to begin anew time and again. It is the source of all divine feelings. I am trust; I am happiness; I am courage; I am hope; I am divine.

I am who I am. The emerald is the key to MYSELF.

It is the strongest healing stone for the emotions.

Emerald . . . . . . RENEWAL
Composition . . . $Be_3Al_2[Si_6O_{18}]$
Hardness . . . . . 7.5—8
Color . . . . emerald-green, green, pale-green, chrome-green
Sources . . . . . . Columbia, Brazil, India, Rhodesia, South Africa, Zambia

Special note: The emerald is permitted to have inclusions, which sometimes define its beauty.

Energy class EXPRESSION OF PERFECTION

SMITHSONITE

CHANGE—GIVING UP OLD PATTERNS

Smithsonite prepares us for new tasks. It encourages us to make changes. This can relate to many facets of life—including partners, relationships, professions, responsibilities, and home. Where change is necessary, fear is not far away. This stone reminds us that change brings us forward and lets us grow.

"Be *courageous*," it says, "*You'll make it.*" In this sense, it is a best friend.

Smithsonite . . . . CHANGE
Composition . . . $Zn[CO_3]$
Hardness . . . . . 4—4.5
Color . . . . colorless, white, gray, yellow, orange, pale-green, pale-blue, brown, red
Sources . . . . . . Europe, Russia, United States, Australia, South Africa

Energy class 2

SODALITE

BREAKTHROUGH TO THE SELF

Its qualities remind us of a promise that we should unconditionally keep—Being true to our self.

Every being has a certain unique quality; This is what determines our personalities. Despite similarities and parallels, originality is our gift to the earth. This is our particular contribution to the planet. The world would not be *whole* if a single being were to give up its special quality. We are ONE; every separate being is vital to this unity.

This is how sodalite encourages us to live these qualities of our very own and make a gift of them to the world. We grow when we give. We should start with ourselves.

Sodalite . . . . . . BEING TRUE TO ONE'S SELF
Composition . . . $Na_8[Cl_2/Al_6Si_6O_{24}]2H_2O$
Hardness . . . . . 5.5—6
Color . . . . navy blue, gray, with white and black
Sources . . . . . . Brazil, Canada, India, Namibia, United States

Energy class 2

SUNSTONE (Aventurine-Feldspar)

JOY IN FULFILLMENT

The sunstone is underestimated. It is an important stone for the new age and therefore an unpopular teacher. It teaches that it is necessary *to share*. As long as we are willing to share, our life is blessed. If not, massive and painful learning processes are waiting for us. God shares his POWER with us. Will we recognize this and use this gift?

Those who open up to the sunstone are willing to share, even when it is reluctantly. We must learn to share. It is a constant learning process for humanity to give and let go. We only receive when we let go of something else. We live in abundance when we share.

This planet will not survive without our willingness to share. When we turn this willingness into action, we will receive every type of help. We must save this planet. The Spiritual World supports every action in this direction. God appoints the helpers of the world. It is a gift of maturity to perceive that *each* of us is a chosen one.

Sunstone. . . . . . JOY OF LIFE
Composition . . . (Na,Ca)[(Si,Al)$_2$Si$_2$O$_8$]
Hardness . . . . . 6—6.5
Color . . . . scintillating orange to red-brown, rarely in other colors
Sources . . . . . . United States, India, Canada, Norway, Russia

Special note: Here we refer to the aventurine-feldspar sunstone. Do not mistake sunstone for the orange-colored aventurine (quartz). It can also sparkle but much less than the aventurine-feldspar. True sunstone is characterized by a very strong gold-orange scintillation when moved in the light. A cheap imitation of sunstone is goldstone—artificial glass with pieces of glitter.

Energy class 3

SPECTROLITE

SERVING FROM A FULL HEART

This stone should come as a present. When this happens, we know that our maturity has arrived. Spectrolite calls us to serve—a word that we often misunderstand!

Serving here means to *live joyfully!*

Nothing fulfills our heart as much as a lasting closeness to God. In order to serve joyfully, we must be filled completely with God.

Spectrolite has an encouraging message.

"Enjoy life to the fullest! Know that God is within you and guides your path. Understand that life is joy when you completely devote yourself to God. Understand that God expects nothing more than your willingness to love.
"Love life with all your strength! Answer all the questions of life with your undivided attention. Fulfill your task by *living*."

The spectrolite reminds us that serving and loving are one. We serve with our *lives*. Nothing more is demanded of us.

Spectrolite . . . . . JOY—SURPRISE—SERVING
Composition . . . (Ca,Na)[(Al,Si)$_2$Si$_2$O$_8$]
Hardness . . . . . 6—6.5
Color. . . . . . . unremarkable gray-black with suddenly flashing rainbow iridescence
Source . . . . Finland

Special note: Spectrolite is an opaque form of labradorite with a particularly strong display of iridescent colors.

Energy class 1

SPESSARTITE (Garnet)

A STONE FOR GREAT SOULS

When we are wholly in despair, when we think that the task God has given us is too big, this stone will come to us.

We master EVERYTHING *when we are connected with God*. With the spessartite come new tasks, there are great things to be risked and a new and eternal trust placed in God. This is a stone that helps us take on our true dimensions, which imparts to us that in our heart we live with God in such harmony that we can never, *absolutely never*, stray from our path.

The souls who require this stone feel themselves to be so much a part of the whole that they always think they do not do enough, do not love enough, and are often so concerned about their path into the Light that they often doubt whether they are still on the right path. God wants to say to them: "As long as you love me as you do now, the earth shines through your presence alone. All human beings and all creatures live in your love. Pause and recognize this. Do not push yourself to fulfill your task until you are tired. Be certain that I comfort you, hold you, and let you know that I love you just as unconditionally as you love me."

This is a stone for great souls who do not recognize themselves in their greatness. It gives them absolute calm and the certainty that they have done everything that has been their task from the beginning until now.

In the light of this stone, these souls finally understand that no, absolutely no, efforts are required for them to move forwards on their path. They have come as far as people can go. They are one with God—much longer than they know.

Spessartite. . . . . HEART'S DESIRE
Composition . . . $Mn_3^{2+}Al_2[SiO_4]_3$
Hardness . . . . . 7—7.5
Color . . . . yellow-brown, golden-brown, brown to red-brown, orange-brown to orange
Sources . . . . . . Sri Lanka, Brazil, United States, Madagascar, Sweden

Special note: I am a great soul when I want to obey God beyond my personal desires. Since this rests in all of our hearts, it applies to all of us. It only depends on when we become aware of it.

Energy class 1

S P H A L E R I T E (Zinc blend)

OVERCOMING BRITTLENESS

This stone helps us see our hidden neuroses. It creates a perception of our reserve and refusal to be accepting. When we have recognized this, we require other stones.

Sphalerite . . . . DEFENSE
Composition . . ZnS
Hardness . . . . 3.5—4
Color . . . . . . yellow, red, green, brownish, black
Sources . . . . . Spain, Mexico

Energy class 2

BLUE SPINEL

REPROACH

Who is going to love a dark-blue spinel? It hurts to be ignored. With this spinel we get a friend that bitterly scolds.

"If you only could *see*! Just as you do not notice *me*, you miss out on half the world! What is it that you see? Illusion! Reflections! You shouldn't be satisfied with this! I love you! I want to help you! Those who love me will understand what I mean."

Then, it speaks a little more quietly.

"I am an example of love—*lost love*. There is so much in the world that could open your heart, and you pass it by. Do you love each other in the same way? Yes. You only want parts of each other. You do not completely accept each other. You cannot live like this. It makes you unhappy."

It changes to a loving tone of voice.

"Take me in your arms and see what I can do. Feel my love, and accept my gifts. Trust that God would like to shower you with gifts. Be open for it."

Those who wear the dark-blue spinel are willing to see a new world.

Blue spinel . . . . . PERCEPTION
Composition . . . . $MgAl_2O_4$
Hardness . . . . . . 7.5—8
Color . . . . blue
Sources . . . . Burma, Sri Lanka, India, Brazil, United States, the Ural area,
Madagascar, Australia

Energy class 1

YELLOW SPINEL

SHINING FLAME

The yellow spinel is the joy of God; it is a gift from other worlds. This brings with it the tasks of reminding us of other worlds. When we give up hope because of what we see, hear, and feel, this spinel builds us up. It knows about *all* worlds and this is what it imparts to us. When this knowledge penetrates into us, it activates an understanding that we normally do not use. We think that we have to deal with our own world so much that we cannot worry about other worlds. This is a mistake. The consciousness of many worlds beyond our own gives us the repose to truly open up to our own world.

With this stone, the premonition of greatness and expansiveness, which is truly indescribable, overcomes us. In view of this inconceivable opening, we become calm. Something happens to us. We experience it as peace.

Yellow spinel . . . GOD AS THE BEGINNING
Composition . . . $MgAl_2O_4$
Hardness . . . . . 7.5—8
Color . . . . yellow-red, orange, yellow
Sources . . . . . Burma, Sri Lanka, India, Brazil, United States, the Ural area, Madagascar, Australia

Energy class 1

GREEN SPINEL

THE PLANT KINGDOM

This spinel has a special task. It protects the plant kingdom. When we wear it, we are connected with the helpers of the plant kingdom. We are informed and taught. At the same time, we get a feeling for this (plant) life that constantly surrounds us, is a part of our life, and yet is so profoundly disregarded by us. Who does not stop in front of a flower and look at a tree in admiration? However, is this enough? No.

With the green spinel we can penetrate into a premonition of life that will make us speechless. We have no understanding at all of the animal and plant kingdom, although we always believe we do. Only in the deepest humility, greatest love, and with the grace of God are we granted a look behind the veil that we have permitted to cover this knowledge.

For those of us who can weep because of a tree, who long for the fragrance of carnations that no longer exist, who know that God's fruit has been robbed of its best qualities, the green spinel is a comforter, a teacher, and a healer for them. For those who feel the pain, the all-consuming, cataclysmic pain, in their breasts because of the human being's destructive exploitation of God's Creation, for them this stone is the only true help.

It will take us in its arms like no other because it knows this pain like we do: it has chosen to suffer this pain. Just as we have. However, it knows why it is important, why it must occur, and what is the purpose of this pain. "Healing," it says, "is understanding. Trust that I will teach you everything that is important for you. One day only the feeling of melancholy will remain within you. One day, there will be love—also for this part of being human. I love you. Trust."

Spinel . . . . PLANT KINGDOM
Composition . . . $MgAl_2O_4$
Hardness . . . . . 7.5—8
Color . . . . dark-green
Sources . . . . . . Burma, Sri Lanka, India, Brazil, United States, the Ural area, Madagascar, Australia

Energy class 1

PINK SPINEL

RELEASING STRICTNESS

We indulge in something good for ourselves with a spinel. It stands for clarity, but still has much more to give. The clarity that it promises us has its basis in the love of God. This stone helps us solve problems. Although it is very powerful, its effect is not quite as strong as that of the red spinel.

Those who decide on the pink spinel should be aware that they are asking God to direct their lives. With this spinel, we subject ourselves to the wisdom of God.

Pink spinel . . . . . CLARITY
Composition . . . . $MgAl_2O_4$
Hardness . . . . . . 7.5—8
Color . . . . pink
Sources . . . . Burma, Sri Lanka, India, Brazil, United States, the Ural area, Madagascar, Australia

Energy class 1

RED SPINEL

GREAT CLARITY

This fiery stone provides us with clarity. It is only meant for strong people who want to walk their path in a very straightforward way. It gives them absolute clarity of perception and the STRENGTH to let actions follow the perceptions. It is a very direct stone. It presents irresolute people with confusion, a condition that leads them to dissatisfaction, from which they ultimately want to free themselves. To do so, there are other stones that help. This is also a path one can take. However, since the gemstones only want the best for us, they would recommend other stones for such people.

Red spinel . . . . . CLARITY—FARSIGHTEDNESS
Composition . . . $MgAl_2O_4$
Hardness . . . . . 7.5—8
Color . . . . strong red, yellow-red
Sources . . . . . . Burma, Sri Lanka, India, Brazil, United States, the Ural area, Madagascar, Australia

Energy class 1

BLACK SPINEL

PERCEPTION OF INNER DEATHS

The special quality of the spinels is clarity. In all clarity this suggests the death within us. There is no change without death and no growth without dying.

We are mature enough to recognize death and life as *one*. As something that is insepa-rable and interdependent. With this spinel, death loses all of its terror. We irrevocably understand that we are immortal.

This is an unnoticed stone that imparts to us one of the greatest truths in life and lets us accept it.

Black spinel . . . . . UNDERSTANDING DYING
Composition . . . . $MgAl_2O_4$
Hardness . . . . . . 7.5—8
Color . . . . black
Sources . . . . Burma, Sri Lanka, India, Brazil, United States, the Ural area,
Madagascar, Australia

Energy class 1

VIOLET SPINEL

(Photograph on page 311)

ENFORCING RULES

Rules are necessary for people to live together. However, this does not refer to rules that have been created by human beings. What is meant are the laws of life that ensure a smooth and happy life together. However, since we resist becoming acquainted with these laws, we are also not successful in living together in peace as citizens of this world.

The violet spinel gives us a profound inner knowledge of the laws of life, their enforcement, and their effects. It is significant for those who have taken over leadership tasks in this age of upheaval. Worn for a long time, it will create a vibration of mercy and understanding, from which these laws of life can also be successfully taught. It is an important stone for people with great tasks who avoid the direct contact to God for personal reasons. For those who let their tasks be given to them directly by God and discuss all difficulties with God, this stone is beautiful but no longer absolutely a mentor.

Violet spinel . . . . . RECOGNIZING TASKS
Composition . . . . $MgAl_2O_4$
Hardness . . . . . . 7.5—8
Color . . . . violet
Sources . . . . . . Burma, Sri Lanka, India, Brazil, United States, the Ural area, Madagascar, Australia

Energy class 1

SPODUMENE

AWAKENING THE FIRE OF LOVE IN THE HEART

The spodumene is a very special gemstone. Although it sometimes has an inconspicuous effect, a very high power lives within it. It reminds us of the love of Christ that has an effect within all of us.

In our human history, we all participate in what Jesus Christ has experienced. His pain is our pain. His love as well. As one of the Highest Masters, he has influenced us more than we know. His teachings of unconditional love live in our heart. We are more deeply connected with him than we suspect.

The spodumene comes to those who feel the power of Christ within their hearts, have called on God, and long to live for God. The spodumene promises the highest level of bliss. God is within us. The love of Christ as well.

Spodumene . . . . LOVE OF CHRIST
Composition . . . $LiAl[Si_2O_6]$
Hardness . . . . . 6—7
Color . . . . colorless to beige-gray transparent
Sources . . . . . . Afghanistan, Madagascar, United States, Brazil, Burma

Special note: Kunzite (pink) and hiddenite (green) belong to the spodumenes. Stones that do not fit into these terms because of their color are just called spodumene.

Energy class 1

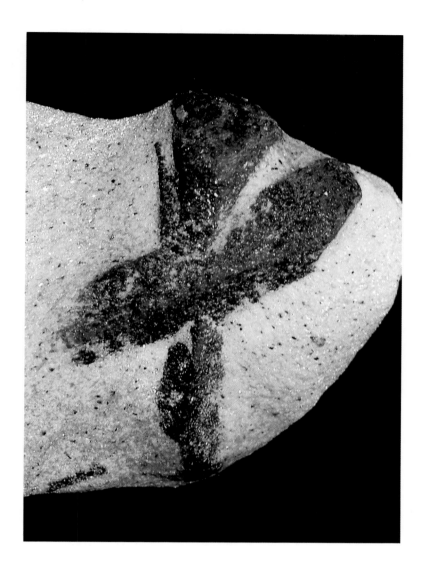

STAUROLITE (Chiastolite)

DELIVERANCE FROM INSECURITY

This is a stone that reminds us of the core of all things—of God. It says "If you are not clear with yourself, then you are not clear with God. God is in EVERYTHING. Search for Him." This stone then *reminds* us. When we want to go on the search, we should take advantage of the help of other stones.

Staurolite . . . . . INITIATIVE
Composition . . . $(Fe^{2+},Mg,Zn)_2Al_9[O_6/(OH)_2/(SiO)^4]$
Hardness . . . . . 7—7.5
Color . . . . red-brown to black-brown to black
Sources . . . . . . Germany, Austria, Switzerland, United States

Energy class 2

STELLARITE

HEALS DESPAIR

This is a stone with a great effect. In its green, as well as in its vibration field, there is much healing energy. It is a stone that imparts courage and hope—courage to live and hope of holistic healing—the healing of our *heart*.

Pain is not what it seems to be. To love pain—that means the learning process that lies behind it—is the most certain path to healing.

Stellarite. . . . . . HELP FOR THE WORLD
Composition . . . Fusion of jasper with chrysocolla, malachite, and limonite
Hardness 6.5
Color . . . . primarily green
Sources . . . . . . United States, Mexico

Energy class 1

STELLERITE

MADNESS

With this stone we find a level within us that we usually deny—madness.

What is madness? Didn't it also take a bit of insanity to have created this earth? Madness also lives within us. Without madness there would be no life. Without risk there would be no luck or happiness. We trust in our life, our visions and faces. Perhaps we are mistaken. However, what a waste it is when everything that we see is truth—and we do not live according to it.

To truly obey God means to love. However, without a trace of insanity we would not be able to do so. Let us train ourselves in the power of differentiation with this stone.

Stellarite . . . . . . MADNESS
Composition . . . $Ca[Al_2Si_7O_{18}]\cdot 7H_2O$
Hardness . . . . . 3.5—4
Color . . . . colorless, white, gray, yellow, brown
Source . . . . Alaska

Energy class 1

STAR SAPPHIRE, STAR RUBY

ENLIGHTENMENT IN THE CHRIST SPIRIT

The appearance of a star (asterism) occurs in several gemstones. It is best-known in opaque sapphires and rubies.

For us, it always means a reminder of enlightenment and the Christ energy.

"Trust your heart. *Obey me*," is what Christ would say. The starlite is a symbol of this.

Star sapphire, Star ruby. . . . ENLIGHTENMENT IN CHRIST

Energy class 1

FRESHWATER PEARLS

ETERNAL PERFECTION

The freshwater pearls are completely different from other pearls. While saltwater pearls give off a strong aura of pain, which means the overcoming of pain on the path to perfection, the larger (!) freshwater pearls radiate in a vibration of pure perfection and joy. For them it is as if the pain with that they were created was no longer important, as if it had never been there.

These pearls teach us that the we can truly heal the greatest pain and the agony of dying. They teach us that we can overcome everything that had once hurt us and that love heals *everything*.

Those who love these pearls in particular have already purified much within themselves and have already understood transformation. The freshwater pearls are a gift for people who long for perfection and give their best in order to achieve it.

This is a gift from nature to loving people.

Freshwater pearls . . . PERFECTION

Composition	84—92% calcium-carbonate, 4—13% organic substance, 3—4% water
Hardness	3—4
Color	light, white-pink, golden-yellow, delicate brown (almost always dyed) with mother-of-pearl shimmer
Sources	Although freshwater pearls exist (the tiny natural river pearls are not meant here), almost all of them are cultivated. The best-known ones are the pearls that grow in Lake Biwa in Japan. They have a particularly good vibration if they are not too tiny.

Special note: These pearls are also created through the animal's pain and its need for compensation. However, they are surprisingly surrounded by a vibration of happiness and joy. We should wear them with reverence.

Energy class 1

SUGILITE

REVERENCE FOR LIFE

The sugilite teaches us GREATNESS. We rarely recognize true greatness since our eyes are tired because of illusions, our heart are exhausted, and we can at best also have a presentiment of its greatness. It purifies the heart and thoughts, it refreshes our soul, and it inspires our mind. We *perceive* and obtain strength from this.

Here we meet a significant gemstone helper. It is one of the first of a series of stones for the new age that the stone kingdom will continue to make available to us.

People who love the sugilite are children of the new age who have already recognized their task. They belong to a circle of helpers for the period of upheaval and the sugilite has called them.

By teaching us *reverence for life,* this gemstone takes over its task of moving people to change their ways. Helpers of the new age support their fellow human beings in this process.

Sugilite . . . . . . REVERENCE FOR LIFE
Composition . . . $Na_3KLi_2Fe_2^{3+}[Si_{12}O_{30}]$
Hardness . . . . . 6.5—7
Color . . . . red-violet, blue-purple to blue-purple, lilac
Sources . . . . . . Japan, South Africa

Special note: Sugilite was discovered in Japan in 1944 but was first traded only in 1975 from South Africa. The stronger the lilac color, is the better. We should avoid stones that contain too much black or gray. When it was first discovered, this stone was also called sogdianite. The sogdianite is a similar mineral but it contains zirconia.

Energy class 1

TANZANITE

GOD IN EVERYTHING—SOURCE OF JOY

The tanzanite is a stone that contains all the divine qualities. Those who wear it are very close to God.

As a symbol of the Light we like to chose yellow stones, as a symbol of love we select the pink-colored ones. All blue stones connect us with the SPIRIT within us and the tanzanite connects us with the DIVINE SPIRIT.

The tanzanite teaches us to *perceive God in everything*.

Those who wear it will become aware of their calling. It is a stone for highly developed beings who have not yet recognized their strength and fearfully close their hearts to it.

It forces us to perceive our path by connecting us directly with God, particularly with *divine perception*. This creates trust and we gradually open ourselves for further energies.

It is at the top of the list of gemstones because it is so important for the coming century for each of us to take his or her place. In order to fulfill our goal as humanity, we must become conscious of our origin and our tasks.

It is easy to say that we are divine. To *feel* and *experience* the unity with God is another level. Those who *know* God in this way will walk their path purposefully, joyfully, and securely. We all look forward to our return home into the Light. However, we have only achieved our true greatness when we are happily and naturally willing to serve humanity and this earth.

"Love the world. Do not separate according to appearance and tasks. Embrace everything that I have created. I am everything that you see."

On the level of subconsciousness, this stone helps us to better come to terms with ourselves. On the more conscious level, it gradually leads us to the perception that we are divine.

Tanzanite . . . . . PERCEPTION—SEARCH FOR GOD
Composition . . . $Ca_2Al_3[O/OH/SiO_4/Si_2O_7]$
Hardness . . . . . 6.5—7
Color . . . . luminous ultramarine-blue, sapphire-blue to pale blue-violet, very rarely green
Sources . . . . . . Tanzania, Africa

Special note: Tanzanites are smoky-quartz-like zoisites that were experimentally heated and then surprised the processors of the gemstones with a splendid blue color. However, because of the heating process they possess a certain brittleness and are sensitive to pressure. A tanzanite is about 585 million years old. There are apparently only very rare tanzanites (zoisites) that are naturally blue.

Energy class LEARNING PROCESSES BEYOND PERFECTION

TEKTITE

QUICKNESS

Tektite brings us very quickly to the truth. Here truth means the understanding of correlations. Unrest and insecurity drops from us when we *understand* a problem. When we comprehend the hidden learning processes behind a problem, the solutions are close at hand. Then we will feel where we should move in order to resolve the challenges in a holistic way.

The tektite likes to come to stern people who are not aware of their sternness. Under its influence, rigidity disappears and the sternness is softened.

A tektite is not a stone for long learning processes. Its quality is speed. Once we see through a problem, other stones help us in carrying out the demands.

Tektite . . . . QUICK HELP
Composition . . . Amorphous glass, mainly of silica acid
Hardness 5.5
Color . . . . dark, sometimes dark-green
Sources . . . . . . Asia, Australia

Special note: Exceptions here are the moldavites, described separately.

Energy class 3

THULITE

MOTHER EARTH

This stone heals all feelings that move us on the topic of *mother*.

It possesses a very earthy quality and is connected with the principal of love.

Thulite. . . . . . . MOTHER
Composition . . . Zoisite containing manganese
Hardness . . . . . 6.5—7
Color . . . . red
Sources . . . . . . Thule Island, Norway

Energy class 3

TIGER'S-EYE

RECOGNITION OF MY MATERIAL WISHES AND STRENGTH TO REALIZE THEM

This is an important stone. However, be careful—for most of us it is too intensely oriented towards the material level.

It is a part of our development to have wishes and to fulfill them for ourselves. Most of us have this behind us. In the coming century, it will be important to learn how to *share* and dispense with wishes that are created by the ego. In this way, we will receive the greatest spiritual gift. Being content is a great gift. However, it has the precondition of maturity and must not be mistaken for refusal.

This stone is good for people who still have to learn to assert themselves. To be on the safe side, it should be used in connection with pink stones.

Tiger's-eye . . . . . MATERIALISM
Composition . . . . SiO_2 with parallel-grain; inclusions of krokydolite, a type of asbestos (harmless)
Hardness 7
Color . . . . yellow, golden-brown, brown (play of colors)
Sources . . . . . . South Africa, Australia, Burma, India, United States

Energy class 3

TIGER-IRON

HEALING BY GIVING UP

This is a good healing stone for the physical plane. It draws inflammations out of the body.

It encourages us to give up an inner defense mechanism and become cured.

Tiger-iron . . . . . HEALING STONE
Composition . . . SiO_2 with bands of hematite
Hardness 7
Color . . . . yellow, golden-brown, brown, red -with hematite
Source . . . . . . Australia

Energy class 3

TITANITE (Sphene)

CAUSES US TO LET GO OF OUR CRAVING FOR LOVE

This stone serves our best interest since we rely on ourselves and no longer *search* for love. Love is a gift that comes from the heart. We can neither acquire nor force love. We will only encounter it when we love.

It also teaches us to perceive our greatness. When we understand who we are, then love is no longer a problem. The more we love ourselves, the stronger is the certainty that there are many types of love and we are permitted to live all of them. We only *pine away* for love when we feel ourselves to be separated from God. If we feel God's love within us, we can also accept and give earthly love with perfection. However, the more we pine for it, the more removed we are from love. Life is rich. The perception of this abundance develops out of love. True perception enlarges our love and love in turn increases our perception. When we trust in God, we trust in our *ability* to love! This is a stone with a short-term effect but it still can deeply influence us.

Titanite . . . . . . LOVE
Composition . . . CaTi[O/SiO$_4$]
Hardness . . . . . 5—5.5
Color . . . . yellow, brown, green
Sources . . . . . Switzerland, Italy, United States, Sri Lanka, Canada, Burma, Madagascar, Brazil
Energy class 1

BLUE TOPAZ

PERCEPTION OF MY STRENGTH—INITIATION

This topaz comes to us when we want to understand our entire life, when we want to know why what seemed to be our greatest wish, our strongest desire, was not fulfilled. Our earthly heart may complain "I have misspent my life." The spiritual heart extends itself in the vibration of the blue Light (blue topaz) and understands for us: "What I have lived is my task, my intended purpose. I may have directed my attention to something else—a hope, an illusion—but I have lived my power, my strength, and my unity with God. I have not noticed this—until today."

The blue topaz permits us to perceive what our true connection with our life looks like, that tasks we have already fulfilled, how we are one with God—and that tasks are still waiting for us.

Connecting ourselves with it means finding peace in our life, peace from the understanding of my greatness, my love and abilities, my all-encompassing love of God. The unique thing about this stone is the intimate connection with the Divine Energy, the joyful losing of oneself in God, the dance with the energy of life. This is a stone for the wise, for those who love this universe, for those who bear the world in their hearts without knowing it, for those who long for God and continually must remember that they already *live* with God and *within* God.

The pain of this world could be healed with this stone.

Blue topaz . . . . . FEVERISH FOR LIFE
Composition . . . $Al_2[(F,OH)_2/SiO_4]$
Hardness 8
Color . . . . blue
Sources . . . . . . Brazil, Rhodesia, Afghanistan, Pakistan, Mexico, Sri Lanka

Special note: The strong blue topazes are almost always irradiated. This frequently also applies for the pink topazes.

Energy class 1

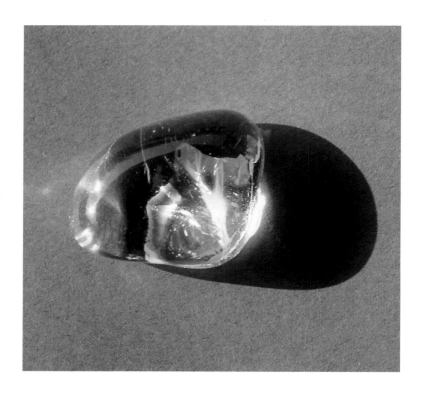

COLORLESS TOPAZ

UPWARD FREEDOM

The direct connection to God—who does not wish for this? This is again a gemstone with which this is possible in the simplest way.

This topaz calls people who want to grow through it. Astonishing: for some very few people this stone is so important that they surround themselves only with it.

The magic of its being lies in the connection of inner strength, willingness for highest love, and boundless rapture for God. This is a mixture that we human beings usually have to work hard at feeling—although it naturally lies within us!

Those who in a certain sense find out that the colorless topaz is their life-stone should not hesitate to furnish themselves and their house with it. A ring, necklace, handstones, and at least two or three stones for the living areas are a must. Happy are those who love this stone.

Colorless topaz . . . . . RAPTURE FOR GOD
Composition . . . . . . $Al_2[(F,OH)_2/SiO_4]$
Hardness 8
Color . . . . colorless
Sources . . . . Brazil, Rhodesia, Afghanistan, Pakistan, Mexico, Sri Lanka

GOLD TOPAZ

ABUNDANCE OF LIFE—JOY OF THE HEART

The golden-yellow precious topaz is connected with the principle of the highest happiness. Those who wear it will be devoted to it in its entire abundance. They will say *yes* to everything that God wants to pour out on them.

The happiness of our life depends on how much we can open up to God's love. The more often we say to God: "I walk *Your* paths, guide me," the more intensely we live according to God's answers, the more we open our heart for *happiness*. The absolute rapture and the joy in God's Creation, with myself as a part of it, flows through our heart only when we have forgiven ourselves for the times when we have denied life.

Promise me, my heart, that you love me. Breathe the Eternal Life. Perform the love of God. Believe in this life. Lead me to myself and let me be the joy that I *am*. Amen.

Gold topaz . . . . . PERCEPTION—ETERNAL LIFE
Composition . . . . $Al_2[(F,OH)_2/SiO_4]$
Hardness 8
Color . . . . golden-yellow to golden-brown to yellow
Sources . . . . Brazil, Rhodesia, Afghanistan, Pakistan, Mexico, Sri Lanka

Energy class 1

PINK TOPAZ

A WAVE OF LOVE FLOWS THROUGH ME

Mercy is a gift of God. The pink-colored topaz is also a gift of God. When we have achieved the highest level of enlightenment, even though we may still have to struggle with everyday life a bit these things are truly no longer important for us because we have seen God. This stone then comes to us. It envelops us with such a radiant, spiritualized, tender love that the duties of everyday life become an absolute pleasure. This is because it also teaches that there is no large and small and that the daily prayer is just as important as washing the dishes every day.

God, in His infinite love, lets us feel through this stone that He is joy, perpetual love, and tender hope. He takes us in His arms and rocks us with a smile. He has given us His smile with this stone.

Pink topaz . . . . . UPLIFTED TO GOD
Composition . . . $Al_2[(F,OH)_2/SiO_4]$
Hardness 8
Color . . . . pink
Sources . . . . . . Brazil, Rhodesia, Afghanistan, Pakistan, Mexico, Sri Lanka

Energy class 1

TOPAZOLITE (Garnet)

(no photograph)

FAITHFULNESS TO LIFE—PURITY

This is a melancholy stone. It does not want to be loved.

A stone shows itself here in the manner in which many people live. They search desperately for love, they run after it—and yet they do not know that they have renounced it. What a tragedy. How difficult life is in this condition!

The topazolite helps us by showing us the troubles we find ourselves in when we do not open up for love. In its impressive manner it represents how desperate we are. However, it is possible to change one's ways. Once we have understood and felt how we have closed ourselves off to love, there are many types of help in order to heal our heart. This stone encourages us to undertake such healing:

Topazolite . . . . . RENOUNCING LOVE
Composition . . . Variety of the andradite
Hardness . . . . . 6.5—7.5
Color . . . . . . green-yellow, yellow
Sources . . . . . Germany, Austria, Italy

Special note: I have only encountered the topazolite in such tiny versions (the size of a pinhead, faceted) that we have done without an illustration of it. As a raw stone, it had the effect of spots of inconspicuous yellowish coating so that we also did not photograph this stone.

Energy class 2

TRAPICHE—EMERALD (Beryl)

UNITY—JOY IN GOD

This unusual emerald strengthens our self-confidence. It exemplifies bonding. Its special quality is unity. What it would like to show is this: "Connect yourself with life, connect yourself with God, connect yourself with *your self* and *you will live happily.*"

Being one with ourselves is easier than we think. However, it requires us to recognize that we are in this state of mind in the rarest of cases and learning is necessary for us to achieve this state. Only when I have learned just about everything about myself, I am capable of being *one* with my self.

Those who are *one* with themselves are one with God and they are one with life. Our development could be so easy, our life as well, if we would allow ourselves to merge with ourselves.

Trapiche-emerald . . . . MERGING
Composition . . . . . . $Be_3Al_2[Si_6O_{18}]$
Hardness . . . . 7.5—8
Color . . . . emerald-green with a dark "cartwheel" sign
Source . . . . Columbia

Energy class 1

STALACTITE (DRIPSTONE)

DEVELOPMENT—PATIENCE

Dripstones (stalactites, stalagmites) give us the hope of a power within ourselves that we can activate. If we are despondent or discouraged, we should remember a life principle—*patience*. What grows in millions of years, we want to create in seconds—this is approximately what the energy with which we approach our tasks looks like.

Dripstones teach patience. At the same time, they assure us that everything that a person dreams of can be created. However, they also remind us that some goals require many human lifetimes in order to be achieved. Time is nothing in the universe. With this stone, we examine our own concept of time. The gift will be *repose*—an understanding of strength and development and the use of our possibilities. This is a stone for the restless when this restlessness results from the fear of perhaps not being able to fulfill their tasks.

Stalactite. . . . . . LIFE
Composition . . . Fine-grained calcite
Hardness 3
Color . . . . white-gray-beige-brown
Sources . . . . . . caves throughout the world

Energy class 3

CONGLOMERATE ROCK

PERPETUAL TRANSFORMATION—GROWTH

With this stone we are reminded: Where there was destruction, there will be a new beginning. Nature heals everything.

What are millions of years? In the universe, *nothing*. This stone speaks of transience and growth. Its history is the demolition of rocks by the forces of nature and the connecting and becoming one again through new rock formation. What was one becomes separated and after the separation a new unity is formed.

In this way, the stone encourages us to develop new things but also to protect what already exists. However, above all it represents the perception that although random destruction will be counterbalanced, this occurs in a period of time that is inconceivable for us human beings. That is why this stone gives us the power to reflect on what exists and feel our reverence for it. Only by honoring the Creation can we save the earth—and ourselves.

Conglomerate rock . . . . . PROTECTING AND GROWTH
Composition . . . . hardness, color and discovery sites vary, but they mostly have SiO_2 and hardness 7. There is jasper conglomerate, landscape marble, and other stones.

Energy class 3

T S A V O L I T E (Garnet)

PERCEPTION OF MY DIVINITY

Clarity of perception, knowledge about love, and understanding for the partner: the tsavolite helps us to live our everyday life with our partner.

When we live together with another person, we enter into a community. When we live together, we have problems to master. This is the way it must be because we grow through problems and an intensive partnership is a quick way to grow. Despite all the love, it can also be a difficult path. In order to be able to perceive myself and the partner, to understand our games and fears, to be able to expose our concealments and denials—the tsavolite helps us during this process. It creates clarity and understanding.

However, since it is a garnet and connected with the principle of love, it supports our love for the other person and helps with his or her growth. If we perceive and love, then we will better understand our partner and many "problems" (learning opportunities) become insignificant. It is therefore a stone for lovers who consciously live their love.

Tsavolite . . . . . . CLARITY—LOVE
Composition . . . $Ca_3Al_2(SiO_4)_3$
Hardness . . . . . 7—7.5
Color . . . . grass-green
Sources . . . . . . Tsavo National Park in Kenya

Special note: Tsavolites are small and sold for collectors' prices. A necklace of dark splinter stones came to me. It only revealed the magnificent green when the stones were held up to the sun. It seemed to be inconspicuous but had the best energy and was quite affordable. It is always important to trust that each stone is within our means and finds its way to us when we need its energy. I have even loaned gemstones or pieces of jewelry or worn those that I have borrowed. Since the gemstones teach that it is important to give up our possessive way of thinking, we should be open for unusual opportunities. It is therefore not always necessary to purchase a stone.

Energy class 1

TURQUOISE

THE STONE OF THE WISE—CONNECTION TO OTHER WORLDS

The turquoise is a good healing stone. It has proved itself in many cultures. The Indians particularly love it. A new discovery is in store for us. This stone will once again become important in relation to the neutralization of radioactivity.

For the current age it is the optimal stone to promote creativity, awaken dormant talents, and heal resistance against these qualities.

The turquoise constantly works with us, even if we do not possess one. It looks care of the preservation of the earth and influences us during our sleep. We should appreciate it more.

Be watchful of extremely plentiful imitations.

Turquoise . . . . . CREATIVITY
Composition . . . $Cu(Al,Fe^{3+})[(OH)_2/PO_4]_4 \cdot 4H_2O$
Hardness . . . . . 5—6
Color . . . . sky-blue to blue-green, turquoise to green
Sources . . . . . . Iran, China, United States, Australia, Brazil

Special note: Select a sky-blue to blue-green turquoise and be sure that it is genuine. There are many turquoise imitations on the market. The turquoise is very sensitive and quickly changes its color when it comes into contact with chemical substances like perfume, soap, and perspiration, for example. Never put it in an ultrasound bath! It can also discolor when we are ill.

Energy class 2

TUGTUPITE

JOY IN EVERYDAY LIFE—TIME FOR OURSELVES AND OUR WISHES

The tugtupite is a cheerful stone. It protects us from self-pity and torments based on a lack of understanding. It gives the proper space to all occurrences. With it we will be able to see certain memories in another light. It dissolves self-doubt and regret. It also protects us from feelings of revenge. This stone is good for us human beings.

Tugtupite . . . . . JOY AND ENTHUSIASM
Composition . . . $Na_4[Cl/BeAlSi_4O_{12}]$
Hardness 5
Color . . . . pink to strong red, sometimes slightly yellow-red and speckled
Sources . . . . . . Greenland, Russia

Energy class 1

BLUE TOURMALINE (INDIGOLITE)

GOD'S GIFTS NEVER END

With an indigolite in the hand, we experience an exultant, jubilant uplifting to God. Under His influence we perceive and pray: "Beloved God, beloved life, thank you for all the gemstones that You have created. Grant me the mercy of my everlasting love to everything alive. Open my heart for the pain of this world and help me to overcome it. Give me a blue tourmaline so that it can heal me."

"I have heard you," spoke God. "Trust."

The indigolite plunges us into the alternating hot and cold baths of feelings. It twirls us upwards into joy. We feel effusive thankfulness and deepest pain at the same time. We feel ourselves torn between perception and a lack of understanding, between moments of enlightenment and apparent senselessness. While the gemstone makes us conscious of these conditions, its healing power starts to work within us.

Blue tourmaline . . . . TRUST IN ME, SAYS GOD
Composition . . . . . $Na(Li,Al)_3Al_6[(OH)_4/BO_3)_3/Si_6O_{18}]$
Hardness . . . . 7—7.5
Color . . . . blue (no other stone has as great a variety of colors as the tourmaline)
Sources. . . . . Brazil, Africa, Afghanistan, Pakistan, United States, Madagascar,
Sri Lanka, Australia, eastern Africa

Energy class 1

BROWN TOURMALINE (DRAVITE)

TRUST IN GOD AND REPOSE

All worries fall away from me, all vexations become insignificant—God is within me.
Like no other stone, the dravite connects us with the primordial trust in God within us.
It works with a great quickness. We hardly hold it—and already feel calmness. We call
to mind what is essential and we feel God. The effect is intensive and the results are
manifold.

For the physical plane, this stone will become very important in the future. *All* illness
can be traced back to our no longer being connected with God and no longer *feeling*
connected.

Brown tourmaline . . . TRUST IN GOD
Composition . . . . . $NaMg_3Al_6[(OH)_4/BO_3)_3/Si_6O_{18}]$
Hardness . . . . 7—7.5
Color . . . . brown
Sources. . . . . Brazil, Africa, Afghanistan, Pakistan, United States, Madagascar,
Sri Lanka, Australia, eastern Africa

Energy class 2

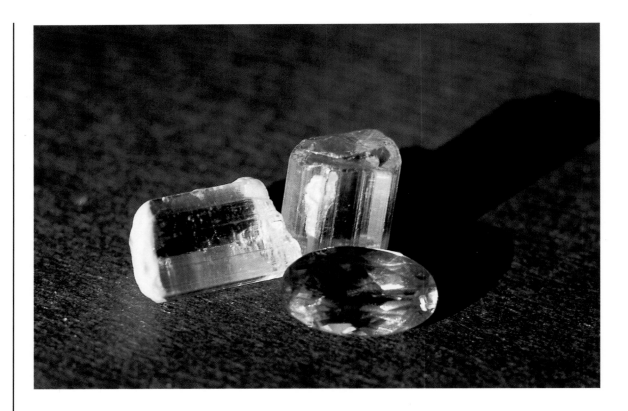

COLORLESS TOURMALINE (ACHROITE)

MOVING INTO SILENCE

Modesty is a quality of this tourmaline. It stands back behind its colorful brothers and sisters and waits to be discovered. At the same time, it does not make this easy for us since it is quite rare.

However, the search is worth it. Here is a tourmaline that loves us so much that it sacrifices itself for our happiness. It says: "Everything you need is within me. Hold me to your heart and understand the meaning of sacrifice. Comprehend that humanity does not understand what sacrifice is. Seek perception. I will wait."

Colorless tourmaline . . SACRIFICE—PERCEPTION
Composition . . . . . . $Na(Li,Al)_3Al_6[(OH)_4/BO_3)_3/Si_6O_{18}]$
Hardness . . . . 7—7.5
Color . . . . colorless
Sources. . . . . Brazil, Africa, Afghanistan, Pakistan, United States, Madagascar, Sri Lanka, Australia, eastern Africa

Special note: The gray tourmaline also deserves dignified consideration. It possesses the same vibration as the colorless but radiates a stronger connection to God.

YELLOW TOURMALINE (TSILAISITE)

SUN OF THE LIGHT—DIVINE JOY

Our highest quality in life is love. The yellow tourmaline teaches us: When we become more open for love, we will become more open for joy and the sun in our hearts. Those who open up to love, open up to all the qualities of Light.

The yellow tourmaline opens within us the door that we usually keep closed because of fear—the door to our inner sun. When we live the inner sun within us, we are connected with *genuine* love, a love that is unconditional, that is born from the Divine Light and that is enough unto itself.

This stone is meant for few people. It demands maturity and a far-reaching renunciation of our ego. It cannot be compared with the other yellow stones that we are familiar with and that are all connected with the principle of the sun and of the Light.

Those who would like to wear a yellow tourmaline should be aware that they are subjecting themselves to the Greatest Sun and the Greatest Love. This love will determine their lives. Those who wear this stone are helpers for the world.

Yellow tourmaline . . GIFT OF GOD
Composition . . . . . $NaMn^{2+}(Al,Li)_2Al_6[(OH)_4/(BO_3)_3/Si_6O_{18}]$
Hardness . . . . 7—7.5
Color . . . . yellow
Sources. . . . . Brazil, Africa, Afghanistan, Pakistan, United States, Madagascar, Sri Lanka, Australia, eastern Africa
Energy class 1

GREEN TOURMALINE (VERDELITE)

HOPE—STRENGTH

The green tourmaline heals the heart. It strengthens our hope for a peaceful and happy life. It strengthens our hope in general. Its gentle vibration spreads into our hearts and promises healing. Enveloped in healing energy and help, we are capable of taking a new look at our lives. We recognize mistakes and denials. We perceive ANEW. This is how it helps us let go of old patterns of thinking and form new thoughts and concepts. We regard ourselves in love and are prepared to heal ourselves.

This tourmaline provides clarity in the area of holistic healing. It is still underestimated in its healing energy.

It is very important for the physical level.

Green Tourmaline . . HEALING
Composition . . . . $Na(Li,Al)_3Al_6[(OH)_4/BO_3)_3/Si_6O_{18}]$
Hardness . . . . . . 7—7.5
Color . . . . green
Sources . . . . . . Brazil, Africa, Afghanistan, Pakistan, United States, Madagascar, Sri Lanka, Australia, eastern Africa

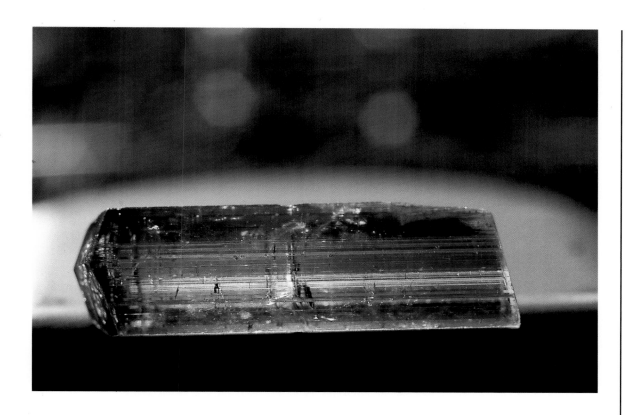

MULTICOLORED TOURMALINE

ABUNDANCE OF LIFE

Multicolored tourmalines bring joy to our heart. They support our growth and remind us of the variety of life and possibilities of developing oneself. Each vibration of the described tourmalines can be contained in multicolored stones.

We should enjoy them!

Multicolored tourmaline . . VARIETY
Composition . . . . Varies according to which colors the stone has
Color . . . . two or more colors layered in one stone (as contrast, see watermelon tourmaline)
Hardness . . . . 7—7.5
Sources . . . . Brazil, Africa, Afghanistan, United States, Madagascar, Sri Lanka, Pakistan, Australia, eastern Africa

Energy class 1

PINK and RUBELLITE TOURMALINE

LOVE OF HUMANITY—HUMANITARIANISM

The pink-colored tourmaline and the rubellite radiate the highest vibration of love among the tourmalines. They are meant for people who bear a special injury in their hearts, for those who can only painfully come to terms with the fact that the earth no longer is a paradise and only few people are willing to do their part in order to recreate this paradise.

It is possible for all of us to live in *abundance*. However, this can happen only when we all subject ourselves to the Divine Wisdom in all of our actions.

RUBELLITE

Those who bear paradise in their hearts also bear God in their hearts. Those who destroy the earth also destroy God. This is our pain. Since God is indestructible, another earth will be created. However, we remain behind with our pain. The rubellite comforts all those who know this. It gives strength to those who want to rise above this pain. It purifies our hearts and gives us insight into God's infinite possibilities. In its more gentle vibration, the pink-colored tourmaline is valued for slower learning processes or we simply enjoy it for the sake of its aura—unconditional holistic love. This vibration is also found in the rubellite but has a stronger effect.

Tourmaline, pink and rubellite . . HEALING—LOVE
Composition . . . . $Na(Li,Al)_3Al_6[(OH)_4/(BO_3)_3Si_6O_{18}]$
Hardness . . . . 7—7.5
Color . . . . rose-pink to deep-rose
Sources . . . . Brazil, Africa, Afghanistan, Pakistan, United States, Madagascar, Sri Lanka, Australia, eastern Africa

Special note: The rubellite is distinguished by a strong rose-colored pink, which sometimes is pink or has a touch of violet. With its color, it reminds us of the ruby. The rubellite is more intense than the other pink-colored tourmalines. See Red tourmaline.

Energy class 1

RED TOURMALINE

ELATION—FIRE OF LIFE

The red tourmaline is quite rare. It dances the dance of joy. It bursts with vital energy. We have to look for it—just like we have to find our joy in life. We only live a fraction of our possibilities. We are destined for more.

With this stone, we become curious about this *more*. We become restless and we search for our vital energy. Dance and Light and joy—this stone imparts these qualities.

Red tourmaline . . . VITAL ENERGY—FIRE OF LIFE
Composition . . . . $Na(Li,Al)_3Al_6[(OH)_4/(BO_3)_3Si_6O_{18}]$
Hardness . . . . . . 7—7.5
Color . . . . rose-red
Sources . . . . . . Brazil, Africa, Afghanistan, Pakistan, United States, Madagascar, Sri Lanka, Australia, eastern Africa

Energy class 1

BLACK TOURMALINE (SCHORL)

CONNECTION WITH GOD

The black tourmaline supports us in its nature of affiliation. Since it brings images from our subconscious to the surface, strengthens memories, and imparts strength to us at the same time, we can heal old wounds with it. It is the ideal stone for working through past lives. When we go through these memories and through our deaths into the Light, we will always perceive our affiliation. We are children of life and connected with all BEING. What happens to us, happens to others; what happens to others, happens to me. The shock of this perception is healed by the black tourmaline.

Black tourmaline . . . . SUPPORT
Composition . . . . . . $NaFe_3^{2+}(Fe^{3+},Al)_6[(OH)_4/BO_3)_3/Si_6O_{18}]$
Hardness . . . . 7—7.5
Color . . . . see Special note
Sources . . . . worldwide

Special note: This tourmaline has a compact black effect. Perhaps most of them are really black. However, a dealer made the effort to have a few of his tourmalines cut wafer-thin. His cross-sections were so thin that they—spread on glass plates—were still very fine. A surprising blaze of colors developed and the cross-sections that I saw were brilliant blue to green edges, sometimes with a delicate black exterior edge. Not everything is as it seems. The stones also teach us this time and again.

Energy class 3

VIOLET TOURMALINE (SIBERITE)

GROWING BEYOND ONESELF

The violet tourmaline teaches about the meaning of sacrifice. At the same time, it supports us in putting what we have learned into action.

In the first place, it teaches us that we grow when we overcome ourselves and that we strive toward the Light by leaving our wishes behind. The violet tourmaline is connected with the highest spirituality and continually teaches us. Among the tourmalines, it possesses the clearest energy for quick growth.

Violet tourmaline . . . BELONGING TO GOD
Composition . . . . . $Na(Li,Al)_3Al_6[(OH)_4/(BO_3)_3Si_6O_{18}]$
Hardness . . . . 7—7.5
Color . . . . violet violet-red
Sources. . . . . Brazil, Africa, Afghanistan, Pakistan, United States, Madagascar, Sri Lanka, Australia, eastern Africa

Energy class 1

ACICULAR TOURMALINE IN QUARTZ

LOOKING UPWARDS TO GOD

This stone settles discord. The acicular tourmaline in quartz is associated with the interrelations of life. To use it means to do something good for oneself because it creates a harmony with ourselves. Rooted in the earth on the one hand, searching for the Light on the other hand—this is the symbolism of the acicular tourmaline in quartz. It is a stone that awakens within us the desire for greatness and connection—connection with life and with our possibilities.

Those who use the acicular tourmaline in quartz take a further step forwards. We often have a hard time with our development. With this stone, we face our development and intuitively perceive that there is no sense in resisting it. Moving *with* our development means harmony and affirmation.

It is a good stone for people who quarrel and do not know why. To use it leads us at some point to the symbolic heaving of a deep sigh and the willingness to reconcile. The acicular tourmaline in quartz is good for everybody. However, those who are older and discover that there is much with which they wrangle need it urgently. For spiritual people the stone is a symbol for love that seeks an alternative. The quartz and the tourmaline are gemstones that normally do not connect with each other. Their connection within this stone shows that everything is possible if we are only ready for it.

Message: "Give love a chance. Rise above your problems. See that there is ALWAYS a solution.
On the physical level, the acicular tourmaline in quartz heals rashes when they are caused by inner struggles. Then it is recommended that you wear necklaces and stones on the body until the rash has healed. (Do not forget to cleanse the stones!)

Acicular tourmaline in quartz . . SOLUTION
Composition . . . . SiO_2 (quartz with enclosed acicular formations—
                                   "needles"—of tourmaline)
Hardness 7
Color . . . . colorless with black tourmaline needles
Source . . . . Brazil

Energy class 3

ULEXITE

ENLARGEMENT

The ulexite gives us a feeling for greatness. At the same time, it reminds us of the obligations that are connected with greatness.
Courage to live requires initiative. There is no greatness without deeds. When we hold an ulexite in the hand for an hour, we come into contact with our next important task. It may then take a few days until this enters into our consciousness.

This stone helps us when we feel ourselves to be aimless or have taken on too much and no longer see a clear course.

It is important for the physical level.

Ulexite. . . . . . . GREATNESS
Composition . . . $NaCa[B_5O_6(OH)_6] \cdot 5H_2O$
Hardness . . . . . 2—2.5
Color . . . . white, whitish, gray, beige
Sources . . . . . . United States, Russia

Special note: Ulexite is also called "television stone": when it is put on top of a printed piece of paper, the text seems to appear on the surface of the stone.

360 | Energy class 3

U N A K I T E (EPIDOTE)

ENDURANCE—STRENGTH

With this stone we box through our own resistance. It reflects the absurdity of resistance and still takes it seriously. It is a good helper in times of stubborness.

Unakite . . . . . . ENDURANCE
Composition . . . . epidote rock (pale-colored quartz): pink feldspar and green epidote
Hardness . . . . . 6—7
Color . . . . mottled pink and green
Sources . . . . . . United States, Rhodesia, Ireland

Special note: Stones and goods made of this material usually sell as epidote (see EPI-DOTE, p. 130).

Energy class 3

U V A R O V I T E (Garnet)

FAITHFULNESS—SELF-DETERMINATION

Every person has a task—a task that differentiates him or her from every other human being. The uvarovite awakens the *desire* within us to find our very own task.

When we want to remain true to ourselves, it is important that we live our task. We feel uneasy to the point of despair when we do not find our task.

The uvarovite, withits fine aura, has a powerful and intensive effect. With its help, we stride forward until we have found our intended purpose.

Uvarovite . . . . . PARTICIPATION IN THE DECISION
Composition . . . $Ca_3Cr_2[SiO_4]_3$
Hardness 7.5
Color . . . . . . deep green
Sources . . . . . Finland, Russia

Energy class 1

VANADINITE

EXAMINATION OF THE HEART

There is no time in which this stone is more useful than during times of upheaval. Old pain flares up—although it had seemed to be healed. Where do we stand? Where are we moving to? Self-doubt strongly influences us.

During these phases the vanadinite helps. It imparts to us that all of life is a test, that we go through purification processes time and again and continually are tempted to cling to the old.

The pain of the necessary leave-taking is healed by this stone. Although it lets memories break open, at the same time it points out the future to us. "Hold fast to YOURSELF," it seems to say. "Trust in YOURSELF. Examine your heart for bonds. Let go of everything that could hamper you. The path to God is simple. Walk it with a light heart. Trust in the LORD and that new doors will open for you. Carefully close the old ones. Remain still in thankfulness for a moment. Turn around and see what is being prepared for you. In the moment of letting go lies the new birth. Trust."

Vanadinite. . . . . EXAMINATION
Composition . . . $Pb_5[Cl/(VO_4)_3]$
Hardness 3
Color . . . . yellow, brown, orange, red
Sources . . . . . . Morocco, United States

Energy class 3

VARISCITE

THE POWER OF FULFILLMENT LIES WITHIN ME

The variscite brings us to the perception: *I have everything within me that I need to be happy!* Every person can be happy. It is just a question of trust. The variscite brings us to the point of perceiving our own ability to be happy. It teaches us that the foundation of all life is *happiness*. The more we develop ourselves, the more we will feel this.

In the daily application, we feel simply lighter and happier with this stone. In order to constantly feel the depth of our happiness, we must either use it over a period of years in the best quality or (preferably) with the help of other gemstones, or forms of therapy and healing sessions to transform our blockades. It is also possible that the variscite shows us our momentary inability to be happy.

Variscite . . . . . . SELF-PERCEPTION
Composition . . . $Al[PO_4]\cdot 2H_2O$
Hardness . . . . . 4—5
Color . . . . pale to emerald-green, also blue-green to colorless
Sources . . . . . . United States, Brazil, Australia

Energy class 3

364

VERDITE

COURAGE OF DESPAIR

With this stone we feel our hesitation, our insecurity, and our despondency. We feel our self-tormented waiting. We could leave it at this if we just wanted to learn something about ourselves. However, when we have finally make up our minds to take a step in our life that we are afraid of and unconditionally wanted to avoid, then this stone can give us the courage of despair.

It can give us such courage and security for a short period of time that we hardly recognize ourselves. It should be used with care and only when we are absolutely certain about the matter at hand. Otherwise, we could harm ourselves.

Verdite . . . . . . COURAGE—ACTION
Composition . . . $Mg_6[(OH)_8/Si_4O_{10}]$
Hardness 3
Color . . . . green with red, or yellow, or brown spots and veins (serpentine rock)
Source . . . . South Africa

Energy class 3

PETRIFIED WOOD

MASTERING LIFE'S DIFFICULTIES

When we take petrified wood in the hand, solutions to problems occur to us. While we are still considering how we should best solve our problems, a feeling of joy and confidence overcomes us. Within this vibration we see everything with greater lightness. Paths appear, doors open up, and understanding becomes easier. This is where the gift lies: When we better understand everyday situations, the optimal solutions occur to us.

In order to be able to enjoy this present, we should use the stone for at least three days.

Petrified wood . . . . . CHEERFULNESS
Composition . . . . . . usually SiO_2
Hardness . . . . 6.5—7
Color . . . . mainly gray, brown, and beige tones
Sources . . . . worldwide

Energy class 3

VESUVIANITE (IDOCRASE)

A STONE WITH HUMOR

Its special task is immersing us in lightness when melancholy wants to descend on us. With it we suddenly perceive that there is no need to worry as long as we feel connected with God.

All the troubles of this world can be traced back to a QUARREL with God. Perception brings healing but only when we let our perceptions be followed by actions. The perception of our love of God is the greatest healer. The perception that we are *upheld by God* is the greatest love, from which everything else grows. The vesuvianite reminds us of this.

Vesuvianite . . . . . SOLUTION OF PROBLEMS
Composition . . . . $Ca_{10}(Mg,Fe^{2+})_2Al_4[(OH)_4/SiO_4)_5/(Si_2O_7)_2]$
Hardness . . . . . . 6—7
Color . . . . yellow-brown, olive-brown, green-yellow, also green or brown
Sources . . . . . . Kenya, Canada, Sri Lanka

Energy class 1

VIVIANITE

A HEALER OF THE FUTURE

We wait all our lives for a certain result; we hope for the fulfillment of our wishes; we do not suspect that they do not fit into our lives. Then comes the heartbreak—slowly and continually.

One day, we will see that all of our wishes were illusions. When we already have begun the process of finally reconciling with the past, this stone comes to us. It will speak to us.

"Look into your heart. Perceive that your true wish from the very beginning was to serve God wholeheartedly, with all your strength and with all your being. Your fantasies were illusions. However, a great future lies ahead of you; fear it no longer. It will be better than you think and it will fulfill you. God's plans for you requires all the strength and attention that you can muster. It will bring you happiness! Therefore, trust. Go healed into the future."

This is a great comforter that removes our fears.

Vivianite. . . . . . TRUST IN LIFE AND THE STRENGTH WITHIN US
Composition . . . $Fe_3^{2+}[PO_4]_2 \cdot 8H_2O$
Hardness . . . . . 1.5—2
Color . . . . blue, indigo-blue, black-green
Sources . . . . . . Germany, Bosnia-Hercegovinia, England, Russia, Bolivia

Energy class 1

WATERMELON TOURMALINE

HEALING—HEALING—HEALING

This tourmaline wants to do particularly well for us. It links the qualities of the pink tourmaline with those of the green. This is its special strength—the principle of *connection*. Love and healing belong together. We become whole when we love; we impart healing energy when we care about others. Our greatest strength is love. In its insistent strength, the watermelon tourmaline reminds us to use this quality for our healing.

This is a very important stone for the physical level.

Watermelon tourmaline. . . REVALESCING AND BONDING
Composition . . . . varies according to the different colors
Hardness . . . . 7—7.5
Color . . . . green rim to a red-pink center
Sources . . . . Brazil, Afghanistan, United States, Africa

Energy class 2

WAVELLITE

HUNGER FOR GREATNESS

When we meet a wavellite, it points to our growth: it is necessary for us to examine where we still resist greatness and expansion.

This stone helps us to the perception that we will always be unhappy and restrained as long as we do not stand up to our own size and do not yet work enough on the fulfillment of our task in life.

The wavellite shows us the impossibility of restrained energy. One day an explosion must occur, an outbreak of our dissatisfaction, our despair, and our sorrow.

"Be who you *are!*" it says. It means well. We can save ourselves from illness and unhappiness when we let it work its effect. It gives us courage and refers us to gemstone helpers that subsequently want to accompany us.

Wavellite . . . . . . HOLDING ONTO THE OLD
Composition . . . . $Al_3[(OH,F)_3/(PO_4)_2]5H_2O$
Hardness . . . . . . 3.5—4
Color . . . . white, pale tones of green, yellow, brown, or blue
Sources . . . . Germany, Czech Republic, England, United States, Bolivia

370 | Energy class 2

ZEIRINGITE

RUEFULNESS

With this stone on the heart chakra, we make a vow to God—we will atone for our neglectful behavior of the past. However, this type of regret has no pain; this is the gift of zeiringite. Therefore, we can feel with greatest sincerity what our refusal has done. Because we do not immerse ourselves in pain, we can see clearly. Because the regret does not make us helpless, we create no new karma through thoughtless promises. This stone means well with us in that it helps us walk our path without the pain of regret. It is a gift for those to whom it comes.

Zeiringite . . . . . JOY ABOUT OUR PATH
Composition . . . aragonite containing copper (see ARAGONITE, p. 62)
Hardness . . . . . 3.5—4
Color . . . . whitish with ribbonlike shadings of pale-blue, pale-green, or blue
Sources . . . . . . Oberzeiring & Styria in Austria, Spain, Greece

Energy class 1

BLUE ZIRCON

ENLIGHTENMENT—CHANGE THROUGH GIVING UP ONESELF

This stone reminds us of the sacrifice of Jesus Christ. It teaches that absolute devotion leads to eternal life.

There is no blue zircon in a natural state. Colorless or blue stones are born through the heating of brownish zircons. By giving itself up in its customary form, the zircon becomes another type of zircon. Through a transformation process it gains in significance. It has elevated itself.

If we wear this stone, we will gradually be prepared to give up our ego in favor of our overall development. With its help, we gain the conviction that every venture, every effort, and every attempt is worth it in order to move forwards on our path and to find God even quicker.

For those who already obey God, an elevation into further Spiritual Planes occurs. When they wear it, they will be closer to heaven than without it. This is a stone that demands sincere changes from us on every level of development so that our path into the Light becomes easier.

Blue zircon . . . . . PREMONITION OF DIVINITY
Composition . . . . $Zr[SiO_4]$
Hardness . . . . . . 6.5—7.5
Color . . . . very pale blue to "most beautiful" aquamarine-blue (artificially colored, see Special note)
Sources . . . . Thailand, Cambodia, Africa, India, Brazil, Australia, Tasmania

Special note: Large and intensely blue zircons are very rare and correspondingly expensive. If brownish stones are heated without the addition of oxygen, they become blue. If oxygen is added, they become colorless or white.

Energy class 1

COLORED ZIRCON

MEANING—IMMERSING IN ENERGIES

The zircon is a joyful stone and it does things its own way. Although there are three special zircons (blue, yellow-red-brownish, and green), it is as if the rest of the zircons would say: appearance is insignificant. No matter which color we have, our effect is the same! It thereby shows that appearance can be important, although it seldom *is*. It would be false to draw conclusions about inner significance based on the external factors. There is certainly a difference between man and woman and that may be of a certain significance. However, external factors like skin color, hair color, form of the face and so on are completely unimportant. Certain qualities, certain memories and dreams may be reflected on our exterior but in our hearts we are all the same. Those who have forgotten this should wear a colorless or colored zircon until they see the people instead of the differences.

The brown, the blue, and the green zircons are an exception. They represent other tasks.

Colored zircon . . . PERCEPTION OF BROTHERHOOD
Composition . . . . $Zr[SiO_4]$
Hardness . . . . . . 6.5—7.5
Color . . . . yellow, colorless, violet
Sources . . . . . . Thailand, Cambodia, Africa, India, Brazil, Australia, Tasmania

Energy class: 1

GREEN ZIRCON

SPECIAL POSITION

The green zircon takes a special position among all the gemstones. It reminds us of disintegration. Nothing lasts forever, everything passes. This stone transforms itself through its own radioactivity. It changes itself through millions of years. It changes its crystal lattice. It gives itself up.

It urgently reminds us to stand up for our tasks even when we—in the human sense—would not survive. To follow our tasks is our highest objective. The accompanying circumstances do not count. What counts is the experience gained, the love that we have lived, and the knowledge that we were able to put into action. Love and knowledge are one. Disintegration only exists in earthly matter. The spiritual world knows only growth. Being a human is different. Here the situation is that spiritual growth cannot be achieved without disintegration and decay. We accept this fact with the help of the green zircon.

Green zircon . . . UNDERSTANDING MY TASK
Composition . . . $Zr[SiO_4]$
Hardness . . . . . 6.5—7.5
Color . . . . deep green
Sources . . . . . . Thailand, Cambodia, Africa, India, Brazil, Australia, Tasmania

Energy class 1

R E D / B R O W N   Z I R C O N   (HYACINTH)

TAKING RESISTANCE SERIOUSLY

When we earnestly examine our resistance, we experience our fears. This zircon honors our recalcitrance but at the same time shows how unnecessary it is. We will receive all the help we need but we must ask for it. This is a law. We are the only beings to have a free will; we can only find assistance when we request it. Some things may come easily to us without any apparent effort or desire; we have also prayed for these blessings—even if it was many lifetimes ago.

With hyacinth, we realize that we belong to God. We receive the revelation that we can ask *anytime* for guidance, gifts, or aid. We can change our lives this way. We cannot change anything through resistance.

Red/brown zircon . . DISSOLVES RESISTANCE
Composition . . . . . $Zr[SiO_4]$
Hardness . . . . 6.5—7.5
Color . . . . brown, yellow-red to red-brown
Sources . . . . Thailand, Cambodia, Africa, India, Brazil, Australia, Tasmania

Energy class 2

CUBIC ZIRCONIA

WRIGGLING JOY

Zirconia is a man made gemstone. Nevertheless, these stones possess an energy.

In its clarity and its gorgeously colored glitter, it leads us to believe in a world of abundance. When we are immersed in its rays, everything in life seems simple to us. However, it is not animated by energy of a deep joy, which is characteristic of earth-mined gemstones. Their effect is very brief and tends to produce unrest. When we lose ourselves in it, we lose ourselves in the world of superficiality. When we desire a mercurial joy and can deal with it, we should lovingly contemplate it.

Cubic zirconia . . . . . DESIRE FOR ILLUSION
Composition . . . . . $[ZrO_2]^{3+}$
Hardness 8.5
Color . . . . colorless, red, green, yellow
Source . . . . artificially grown crystal

Special note Zirconia crystals grow in "farms" of intense heat & pressure. They are used as imitation diamonds, because they have a peculiar sparkle.

Energy class 3

CITRINE

HIGHEST ENLIGHTENMENT

The citrine is astonishing! In connection with the amethyst, it helps beginners achieve a certain understanding of gemstones. Together they create a path to the feelings of the person using the gemstones. However, they can also bring us *highest enlightenment*. Both are great stones and both are simple.

The citrine is considered capable of helping us overcome our timidity in approaching God. God is love. We forget this time and again. With the citrine it seems that He is showing us the reflected glory of the heavenly kingdom and asks us to enter into it. He says: "Since you are a child of God, God has a table prepared for you. You can rest and relax. Come closer and recognize the love of God. Comprehend that you did not know what love really is. Learn to give that part within you that prevents you from living perfect love. Perceive for a moment where the abandoning of all wishes leads us. *Trust in God*."

The angels who guard our transformation, who protect us from obstinacy and defiance and who accept us into the school of initiation are connected with citrine.

This is a stone that asks nothing and yet can demand the highest concentration. It can even have a trailblazing effect. Its healing aura lies in the acceptance of our path to God and its help in this process. It is a helper that we will require time and again on our evolutionary path.

Citrine . . . . PEACE WITH ONESELF—HIGHEST ENERGY
Composition . . . SiO_2
Hardness 7
Color . . . . all tones of yellow
Sources . . . . . . Brazil, Africa, South Africa, Madagascar, Spain

Special note: Natural citrine occurs in a rather reserved yellow; sometimes it can be nearly brown. Yellow citrines that radiate magnificently are all artificially heated amethysts. We enjoy both of them.

Energy class 1

LEMON CHRYSOPRASE

FRESHNESS AS SOURCE OF LIFE

This is a stone that brings us freshness, freshness for our thoughts and for our soul. When we feel exhausted and sad, discouraged and alone, then the lemon chrysoprase helps us. It gives strength in its inimitable way and trust in our inner strength, which will ultimately allow us to overcome everything.

This is an ideal stone for times after a long period of illness or when the hope of healing has deserted us. When it is worn for three weeks, life seems to be renewed and worth living. It takes effect practically from the first hour.

Lemon chrysoprase . . . FRESHNESS
Composition . . . . . . Magnesite containing nickel (see MAGNESITE, p. 200)
Hardness . . . . 4—4.5
Color . . . . lemon-yellow, yellow-green
Source . . . . Australia

Energy class 2

ZOISITE

JOY—DISCOVERY

The zoisite is an adventurer. It leads us into the adventure of self-discovery. Its task is making conscious an aspect of our self that deals with our childhood. It points out where we had already been clairvoyant as a child in this life. When we remember these capabilities as adults, we regain a piece of our dignity. We understand that we knew more as a child than the adults wanted us to believe. We comprehend that we have suppressed sources of strength because we thought we had to protect ourselves. Now we discover to our pleasure that these capabilities are still within us and that we can live them. We gain in strength and confidence and we integrate our strength as a child.

Like so many types of help given to us by gemstones, this can also occur in the subconscious or enter into our daily understanding. When we use it for an adequate period of time, we will in any case feel stronger, more joyful, and more whole.

Zoisite . . . . DISCOVERY
Composition . . . . . . $Ca_4Al_3[O/OH/SiO_4/Si_2O_7]$ and ruby
Hardness . . . . 6.5—7 (zoisite), 9 (ruby)
Color . . . . green with black dots and pieces of ruby
Source . . . . Tanzania

Special note: We use this mineral as if it were one unique gemstone. If you want to use only the energy of the ruby, you should separate the ruby from the zoisite.

Energy class 3

FIVE EXPERIENCES WITH GEMSTONES

THE SAPPHIRE

When the sapphire entered my life in 1987, I was making preparations to travel. In my rush I decided to acquire three stones for this trip, one of which should be a sapphire. I had a little less than $200 available for the purpose.

After I had purchased two of the stones in a mineral store, but could not find a sapphire, I drove to a wholesale gemstone dealer. The neighboring store was a boutique and so I first browsed around. I was thrilled! Three wide blouses particularly appealed to me. Together they cost about $200. Would it not be better to buy clothing? I had been invited to work as the leader of a seminar at a therapy center and with these blouses I would look chic—an attractive reincarnation therapist! I must admit I had a hard time parting from the blouses and eventually went to the wholesaler dealer.

"I'd like to see sapphires," I said. It was the first time that I looked at cut stones. The salesman silently set up five sapphires in front of me. In my eyes they were tiny and very dark. The dealer stood in front of me as I took the stones in my hand. Nothing happened. I became nervous. I wasn't used to feeling the energy of the stones in public. The salesman was watching me and I found this irritating. To make matters worse, the third stone had nothing to say to me at all.

As I took the fourth one in my hand, I heard clearly: *"I will serve you faithfully."* I stared at the stone in surprise. It was small and inconspicuous as it laid there. How could it have the ability to do this? "What does this one cost?" I asked reluctantly. "$330," answered the salesman. "What?!," slipped from my lips, "so much money!!!" The man remained silent. I reluctantly moved the stone in my hand. I didn't like it. However, its message was clear. I thought of the blouses. And besides—I didn't even have that much money. At the same time, I totally forgot about the $350 that I had with me to buy the ticket for my flight. "I have to think about it," I finally said and left.

It was November. A ray of sunshine fell on the front door of a building. I sat on the doorstep and thought things over. I never have enough money! Everything is always too expensive! I can never afford to buy what I want. A wave of self-pity swept over me and I was close to tears. A small dog trotted by and looked up at me. Now I was really crying.

After a few minutes a thought occurred to me. Hadn't I always had money when I *needed* it? Hadn't I already experienced my wonders? Would it not be easy for the universe to quickly create a few patients for me? I wrinkled my forehead. Money. Was money my problem? No. What was the problem then? I thought about it.

Yes, money had somehow always been there, even in the difficult period of upheaval and intensive learning, the new beginning. *So what was actually the problem?*

Trust. TRUST! That was it! The problem was not money, *but whether I trusted my feelings!* The sapphire had said: *I will serve you faithfully.* Here was the test. I thought of the stone. Was it a sapphire? Couldn't it also be a piece of glass? If I now held it in my hand

and—*snap*—maybe it would be gone. Who can tell me that it is genuine? Who can tell me *that it will have an effect?*

Life wants me to trust and listen to my inner voice. It wants me to believe in wonders and take this stone seriously and trust it. *I should believe in the stone and its message.*

At that moment I saw an angel in front of me. It smiled at me. Tears veiled my eyes. Yes, this is my path. The angel pointed to the left. I followed it. We turned left, and I saw a church. The door was open, which is rare in Berlin. I went into the church and prayed. I renewed my trust in God and I thanked Him for the test. Then I went out and bought the stone.

I wore it for three months during a very difficult period of my life. The sapphire strengthens our faith. It connects us with God. I have this stone to thank for my intimate relationship with gemstones and their effects. My trust was rewarded.

Note: A good raw sapphire stone can be purchased at a mineral exchange for about $8. Particularly large cut stones can cost far more than $800,000.

THE BRILLIANT CUT DIAMOND

In the summer of 1988, three-quarters of a year after the purchase of the sapphire and urged on by a girlfriend, I drove to Idar-Oberstein for the first time, .

Shortly before I left, I discovered that I was to buy about twenty stones. After some initial resistance, since I had not even paid for my last training course yet, I borrowed the money for the purpose. I was then also very much surprised to learn that I should buy a brilliant for my protection and growth.

According to the information that I obtained with the pendulum, it should be 1/2 carat and cost over $1000.

Using the pendulum itself was actually new for me. For example, with it we searched for a fire opal. The woman serving at a gemstone company said: "There are none in this room." I looked at my pendulum, which I had held loosely and was now swinging a vehement YES. While I looked at my pendulum, a man entered the storeroom. "The fire opals are on the first floor, are not they!?" said the woman to him. "Why?", he asked. I turned red since I still didn't like to use the pendulum in public. "My pendulum thinks they must be in this room," I murmured. The man looked at me in disbelief. Then he went to a cabinet and placed a few plastic containers in front of me. "These have been here since yesterday," is all he said.

At this point I would like to give a clear warning: Using the pendulum often led me into learning processes that were, in part, extremely painful. It is important to me to be able to rely on my feelings, to hear my inner voice, and to trust in God. I no longer use the pendulum.

In any case, at that time we dealt with our brilliants immediately afterwards. My girlfriend also wanted to look for one. We were led into a small room and sat down. Two of the company's employees sat in front of us. On the table between us they put a small box in which there were white little paper packets containing brilliants. We stated our wishes. We thought that the brilliants that were shown to us were tiny. The pendulum always said NO. When we had seen so many that it was already quite embarrassing for me, I gathered my courage and asked: "May I use the pendulum on the small bags?" I was permitted to do so. The pendulum finally showed YES. We were disappointed. The stones were far less than half a carat, but they were flawless. Only later did I understand what the pendulum wanted to say: Purity is important. *Risk more!*

The salesman finally got a new small box. "Perhaps this is something for you." He opened a small bag and two larger brilliants were in it. "Like twins," said Adelheid. "Do they want to come to us?" I took a brilliant in my hand. *I will stay with you*, it said. At the same moment, I heard the price—almost three thousand dollars. Outraged, I put back the stone. How could the stone claim to stay with me when I didn't even have the money!

In the meantime, my girlfriend was lost in thought as she looked at the stones. I was resentful. I finally pulled myself together. She had money. I could at least help her. I took the other stone in my hand and heard: I *want to go to Adelheid.* I reluctantly gave her the brilliant and said: "Feel this."

Then I observed how her fingers closed around the stone in a slow-motion tempo. I whispered: "It wants to go to you." "What?" she asked out loud, "you've received messages?" "Yes," I admitted, moved with embarrassment. "It is meant for you and the other wants to stay with me. However, that can't be true!" I added, somewhat irritated. She sat up straight. As still and reserved as she usually was, she now said very loudly: "if the stones want to come to us, then you must tell me about it! I'll take care of it!"

"But, no," I whispered, "I do not have any money." Confessing to the listening salespeople: "I have debts! I cannot afford it." "It is all right," she said and patted my hand. "What do the stones cost? Is there a discount? Can I pay by check?" Speechless, I listened while she negotiated. I stared at the brilliants. They looked white and lifeless. The company hadn't even made the effort of installing light for brilliants. The special thing about brilliants is their colorful sparkle. These didn't sparkle.

"Please," I begged her, "let's think about this!" "There's nothing to think about if they want to come to us." "Please," I continued to beseech her, "I don't have any money, I have to pay back debts. I don't know when I can pay you for the brilliant!!!" "It is all right," is all she said. Tears came into my eyes, and I squeezed her hand. While she took care of everything, I stood off to the side.

Am I crazy? I asked myself. *What am I doing?* The stone looks colorless and dull. What effect will it have on me at all? When will I be able to pay back the money? What have I gotten into? I felt awful.

When everything had been take care of, we drove to a park. We sat in the sun. A white feather lay in front of me—a swan feather. "How beautiful," I cried out in delight and picked it up. This is also how I had reacted when I discovered some tiny jade turtles a short time before. They had cost $3.50 a piece and I had purchased two of them for us.

Now we took out the brilliants. We opened the small packet—and the most magnificent brilliants that I had ever seen sparkled in the sunlight with a size of 0.57 carats. Deeply touched, I stared at the stone. It had been the right thing to do. It had been worth it.

We rested. I loved the stone and listened to what it had to say to me. I put my other treasures next to it—the feather and the turtles.

Suddenly I understood. Because I loved *everything*—without paying attention to the "value"—the brilliant had come to me. I was permitted to have it. The matter of the money would take care of itself. I could trust.

The brilliant proved to be my greatest teacher. I wear it all the time.

THE TOURMALINE

The larger part of my current life was determined by my desperate search for 'my' man, 'my' beloved. This motivated the beginning of my spiritual development.

In the years of most intensive reincarnation therapy, I experienced that up to this point in time I had searched for a soul I had known from previous lives and absolutely wanted to meet again. I had secretly threatened God: either this soul—or none at all! Since God does not let himself be blackmailed, I met none at all. Stated more precisely: I met men. However, no relationship lasted very long.

After I knew the reason, it took me three further years until I could let go of this soul. However, since I had experienced a deep spiritual development in the meantime, we were permitted to meet. Then I realized that this soul—also a man in this life—did not at all harmonize with me and my present life.

I had received many messages in the meantime that the true man for me was close by, that I would meet him, and that we would be happy. Being as I was—I longed for this...

Longing costs energy. Longing stands in the way. Longing is always associated with sorrow. However, God wants to see me free of bonds. He would like to know that I am *happy* to the same degree with or without a man.

So it happened that a green tourmaline, a raw stone, entered my life. I found it especially beautiful and particularly affordable. I loved it. I carried it with me for three days and nights. On the fourth day, I went for a walk. It was snowing and I felt myself at peace. Then time stood still, and the tourmaline gave me a great perception:

I love life for itself—and not for what it promises me!

There was a deep peace within me. The promised man would come and, until then, I could develop myself with joy.

It was as if a burden had been taken from my shoulders. The tourmaline had given a new direction to my thoughts. I wanted to savor this, and so I went to the jewelry store the next day to enjoy myself and to 'bathe' in the stones. In the process, my attention was drawn to a brilliant ring, magnificent and beautiful and in the shape of a star. I sighed. I didn't have the money for it. I had become involved in a conversation with the saleswoman and also showed her the tourmaline that I held in my hand the whole time. Afterwards, I left the store in an elated mood.

As I walked out, the tourmaline jumped out of my hand in a high arc! Frightened, I stopped: had I been careless? I picked up the stone, of which a tiny piece had broken off. I was stunned as I looked at the tourmaline. I was so sorry about it! Why had this happened?

I have served you. You do not need me any longer.

I must not have heard right. I didn't want to believe it. Silence. The tourmaline no longer spoke to me. My God, what should I do? I asked for help.

It seemed to me that Christ was standing in front of me: *Go in there and give it to the saleswoman.*

My stone? *My* tourmaline? Jesus was silent. Everything inside of me protested. I had just learned to love the stone; it had helped me so much. And now I was supposed to give it up already? *No!* Everything inside of me screamed *no*.

Once again, I prayed for help. It was as if Christ now stood in front of the door to the shop. His face was serious, and he pointed into the store—*go!*

The serious face made me feel dismayed and I missed his smile. I knew that it *was* serious. I went to the saleswoman, willing and reluctant to the same degree, and gave her the stone.

It took months for me to get over this. I had also understood the lesson: nothing really belongs to us. Life gives to us—people, animals, things, and much more. However, life is also change, and separation is something natural.

After I had really and truly let go of the tourmaline, I saw it in my meditation one day and at the same time I had the feeling that it wanted to come back to me. That was one year after my visit to that store.

A few days later I was on my way. I had saved money to buy myself a new couch and wanted to go to the city anyway. The furniture store I planned to visit was closed, which was quite unusual, so I went to the next one. The saleswoman telephoned for hours before she suddenly said clearly and distinctly: "Not before Christmas." Something touched me. The closed store and this *not before Christmas*. It was a message for me. I noticed that I should not buy my couch before Christmas. Somewhat surprised, I visited the jeweler where I had given away the tourmaline.

The same saleswoman was actually there and so I asked about the stone only to learn that she had never used it. "You know," I now said, "I have the feeling that it wants to come back to me. What do you think about that, would it be all right with you?" She was naturally surprised. "I believe that I was just supposed to learn something. Perhaps a therapy session would be good for you, as compensation, so to speak." By then, we had also briefly talked about my healing work at that time.

Then something occurred to me: "Do you still have that ring with the small brilliants in the shape of a star?" "Yes," she replied. I tried it on and in doing so I realized that it wanted to come to me. It cost exactly as much as I would have spent on a new couch.

At Christmas I sat on my threadbare sofa. The green tourmaline was with me and the ring as well. The ring is connected with the Christ energy and has the effect of a guardian angel. God is great. I had often dreamed and heard: *Everything important will come back to you.*

Yes, everything IMPORTANT comes to us—and back to us as well. When we finally can let go, life gives us even more!

THE PARAIBA TOURMALINE

When I looked for a publisher for this book, it contained the description of about 150 gemstones. Shortly before the final deadline, I traveled to Idar-Oberstein with a photographer to take what were to be the last photographs. At the time, I didn't feel well at all. I had terrible headaches, and when I asked inwardly about the struggle going on inside of me the answer was—*money*.

On the very first day in Idar-Oberstein, I discovered a ring with a green Paraiba tourmaline which was almost three carats (the cause of my headaches). I ignored it steadfastly. After I had paid back my first loan on time, a further loan was necessary in connection with this book and I simply couldn't imagine that I now should undertake such a major expense. While the photographer encouraged me intensely, I felt my negative response—*I do not want to have to ask again*, and *I finally want to live without debts*.

Later, I asked her to read me the text for the Paraiba tourmalines. While she read, tears ran down my face. During the years of my healing work I had exhausted myself, the constant poor posture at the treatment couch had produced symptoms, my glowing enthusiasm for my spiritual path had let me forget my body and my other needs to a large extent. Even before I had heard the entire text, I knew: *If I believe in everything that I have written in this book, then I must acquire this ring. This is where my help is.*

And so the decision was made. However, at this time I had only written the general text on the Paraiba tourmaline. I did not yet know that the green tourmaline fulfills our "wish for further, uninterrupted growth." In return I experienced an expansion of this book in leaps and bounds. This meant purchasing new minerals, making additional trips in order to be able to borrow gemstones and have them photographed, and a long-term closing of my practice because time was running out. Above all, this meant that I was forced to take out further loans. At the same time, I encountered people who had listened to their "inner voice" and had failed dangerously as a result. Doubts and fears struggled within me. How was I different from them? There was only one thing left for me to do—to throw myself even more intensely into the arms of God and check time and again whether I was still operating within the realm of reality.

One day I heard someone talk about an acquaintance. "She has more debts than she can pay back in this lifetime!" This made me curious and so I asked what the amount was. It was the same sum of money which I owed and I mentioned this. "It is different with you," I was told, "you can reckon with income from the book." I remained silent. What I had encountered here is very typical for most people and the modern age. We do not have enough confidence. *We do not have enough confidence in God.*

Most people still follow their own will. They do not listen to their inner voice, even though they sometimes think they do. When we truly listen within, we are protected. The challenges still exist because we are meant to grow. Had I had money, I would have simply spent it. I would never have been able to develop myself in such a tempestuous manner. This is why I had to overcome fears once again, heal doubt, and perceive that trust in God is of elemental importance, but it was now my learning process to strength my self-confidence. Above all, I once again learned to trust in gemstones! I tried out many new energies, and all of them fit my respective condition exactly. Over a long period of time I carried an andradite (forwards!) and a prehnite (encouragement, with the emphasis on: *You can do it*) with me. At night I slept with stones taped on me, which gave me important dreams or comforted me. I was always aware that everything occurred for my benefit and my speedy growth. I was informed that this strenuous time was triggered and advanced by the Paraiba tourmaline, which exuded healing energy at the same time. I can also thank it for the dramatic memories of a former life in which I belonged to a group of people who destroyed people and animals through the manipulation of gemstones. This memory caused my immune system to break down immediately, bringing with it a massive cold. I healed my oppressive guilt feelings about these memories and was then very thankful to the Paraiba tourmaline. However, without the help of the other gemstones I would have not been able to walk my path as quickly or as intensely.

My most important advice to other people will always be: *Everything is possible when we listen to our inner voice.* Learning processes are a part of our growth. Those who do not listen within and accumulated debts as a result always get another chance *if they ask God for help.* The answers may not exactly be to our taste. For example, let us consider that a woman, one I had actually heard about, had a fast-food restaurant offered to her. It is very probable that she would recoil from this opportunity. There is perhaps a matter of pride involved here, a struggling with the circumstances and convenience to be overcome, or whatever her learning process may be at the moment. I only know one thing—if this was her truth and she had opened up to it, she would have been able to pay off her debts in the shortest amount of time. Afterwards, God would show her new paths. In recent years I have had to let go of my healing work a number of times—only to experience that there was subsequent enhancement.

As far as I'm concerned, this time the Light said to me: *With this book you have proven that you are a master. However, we would like you to see the coming two years as years of apprenticeship.* Examples for this were shown to me. Whatever situations we may encounter, they are only challenges through which we are meant to grow. In this process, the gemstones are invaluable helpers that support us in every respect. My debts also proved to be great helpers. In response to the question "How can I earn money outside of my practice in order to pay off my loans?" the Light pointed out my talents and that I should work with managers, as well as in that way. Since I perceive energies and can look into the heart of a person, I can tell that a particular department of a company is ruled by which specific energies, how these impede the work processes, and which people are best suited for a certain job. At the same time, I can advise a department head on how to deal with the people entrusted to him or her in order to achieve the best-possible solution for the individuals and the business. I can also show managers their unconscious blocks. I can encourage them to follow their hearts. As long as a businessman thinks that he must separate the heart and the task, he will never be truly successful—and is in increased danger of a heart attack. I had known about my task in the business sector, but I had considered it to be a project for the future. The external financial pressure and the multitude of gemstone energies let me grow very quickly and said to me: Start *now*. As always when we risk taking on a new tasks that is predestined for us, I was filled with much joy and thankfully felt the burdensome pressure of times past to be a clear guide.

It is also interesting that a colleague of mine insisted that I take some firestones that were the size of the palm of a hand with me before I drove to the publisher to deliver all the material for this book. Before this trip I was afraid that I would be absolutely exhausted when I returned, to a certain extent as a reaction to the excessive stress to which I had subjected myself. Just one day before, I would have preferred to have rewritten the entire book. I suspected that the firestones were meant to help me.

When I returned to Berlin, I stayed in bed for a day. Twice I placed the firestones on me and around me for an hour at a time. I felt no effect but kept one oversized stone at the foot of my bed. In the following days, the book was so distant from me it was as if I had never written it. I couldn't imagine taking care of the rest of the work for it either. Instead, I happily attended to a bit of housework, spent much time in bed, and relaxed completely. Finally, I took up contact with the firestones because I felt so conspicuously *different* than before—namely, positively *good*. The firestones let me know that they had led me to what was *essential*, which was rest and harmony in this case. I love this experience and take it as a 'joke' by the Spiritual World that let me write a book about gemstones and then has elementary help come to me through simple natural stones.

THE EMERALD JEWELRY

The most important stone for my present life is the emerald. It leads me into the greatest depths and lets me perceive what is still concealed within me and what people are made of, independent of what they show me of themselves. It is perhaps astonishing then that I only possess one inconspicuous stone, a stone which I also seldom use.

At the beginning of my gemstone work, I was not interested in old jewelry. I had found out that it is seldom acquired for its own sake but usually because it connects us with memories that we are meant to heal. In addition, jewelry that has been worn very frequently tends to have a destructive energy because it has hardly been cleansed energetically.

Some years ago I gave a seminar in Geneva and discovered wonderful stones there. While in a store I requested permission to hold a certain emerald. I didn't feel good about it because the salesman watched me with mistrust. Still, he told me the age of the ring that I held and from where it came. I only saw the emerald and was disappointed that it apparently had nothing to tell me. I finally said good-bye.

After a few steps, I unexpectedly started to cry. Time seemed to stand still. I felt a repose that I had never before experienced, a peace that I had not known up to that time, a state that was foreign to me—*I was allowed to experience what it is to BE.* My silent weeping occurred out of deepest emotion.

Unfortunately, this state of being cannot be described. In addition, I also cannot call it back into my memory. I was allowed to *experience* it for a moment. However, what I had deeply learned was the following: Some stones are so perfect that they are not influenced by the energy of their owner, not by the owner's moods or diseases or a lack of cleansing.

Because of my love for emeralds and this experience, I had always desired a special emerald photograph for this book. Astonishingly enough, all attempts failed. At the last moment I heard of a man who had a passion for emeralds and possessed a few of them. I called him, told him about the book, and asked whether he would make a stone available to me for the purpose of photographing it.

Shortly thereafter, he visited me in my practice. He showed me three pieces that were very lovely but not typical. Then he opened a jewelry case and placed it in front of me. It took my breath away! I was almost shocked as I looked at the jewelry. I saw a piece of jewelry made of diamonds and emeralds. The emeralds stood out in such an intensive green that they looked unreal to me for this reason, as well as because of the amount of diamonds. I was immediately touched, but still couldn't believe my eyes.

While my visitor explained how this piece of jewelry could be divided into individual pieces and spoke about the excellent handicraft and old pieces of jewelry, I was permitted to hold one of the stones. In turn I talked about my work and my experiences. Towards the end of his visit, I had held the most intensive stone in my hand for more than half an hour and looked at the jewelry time and again. I finally brought my guest to the door. Before I had even closed it, I heard within me: *Lay down and put your hand on your body.* I immediately obeyed.

I had hardly done this when I began to sob with great emotion. I wept bitterly, which I had not done for a long time. While I cried, I did not ask any inner questions but when

I felt better again, I understood the reasons behind what had happened. The emerald had made a realization possible for me. A few months before I had experienced the grace of being allowed to comprehensively understand the past ten years of my life. Now I was permitted to perceive that the last *twenty* years had represented a special test and that I had passed it. As I cried, I had not yet been able to recognize this gift because I was once again connected with the pain I had suffered. In the meantime, I cried because I was deeply grateful.

An explanation is important here. Let us assume that we compare our path in life with a stretch of highway. This broad street has many doors standing close to each other that we must open and pass through in the course of our life. Towards the end of our life path, some mighty doors are to be found and we normally open one door after the other.

There are so-called great gemstones. This means gemstones that show an extraordinary size, purity, and quality for their kind and therefore possess a much stronger aura than a stone in the usual construction. When we are permitted to hold such a stone, it is as if it ignores all the doors and opens one of the last large ones for us. Then whatever is important for us at this moment—and for which we are prepared—can happen.

Gemstones with these outstanding qualities shake us down to the very core of our being. My little emerald would need years to achieve what these immense stones can do in thirty minutes. If we should be lucky enough to come into contact with this type of exquisite stone at certain times in our life, it will always have a lasting influence on us.

It should also be added that with such stones—should we possess one and frequently carry it with us—we can experience an outstanding development. However, this does not mean that I would constantly find myself in the state that the stone in Geneva has granted me. This emerald would have the effect that I would gradually be forced to let go of my entire ego, incomparably more quickly than would otherwise occur in my life. As a result, I could then take on completely different tasks. It would impart great moments and deepest insights to me, but it would perhaps have permitted this incomparable state of being, next to which nothing else matters, a few more times; I presumably would not have completely achieved such a state as a permanent condition in this life, not even shortly before my death. Large stones give us outstanding experiences. However, most of the time they only work intensively with us—in a way that could, however, completely change us.

The emerald jewelry presented me with a further perception: gemstone photographs may prove to be effective and touch us. However, there are certain stones that need to be *seen* in order to grasp them. There are some gemstones in which we can *immerse* ourselves. Their beauty is so unbelievably impressive, their depth cannot be reflected by a photograph or a description and their *life* cannot be documented. As effective as an illustration may be, it can never convey the energy of a stone. Photographing the emerald jewelry was a disappointment. The picture looked flat and in no way reflected the aura of the stones. If we want to get to know gemstones, only living contact helps us. Look at the stones, feel them, and wear them. Perceive that the stones are *alive*.

THE LIFE PLANS FROM GEMSTONES

Gemstones love us. They want us to understand them. When we ask them for help, they will help us.

After I had purchased "my" brilliant, I became involved in intensive learning processes. The cleansing took place on all levels. However, at the same time, an unimaginable possibility opened up to me. With the help of the brilliant, I pressed forward to my deepest task: LIVING with gemstones. Only when we truly let something into our life can we understand it. I had permitted the stones considerable influence upon my life. This is why they chose me to understand their essence—a task that other people can do as well of course. This ability is available to all people, in case they want to make use of the opportunity.

When we gain insight into the essence of the stones, we recognize their possibilities to influence people. When an even deeper insight into the nature of human beings is granted us, we understand that a stone will have different effects for different people and that the same stone frequently has a different effect for the same person at different times in his or her life.

I now know that there is no sense in choosing an aventurine when we want to be happy just because it is connected with the principle of happiness. I always ask myself: Which stone is particularly good for me at this point of my life? In doing so, I accept that my Inner Knowledge sees *further* than I do. Perhaps sorrow is on the agenda at this point in my life. If I ignored it, it will have a painful effect inside of me and can create illness and despair, stagnation and death. However, when I hear: the pearl is good for you now—and I use it and it has the effect of sorrow within me for several hours, which I perceive very consciously and can therefore release its causes, then I will perhaps be happy *afterwards*.

I dispensed with my notions regarding gemstones and *trusted* them. In return they gave me a task that goes beyond my seminar work with gemstones.

They gave me the possibility of finding out for other people what their tasks in life are and how they can optimally master these tasks with the help of gemstones. Gemstones are definitely our helpers—if we want them to be—and they have messages for us. These messages are universally valid.

In addition, in their helper function, they give messages to individuals when these people want to listen to them and work with the stones.

In this way, the so-called life plans from the gemstones are created. In such a plan, I list the stones that are important for the entire life of a certain person. At the same time, I write down the very personal message of the gemstones to this person. These messages contain advice about the person's tasks in life, about the abilities that he or she should realize in this life, about the types of help required for this purpose, and about releasing resistance.

The stone world assume that a person who possesses the recommended stones, who uses them and meditates on their messages, can more easily fulfill his or her tasks. Moreover, this makes it easier for many people to select the best stone for themselves from the variety of stones and information. Those who have acquired the recommended gemstones will also have more certainty in making the daily choices.

I am convinced that we always make the right selection for ourselves *when we listen to our feelings*. However, for beginners and those who are in a particular hurry on their path or seek a greater depth, such a plan can be of significant help.

As a result of this, we also perceive how much effort the world of gemstones makes to constantly enter into contact with us in new ways. A deeper contact with the stones is created when we love them. The stones also love us. Their gifts are immense. We should thankfully accept them.

Gemstones are God's helpers.

AUTHOR'S COMMENTS

ABOUT THE PHOTOGRAPHS

Gemstones and minerals are almost always photographed with artificial light. Most photographers consider it impossible to photograph in sunlight. It was particularly important to us to photograph the stones where they are at home—in nature. Many minerals increased in beauty with the sunlight while for others there were difficulties in reproducing the color. For example, some green tones did not photograph properly.

In any case, we would like to encourage hobby photographers to take more pictures of stones in direct sunlight. Both of the photographers for this book even used weak rays of sunlight that fell into a room and created wonderful photographs as a result.

Some of the pictures have stories behind them. The chrysopal was photographed at Lake Constance, the epidote on a mountain wall which had water rippling down it, and the ruby in water because its growth lines can be more easily seen there. The dioptase simply did not work in color. We finally even decided to use the green that had the least similarity to the true color because we gave priority to the intensive light reflection. The stones gave us many "little stars," but this frequently occurred on pictures which were not suitable for this book. We were happy about every light reflection—which professional photographers often add or remove artificially. Almost all the professional photographers we asked discouraged us and tried to convince us of the folly of our plan. The stones themselves encouraged us, led us into learning processes, and rewarded us richly. This message has been important time and again: *Trust your feelings. Listen to inner instructions. Do not let yourself be impeded by external difficulties.*

The loveliest photos were created when the photographers took the time to connect with a stone before they photographed it, when they asked it for help, and when they followed their feelings. Those who photograph stones can experience much joy. The viewer as well. But most stones must be held or looked at in order for their true beauty to open up to us. A photograph can touch us—the living stone will give so much more.

ABOUT THE COMPOSITION OF THE GEMSTONES

Finding the chemical formulas proved to be quite a large-scale undertaking. People told me that most formulas in the books are based upon the work of two famous scientists. As I considered using their formulas I began to understand that some of the information had become outdated in the meantime and the newer gemstones were not listed. The same formulas are sometimes also written in different ways, ways which cannot always be distinguished by nonprofessionals. I finally decided to use many formulas from the book *Das große Lapis Mineralienverzeichnis* (The Large Lapis Mineral Index) by Stefan Weiss (Christian Weise Verlag). However, for special cases, degrees of hardness, and places where they are found, I refer to the information and documentation from the company Ruppenthal in Idar-Oberstein, Germany, as well as the book *Gemstones of the World* by Walter Schumann (Sterling Publishing) and information from various gemstone dealers. For the American translation, please refer to the Bibliography on page 398.

Since I continuously received greatly differing information, I can only advise: Those who are seriously interested in the chemical composition of gemstones should verify the data in this book to be on the safe side.

ASSISTANCE

Various kinds of help were given to me for this book especially in the last phase of writing prior to production. My Spiritual Helpers accompanied me quite perceptibly the whole time. But I am also thankful for the support through information, for the loan of gemstones, for work at the computer, and for some financial assistance. From the bottom of my heart, I once again thank all of these people that helped make it possible to create this book.

SOURCE OF PHOTOGRAPHS

Adelheid Siebenbaum, Berlin: Almandine, amazonite, amethyst, andradite, aragonite, aventurine orange, bornite, calcite, chalcedony, chita, chrysoberyl, chrysocolla, chrysopal, dripstone, fire opal, fluorite, girasol quartz, goldstone, hauyn, hawk's eye, hematite, herkimer quartz, honey calcite, jade/jadeite, kunzite, labradorite, leopard jasper, malachite, marcasite, melanite, mookaite, moonstone apricot, moss agate, mother-of-pearl, objects, parrot-wing, peridot, purpurite, pyrite, rhodochrosite, rhyolite, rocks, rose quartz, rubellite, serpentine, smithsonite, spinel pink and red, starlite sapphire, sugilite, tiger's-eye, topaz colorless, tourmaline green, unakite, vanadinit, variscite.

Gerd Becker, Idar-Oberstein: Onyx

Glanz-Licht Studio, Berlin: Paraiba gray

Sabine von Neubeck, Berlin: All other photographs in this book.

DEAR INTERESTED READER

Every mineral possesses a certain quality. Beyond the scope of this book, I am certainly interested in other minerals, their vibrations, and their appearance—but more particularly in their tasks and messages. However, since there are more than three-thousand known minerals I would certainly appreciate a particular kind of help:

I am looking for a mineral collection with which I can work. That is, I would like to be permitted to hold the minerals in my hand and to photograph them.

Gemstones with a special presence are a deep personal desire of mine. I am grateful for every opportunity to hold a truly great stone in my hand, meditate with it, and listen to its message.

If anyone of you is willing to give me the possibility of visiting a mineral collection or a special gemstone for this purpose, please write to me.

INFORMATION ON

INDIVIDUAL WORK
LECTURES
SEMINARS
TRAINING FOR PAST-LIFE REGRESSION
LIFE PLANS FROM THE GEMSTONES
PERSONAL CONSULTATION
MANAGEMENT CONSULTATION
THE RADIANCE TECHNIQUE®

can be requested in writing from:

LOVE OF LIFE
Institute for Positive Development
Renate Sperling
Zoppoter Strasse 11
14199 Berlin, Germany

BIBLIOGRAPHY FOR THE AMERCAN EDITION

Matlins, Antoine L., and Bonano, A.C.; *Jewelery & Gems: The Buying Guide*; GemStone Press: Woodstock, 1993
Encyclopaedia Britannica, 1959
The Encyclopedia Americana, 1941
Schumann, Walter; *Gemstones of the World*; Sterling Publishing: New York, 1977
Schumann, Walter; *Minerals of the World*, Sterling Publishing: New York, 1992
Cipriani, Curzio, and Borelli, Alessandro; *Guide to Gems and Precious Stones*; Simon and Schuster: New York, 1993

INDEX OF GEMSTONES